# On Ancient Roads

Recollections, History and Folklore
of County Meath

## Anthony Holten

# On Ancient Roads

## Recollections, History and Folklore
## of County Meath

**Anthony (Tony) Holten** was born near Tara in 1945. He travelled extensively during his marine engineering days in the Merchant Navy prior to continuing his career working on offshore oil and gas fields worldwide. He is the author of several books, including; *A Stroke of Luck* and *Where Toll Road's Meet.* He has three grown up children and lives in County Cork.

ISBN  978-0-9569911-0-2

Additional editing: John Holten
Cover design: edit+ www.stuartcoughlan.com
Design and setting: Anna Marie Holten and Stuart Coughlan
Set in Adobe Garamond Pro
Printed, in Cork, by City Print Ltd

# Contents

# Acknowledgements

I sincerely thank the following people for the assistance they provided in putting together these writings of the area, which is undergoing tremendous change in these times of great progress:

❖ The staff of Navan Library, especially Frances Tallon, who kindly reviewed some of the manuscript and previously introduced me to Larkin's Map, without which it would have been well-nigh impossible to disentangle many mysteries from the past.

❖ The staff of the National Library and National Archives – Noel French of the Heritage Centre in Trim.

❖ Local historians Michael O'Brien of Johnstown, Michael Slavin of Tara, Liam and Bernie McCarthy of Garlagh Cross, Sean and Mary Finnegan of Somerville, Alfred and Kathleen Woods of the Bolies and Paschal Marry of Balrath, who provided documentation, some old photographs and generously shared their extensive knowledge.

❖ The following people who provided me with anecdotal information and many clues that helped me out:  Noel Devine, the late Don O'Brien and his wife Elizabeth (nee Teeny Allen), Colm Powderley, Dodo Flanagan of Corballis Vale, Tommy Hamil, Brendan Farrelly, The Bowens family of Blacklion, Mickey Creighton, Dan and Moira Norton, Brenda Ferris, Nancy Farrelly, the late Ita Maguire, Jimmy Foley, Greg Murray, Paddy McLaughlin (the gardener) Balrath, Ray Mooney of Danestown, Oliver Duane of Balgeeth,

Liam Barry, John Hynes, Tommy (the Bundy) Callahan, Seamus Duffy, Richard and Geraldine Farrelly of the other Balgeeth, Malachy Oakes, Mickey Morris, John and Donal Bradley, the late Maureen Fox, Stephen Ball, Padraig and Pauline Clarke of the mill farm in Lismullin, Val and Cora O'Brien, Francis and Emer Steen of Odder, Rev. Fr Holloway, Sister Rose D. King, Larry and Mary Clarke of Brownstown (Daly's Mill), Joan Gallagher of the Borrowaddy Road, Joe Maguire, The staff and patrons of *The Yankee Connells* & *Fox's* pubs in Skryne. Annette Peard of Belper, Vincent Callan of Ballymagarvey, my brother Tom and his wife Pauline, my sisters Breda, Kay and Margaret and my cousin Mairead. Vincent Mulvaney, Donie Halpin, Shiela and Patsy Sheridan of Robinstown.

❖ John Long of Co. Tipperary for his help and encouragement and Ellen and Michael Hurley of Iskanafeelna Glengarriff, for their hospitality. Breda and Peter O'Leary for the view over Bantry Bay while I was writing.

❖ To my wife Marie, my son Joseph, and my daughter Anna-Marie and Stuart Coughlan for their time and patience.

❖ Special thanks to my son, John, for his help with editing, structuring and preparing the book for publication.

❖ And last but not least my Mam and Dad who passed down the folklore of the area from Tara to Kilcarn, which filled my young mind with insatiable curiosity and a desire to discover more.

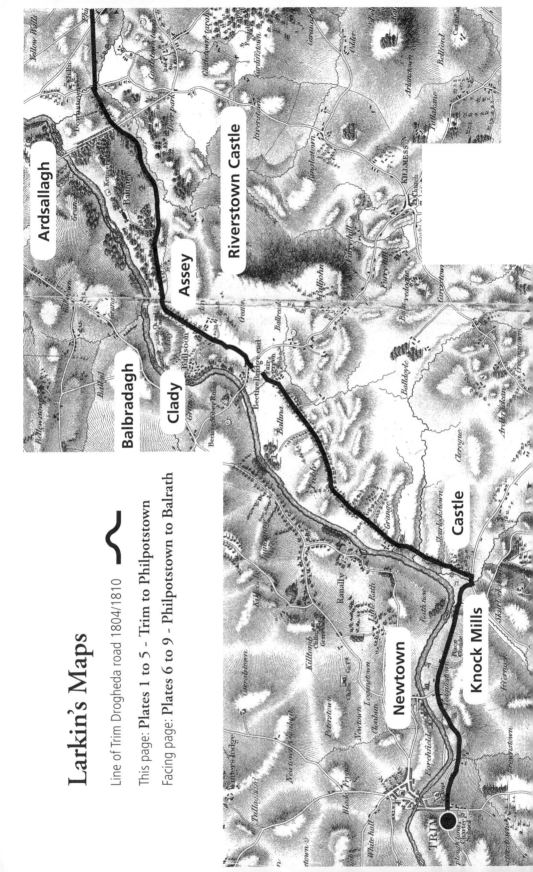

# Larkin's Maps

Line of Trim Drogheda road 1804/1810

This page: Plates 1 to 5 - Trim to Philpotstown

Facing page: Plates 6 to 9 - Philpotstown to Balrath

Ardsallagh

Assey

Riverstown Castle

Balbradagh

Clady

Castle

Newtown

Knock Mills

TRIM

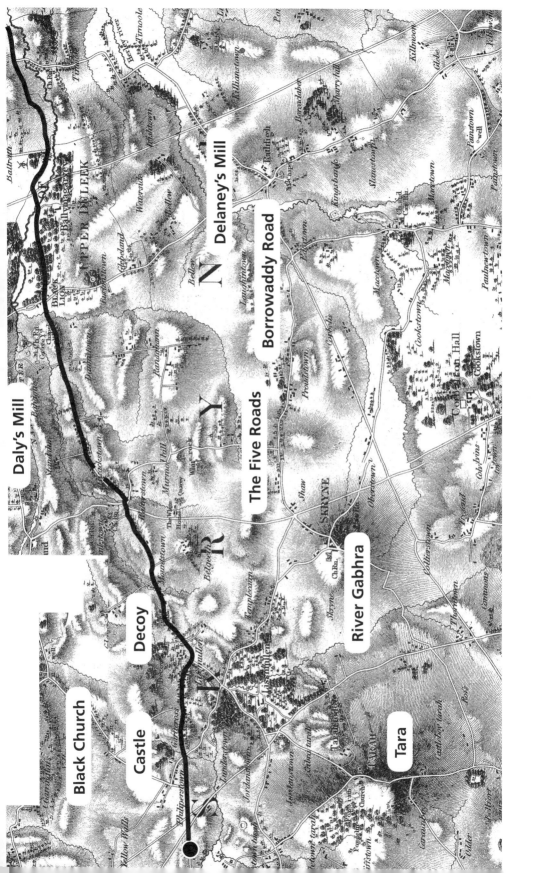

Daly's Mill

Delaney's Mill

Borrowaddy Road

The Five Roads

River Gabhra

Black Church

Castle

Decoy

Tara

# Introduction

*Those childhood days we spent playing by the roadside were very special and provided us with a rich lode of memories. In rural parts in those times life was very simple indeed and excitement was scarce enough, so in some ways we were easily amused. The roadside was our contact with the outside world, that great unknown place we heard so much about but had seen little of. The simple dusty country road of our childhood where we played our games and watched life pass by, was in the future to become our escape route to this great other existence. A highway that was to take us far away from the places, people and things we loved so much. But we didn't know this then, so we played our simple games and dreamed our dreams by the roadside in Dowdstown, so long ago.*

My birthplace is Dowdstown near Tara in county Meath, where during my youth our family resided in a house alongside the Trim/Drogheda road. The foregoing paragraph is an extract from a series of childhood memories I penned recently and purports to illustrate the importance of this road to our young lives – though we didn't realise it then. Looking back on those years through the misty window of time and with much wiser eyes, I note the impact country roads made on our lives. We used the road to do so many things, from playing hopscotch, marbles and skittles, to hauling firewood, travelling to mass, to school and in later times going to work and out to sporting events and cinemas in the local town. In later years this road of our childhood became the route to both adventure and sorrow; our path to emigration. But equally it provided many joyful homecomings. Such is the road of life, with numerous emotional humps and hollows along the way – however, journeying along life's path is like traversing the country roads of yesteryear and should we seek hard enough a bridge could be found to carry us over most troubled waters. Outside the environs of our home life nothing much could be done without passing along these roads. Hence they were an integral part of our lives, and remain so, although most of us scarcely realise this, living as we do in the time famine of modern times.

The coming of the M3 motorway to Dowdstown and the environs of Tara prompted me to record some of my early memories of the place – ere the peace and charm of the area was lost forever amidst the discordant clamour of the super highway. This in turn provided me with the notion of compiling a book on the Dublin to Navan turnpike road, which once passed by our old home in the valley. The few remaining traces of the ancient route now lie buried beneath the new motorway, together with my fields of dreams but not my many happy memories thereof. Researching and writing the book copper-fastened in my mind the realisation of the rich lode of ancient history hidden alongside the routes in the area, especially around Tara and the Boyne Valley. The road from Scurlockstown to the well of the Deenes, near Duleek, is especially endowed with historical sites such as Scurlockstown, Grange, Trubley (Tribley), Bective, Asigh, Balsoon, Bellinter, Dowdstown, Riverstown, Tara, Garlagh Cross, Lismullin, Kentstown, Rathfeigh and Balrath, to name but a few. During boyhood some of these areas were practically our playground, places which in olden times were the crucible of our ancient culture. Whilst a great deal is known of older and medieval times, much of the more recent history and place names seem to have faded and all but vanished from people's awareness. Many items of interest such as Scurlockstown and Riverstown castles, Bective mills, the ancient churches at Balsoon and Clady – Asigh (Assey - Assy) castle, the Bellinter arches, Dowdstown lakes, Black Lion Inn, the three mills on the River Gabhra and many other such places are rapidly being erased from public awareness. To illustrate this point, the name of Black Lion no longer appears on the latest Discovery maps and Dillon's Bridge has been demolished during construction, or destruction work for the M3 motorway – perhaps its name will join the ever lengthening list of disappeared place names. The well of the Deenes is now overgrown and almost closed up, practically no trace remains of the beautiful spring well where in earlier days we slaked our thirst during frequent cycling trips through Duleek. Many people assume that the road ran on its present course, but research shows otherwise – should you read on, you may be surprised at the routes the road took in the relatively recent past.

My main intent in this book is to trace the evolution or disappearance of ancient routes in this very interesting and historic area – and to relate some of the more recent history and folklore of places en route. Many old roads were known anecdotally and the knowledge passed down through the generations, but some merged back into the landscape, the ruins of an old bridge or crumbling wall perhaps the only remaining clue to their former presence. For those who are curious about such things and wonder why a peculiar bend or ditch is sited on a particular road, this information may be of some interest?

The Trim/Drogheda road to Duleek passed through the environs of the Hill of Tara and intersected most of the routes traversing the historic hilltop. The process of unravelling the origins of the more recently constructed roads in this area is, therefore, most revealing and provides glimpses of the five ancient roads of Tara emerging from the mists of time and history.

Our generation lived through a period of great change, during which the Ireland of old interfaced with the new progressive Ireland – its passing signals the end of a particular era, people being more mobile nowadays, the acquisition of local knowledge is becoming increasingly difficult. I consider, therefore, that we are but paying our debt to posterity by relaying such folklore to future generations.

## The Barony Maps

These maps were first compiled during the Down Survey of 1645/1646 (conducted by Sir William Petty); the purpose of which survey being to map the lands, seized following the rebellion of 1641; so that they could be reassigned to soldiers and mercenaries of the Parliamentarian Army for services rendered during the said rebellion. The two maps show parts of the Baronies of Lower Deece and Skreen, through which passed most of the routes covered in this book – these maps have an East/West – West/East orientation. On an historical footnote, legend says that in ancient times, the tribes who inhabited the Baronies of Upper and Lower Deece had a dispute with the High King of Tara and were expelled to East Munster – thus giving rise to the nickname *The Deise*.

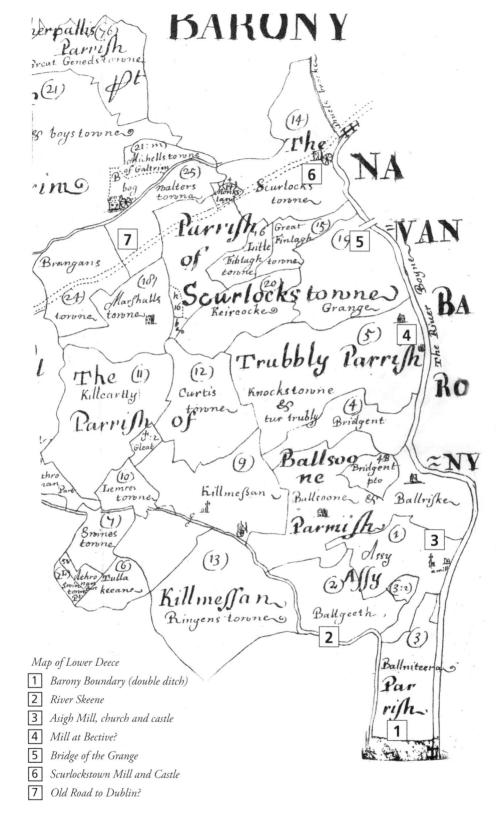

# BARONY

The NA VAN BA RO NY

verpallis (76)
Parrish
Great. Genedstowne
(21)
boystowne
(21: m)
Michellstowne
of Galtrim
bog (25)
malters towne
Monks land
Scurlocks towne

(14)
The
6

Parrish
of
Scurlockstowne
7
Brangans
(18)
Marshalls towne
(24)
towne
h 16
Keircocke
Scurlocks towne Grange

16 Great Finlagh
Litle Fihlagh towne towne
(15)
19 5

4

The
Killcartly
Parrish
of
(11)
(12)
Curtis towne
Killmessan

Trubbly Parrish
Knockstowne & tur trubly
Bridgent
(5)
(4)

H. 2 Gleab
(10)
Liemres towne
(9)
Killmessan
Ballsoo
ne
Bridgent pto
4 B
Ballsoone & Ballriske
Parmish
(7)
Sroines towne
(1)
3

(6)
Athro Tulla Sroinan towne keeane pt
(13)
Killmessan
Ringens towne
Assy
(2) Assy
(3:2)
Ballgeeth
1

2

(3)
Ballniteera
Par rish
1

## Map of Lower Deece

1  Barony Boundary (double ditch)
2  River Skeene
3  Asigh Mill, church and castle
4  Mill at Bective?
5  Bridge of the Grange
6  Scurlockstown Mill and Castle
7  Old Road to Dublin?

Map of Skreen Barony

1. Later Day site of Oak Lodge
2. Philips Town – site of Moate and Bailey unearthed in 2006
3. Skane Gabhra confluence
4. Philpotstown Castle?
5. Ancient Road to Dublin via Trevet

# 1

# The Road From Scurlockstown to The Well of the Deenes

The road from Trim or *Baille Ath Troim, The Ford of the Elder Tree,* to Duleek, followed several different routes in times past. Nowadays in 2007/9, with the exception of a few realignments here and there, the route is much the same as it was during my youth. Previous to the realignment of the section between Newtown and Connell's Cross (Bective Cross); the main route followed the Navan road and passed over the old railway bridge near Newtown (Peterstown Bridge) spanning the now defunct railway line from Kilmessan to Trim and Athboy: it turns southwards at Connell's Cross and crosses the Boyne at Bective Bridge. Taking a left turn in the village and running through Balsoon, Asigh (Assey) and Bellinter, the route continues onwards through Dowdstown and Philpotstown Cross (Garlow Cross), the Decoy and Walterstown. From here it passes through Mountown (Monkstown) and wends its way along the valley of Slanduff (The Black Glen or Dark Slope) to Black Lion and Balrath Cross. Crossing the River Nanny on the triple arched Ballymagarvey Bridge; it runs past the old mills and onwards to the White Cross and the Well of the Deenes to Duleek.

This route is part of what we came to know as the Trim to Drogheda road and I assumed the road always passed this way. Research shows otherwise and reveals that at least three other main routes were used during different periods. The present day route evolved over many years and came into being because of three major developments dispersed over one hundred and fifty years. These included inter alia construction of Bective Bridge across the Boyne, building a new road and bridge over the Rivers Skane (Skein) and Gabhra at Dowdstown and major realignments to the road network between Bellinter and Black Lion – more details of these are included in later chapters.

John O'Donovan's letters and field notes of 1836 contain several references to another main route between these towns, which traversed the following course. Starting from Trim it followed the route of the Dublin turnpike road (towards the Blackbull) to Batterjohn crossroads (Big) or what is nowadays the Grange Farm crossroads. Here it joined the main route from Summerhill to Drogheda, which ran eastwards, crossed Dunsany Bridge over the River Skane near the Black Lodge and passed through Dunsany village, Ross Cross, Oberstown and onwards to Rathfeigh. From here on I'm uncertain of the route, but it may have continued on through Timoole (Tymoole) and rejoined the present day line near Nanny Bridge. Alternatively, as the main Dublin to Slane road then ran through Rathfeigh and Somerville Demesne, the Trim to Drogheda road could have joined it at Rathfeigh and ran northwards to rejoin the main route at Black Lion (Burtonstown). Further details of the road from Batterjohn to Rathfeigh are included in chapter 14. Another and older route, mentioned in the Grand Jury records, was via Peterstown to Bective crossroads (Connell's Cross), then through Cannistown, across Kilcarn Bridge to Johnstown and onwards to Kentstown. I will discuss various aspects of these other routes where they interface with the main route under discussion.

In earlier years, previous to the construction of the bridge over the River Boyne at Bective in the late 17th or early 18th century, it's likely that one of the main routes ran from Scurlockstown to Bective and onwards to Duleek. It is said that this road was part of a main route between Athlone and Drogheda. There is evidence that a road passed this way in earlier times – Oliver Cromwell's marauding armies reputedly travelled this way to Trim following the sacking of Drogheda. The road then would have been vastly different to the route as previously described.

The present day Bellinter crossroads and Dowdstown Bridge didn't exist, nor did Philpotstown Crossroads (Garlow Cross), the 'new Walterstown crossroads' or Balrath crossroads – the roads then followed the traditional routes of the ancient *Slighte,* many of them running along the ridges and not in the valleys like nowadays. Thus the way was most likely narrow and winding with many steep hills, unsuitable, therefore, for the larger wagons and carriages coming into increasing usage. The following chapters outline some of the many changes, which occurred on and alongside this road over the centuries.

Thankfully, the highways and byways weren't always used for warlike purposes and to inflict mayhem on the populace, as was their supposed usage during the Cromwellian and Williamite wars – they were the focus of much more pleasant and less bloody occupations from time to time. During the 1840s, Sir William Wilde, father of Oscar Wilde, travelled parts of this route whilst writing his famous book *The Beauties of the Boyne and the Blackwater,* a marvellous descriptive work of the area and its historical sites.

HANLON

*Scurlockstown Castle - Built circa 1180 - a towerhouse of the pale. From a woodcut depicted in William Wilde's* The Beauties of the Boyne and Blackwater *(1849)*

# 2

# A Coach Journey in Olden Times

To illustrate how I visualise the route of long ago, at this juncture let us take an imaginary trip along the road in times past. Commencing our journey in the summertime of 1790 and journeying from Trim to Scurlockstown crossroads; then travelling eastward to Duleek. The distance is about twelve Irish miles and our conveyance is a small coach drawn by two horses.

Leaving Trim we passed the ruins of an old monastery near St. Peter's Bridge, which crossed the River Boyne at Newtown, where, downstream of this ancient edifice we observed a corn mill on the riverbank to the left of our road. Immediately adjacent was a tuck mill, the loud thumping of whose wooden hammers could be heard above the clip-clopping of the horses' hooves upon the dusty road. About a mile from the town we drove by the racecourse on our right, then past the water mill to the west of the road – its overshot wheel driven by the waters of the Knightsbrook River. Nearby was an old church and motte on our left, with another mill on the Boycetown River standing out in the foreground. In the background the dark bulk of Scurlockstown Castle overshadowed the entire area – this memento of a bygone era, an ancient *watchtower of the Pale,* commanding the nook formed by the big bend in the River Boyne. The great loop in the river resembling a crooked elbow embracing these three relics from different epochs of history. Arriving at the crossroads we turned left, heading eastwards along the beautiful banks of the Boyne.

The narrow road wound between the castle on the right and the mill on the Boycetown River down below us in the river valley and almost on the Boyne's Banks. Scurlockstown Castle stood on the edge of the road and towered above it in menacing fashion – the gaunt stone structure, with its cracked eastern wall, cast a dark shadow over the road on the bright warm day. Shivering in the sudden chill whilst passing through its gloomy shade and gazing up at the few narrow embrasures overlooking the road, I wondered what dark deeds were perpetrated there since its construction in the 1180s. Thankfully, this was but a brief interlude on a lovely sunny day and soon we were back out in the bright sunshine once more, travelling on the banks of the river towards Grange, where once an ancient bridge spanned the Boyne.

Our road passed close to the big river, it dipped into a little vale, crossed a small brook and climbing the far bank headed slightly away from the Boyne. We passed a hill known as *Cromwell's Hill* and wondered at the name. Now the ruins of Trubley Castle loomed to our left – perched upon the banks of the Boyne close by the castle were the remains of a small church. Then we crossed a brook known as the Versheen River, flowing from a townland whose name translates to *the town of the plovers*, the stream passed beneath the road and powered a small mill ere mingling with the Boyne waters below Bective Bridge. The small townland of Ballina (Ballyna) lay between our road and the Boyne, whilst directly to the south was the famous *Fair Green* of Bective, with several thatched buildings clinging to its southern edge. Then we came to the crossroads of Bective or Bridgend, around which clustered a number of houses forming a hamlet known as Bective village.

The village was fair sized, sitting astride the main road from Ballbraddagh to Kilmessan – about thirty stone and mudwalled thatched dwellings were scattered around, with many of them forming a street leading down to the bridge over the Boyne; the outline of the old Cistercian Abbey on its northern bank providing a medieval backdrop to the scene. Though a fine hostelry overlooked the crossroads we didn't tarry long, our coachman being anxious to reach our destination ere the dark shades of evening fell; we bade farewell to this picturesque place and continued eastwards towards our destination.

The road meandered through many curves and between high hawthorn hedgerows – we passed near the old church and ruins of Balsoon Castle to the left and close to the riverbank. Topping a hill we saw the remains of another *watchtower of the Pale* close by the ruins of an ancient church: this place was named Asigh (Assey) or *The Ford of Sighe*, an ancient crossing place of the Boyne. Nearby, where the road wound through a little vale, a laneway led off to the right, passing along what appeared to be the remains of an esker. Crossing a small stream we climbed again and travelled between some flat pastures before entering the darkly wooded expanse of the demesne at Bellinter. Now we caught our first glimpse of the Hill of Tara; a low hill off to our right, the tip of the tree-clad hilltop could be seen above the great woods lining the valley to the south.

For some distance our coach drove beneath the shade of the overhanging trees, growing in profusion along the grassy banks on both sides – the bright sunlight penetrating through the dappling leaves giving a delightful display of colourful light and shade, the likes of which I had seldom seen. Having passed the entrance gates, we observed the bulk of Bellinter House through the trees to our left. The house was designed by Richard Castle and built for John Preston in the 1750s, grandfather of the present owner, another John Preston.

Now we were driving along the valley of the River Skein, enclosed on the northside by the road and the Bellinter Woods and on the southside by the dark menacing looking stretch of the Cluide Wood and the great deal woods over by Balgeeth. We drove on for a mile or so along the banks of the meandering Skein, until the stream veered off to the south and away from the road – then we came to the mearing between Bellinter Demesne and Dowdstown. This boundary comprised a deep ditch to the west and a high stone wall on the Dowdstown side, it was built rather like a haw haw or sunken fence; through which a gap of a few perches permitted the onward passage of our road.

Passing through the opening in the great wall, we left the woods of Bellinter behind and entered the open parklands of General Taylor's estate in Dowdstown. Now we had a magnificent view of Tara, the famed hill together with The Hill of Skreen, commanded the flat plain hereabouts and were the only significant eminences to be seen from the coach. The road remained on the firmer higher ground above the swampy river valley and gradually swung to the northeast towards Dowdstown Hill. In a little graveyard on the hilltop could be seen the old ruined Cistercian Church standing out clearly in the bright sunlight. Our immediate destination was the Dublin to Navan turnpike road, a threadlike track winding its way by the churchyard towards Kilcarn.

We came upon the turnpike at a forked junction, just before crossing the old stone arched bridge spanning the waters of the rivers Skein and Gabhra, which mingled a short distance upstream. This was a beautiful spot, a place of shady wooded nooks and rippling water, profuse in wildlife and birdsong; where the clip-clopping of horses's hooves echoed from the stone walls of the ancient bridge to blend with and enhance the harmony of the scene. Driving along the smoother and wider highway was a luxury indeed compared to the bumpy ride along the road from Bective. Alas, our newfound comfort was short-lived, as we soon came upon the road junction just below the ancient churchyard; where the turnpike road joined the other highway from Dublin that ran through Ratoath and Skryne. Turning to the right and leaving the turnpike, we set off eastward along an equally bumpy road traversing the flank of the ridge and heading towards Skryne.

A spectacular vista unfolded as we departed the valley of the three rivers, where the Hill of Tara commanded a pastoral scene of great beauty, appealing to the eye and refreshing to the spirit of the traveller. Beyond the ridge, our coach continued eastward towards Lismullin in the Gabhra valley, which was overlooked by the Hill of Skryne. Next we topped a small knoll and descended towards Garlagh Cross, which nestles in a little glen beneath Clonardran.

This was a *four road* crossroads, the road to the left leading back to the turnpike at Dowdstown – en route passing a junction with the Gilltown road, which branched to the right and continued on past Gerrardstown Castle towards Slane. The way straight-ahead was but a rough track and unsuitable for the coach. Our route now was part of the Dublin road through Skryne, which veered to the right at the old crossroads and took the traveller through Lismullin towards the Hill of Skryne. Turning to the right past the old Inn by the bridge, we drove on towards Lismullin, or 'the fort of the mill'.

The Skryne road wended its way through a wooded glen, home to the stream known as the River Gabhra – a little river of great significance to lovers of ancient Irish folklore. We passed an old Smithy opposite a little laneway leading to the mill from which the district derived its name. This mill stood on the banks of the Gabhra, directly across the stream from *the hill of the fox, or Cnoc an t-Sionnaigh* and was reputedly built by Cormac Mac Airt, the High King in Tara. The mill was powered by water from the River Gabhra, which was diverted through a headrace and clearly visible from our road. The mill was still in use grinding corn, as evidenced by the number of grain-laden carts trundling along the roads. Passing through the wooded glen, we emerged at a crossroads where the road from Tara left the demesne of Lismullin and crossed the Skryne road. Here we turned left, driving up the same road supposedly travelled by King Billy one hundred years previously following his victory at the Battle of the Boyne in 1690. At the Decoy of Lismullin we came upon the other end of the muddy laneway leading up from Garlagh Cross and turned right to continue our journey towards Duleek.

The coach was heading directly east again and passing over several small streams and some low rolling hills. Beyond the Decoy, our road swung to the right and climbed gradually to the ridge top that commanded a view across the valley leading to Mountown and Slanduff. We passed close by a local manor house and hamlet in Belgeeth and shortly thereafter a small laneway to the left led to another hamlet known as Glean Uaigneach, or 'the lonely Glen'. The narrow road climbed higher over the ridge and then descended into the valley to the crossroads at Cusackstown.

Two roads formed a *four way crossroads* in the picturesque little glen; where a hamlet comprising of a roadside Inn and some dwellings straddled the brook. In the near distance an old ruined castle brooded over the little vale, yet another former *watchtower of the Pale*, but now with no sentry on the parapets; its empty windows and doorways open to the elements. We drove across the hump backed stone arched bridge spanning the stream and pulled up at the Inn. Whilst the horses were being fed and watered we entered the cool shade of the hostelry and partook of boiled mutton and quaffed some ale – then boarded the coach and set off on the road to Duleek once more.

From the brook side Inn at Cusackstown, the roadway climbed a steep hill and headed eastward along the ridge forming the southern rim of Slanduff valley. Soon our coach passed by a narrow laneway on the left leading to a house and some offices nestled in the middle of the long glen – these buildings were located some distance east of the old church and graveyard of Mountown. Further on we could see the ancient Rath and ruined church in Danestown graveyard across the valley – the old church supposedly dated from Norman times with the Rath being a relic of more ancient times. Continuing on, our route crossed a little road leading from Ranaghan to Kentstown, then followed the high ground towards the woods of Somerville and the main highway from Dublin to Slane. Descending again and crossing a stone arched bridge over a small stream, we sped through a hamlet and passed a mudwalled chapel on our left – then, emerging from the shady woods we came upon the great road to the north at the crossroads by the Black Lion Inn.

The Inn stood on the southeastern corner of the crossroads and was a fine hostelry with a freshly thatched roof, its yellow straw gleaming brightly in the strong sunshine. A squeaky sign swinging above the front door portrayed a rampant black lion and proclaimed in bold white lettering that this was indeed the famous Black Lion Inn.

We did not tarry here but crossed the great road and wound our way down the hill into the valley, passing by the ruined church of Ballymagarvey where we traversed the Nanny water on a wide triple arched stone bridge. For some distance our way now followed a twisty path through the swampy valley of the River Nanny – the erratic course of the road being to take advantage of the higher ground. The route crossed a twin arched skewed stone bridge spanning a millrace and headed into a tree shaded glade. Near a junction with a narrow lane leading off to the north, we passed a big water powered mill close by the right hand side of the road and near the riverbank. The millrace running to the south side of the road led to the mill and powered its big undershot waterwheel, which could be heard thumping and splashing as we passed by. To the left a large stone windmill peeped through the trees, its four huge sails turning lazily in the gentle summer breeze.

Further on, topping a hill we came upon the White Cross standing by the roadside opposite a small laneway leading to Athcarne Castle off to the south. Shortly thereafter, our coach arrived at the junction where the well of the Deenes lay hidden beneath the roadway. The adjoining road led to the south and crossed the Nanny on the Bridge of the Deenes, located just downstream from where the Herley River had its confluence with the Nanny. Here we disembarked and met our friends at the crossroads. The coachman drove on to seek lodgings in Duleek whilst we mounted horses provided by our friends and set off to complete our journey along some bridle paths and country lanes.

The journey just described is fictitious, merely a figment of my imagination and it's told in the idiom of today rather than of times past. But the described route derives from extensive study of maps, local knowledge and much research. People familiar with the area will notice that I omitted some features of the present day route – the reason for the omissions is simple, they didn't exist in 1790. In the following chapters I will discuss and analyse the route, section by section.

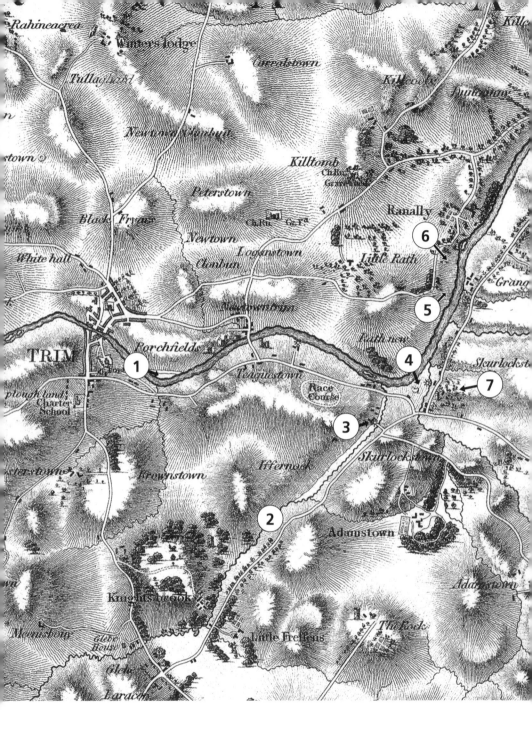

Larkin's No. 1 (Items 1 to 7)

1. Magee's Island
2. Knightsbrook Bridge
3. Knock Mills
4. Scurlockstown Mill (Cassidys)
5. Bridge of the Grange
6. Rathnally Mill
7. Scurlockstown Castle

# 3

# From Trim via Scurlockstown to Bective

The Drawbridge and Magee's Island – Keely's and Smart's Weirs and Boyne Canal – Peter's Town and the abbey – Knightsbrook River and bridge – Knock Mills – Scurlockstown Castle, church and mill – the ancient bridge at Grange and Tribley (Trubley) Railway Bridge – Rathnally Flourmill and canal locks – Cromwell's Hill and Tribley Castle – Harvey's Mill and the town of the plovers.

During my younger days I was involved in amateur cycle racing for a number of years and so became familiar with the road between Scurlockstown and Trim. Oftentimes of a summer's evening following our day's work, I met with several other members of the cycling club and went for a training spin. One of our favourite routes was a circuit comprising of the road from Navan to the Blackbull Bridge and from there to Trim via Scurlockstown and onwards to Navan, returning home to Dowdstown by old Kilcarn Bridge and Garlow Cross; the round trip being a distance of about forty miles. This route became known to most cyclists of the period as *going around the bull*, and, together with various members of Navan Road Club, I rounded the bull many times during those days. When training for shorter races, we used the triangular circuit alongside the Porch Field and around by Newtown Bridge, sprinting up the hill by Regan's pub at the old bridge, then turning left near the now defunct railway bridge (Peterstown Bridge) on the Navan road and back

*'The Drawbridge' - Porch Field, Trim, 2009*

around by Trim. Some evenings we might complete this circuit up to twenty times and became so exhausted that we were scarcely able to turn the pedals to ride back home. Hence, I came to know the area well and developed a great fondness for the place.

In 1968, following completion of *An Ras Tailteann* in which event I rode for the County Louth team, we took part in one of the early Olympiads held in the yard of the old mill at Iffernock on the Knightsbridge River. Following the cycling event and other sporting activities, a shindig was held in the yard and a great time was had by all. It was such a novel occasion I still recall the event forty years later.

But I have digressed a bit down memory lane, so back to the main objective – the discussion of the old road between this enchanting place and the village of Bective.

First I'll give a brief description of the once beautiful section of the River Boyne, alongside which the road to Scurlockstown runs for about a mile and a half. Several years ago a bridge was built to carry a new ring road across the river just below the castle in Trim. Looking downstream from this bridge, a single stone arch can be seen standing on the riverbank and people wonder what its purpose was in times past. This little structure is known locally as *The Drawbridge*, but it had nothing to do with the nearby castle, being once part of the uncompleted section of the Boyne Navigation Canal intended as a water transport link between the towns of Navan and Trim. The drawbridge provided access to a tiny portion of land (1.408 acres) referred to colloquially as *Magee's Island* – it was located on the opposite side of the Boyne to the Maudlins. The tiny islet being formed by a short section of canal, cut to bypass a weir called Smart's Weir, which in olden times diverted the Boyne's waters to power a Tuck and Corn Mill of the same name. This canal section had a two-lock system designated as number eight lock.

The number seven lock on the system was located further downstream, below Newtown Bridge: this lock bypassed Keely's Weir, which provided water to Keely's Tuck and Corn Mill. I believe that a family, named O'Keefe, were the last operators of Keely's mill, supposedly they moved to Athboy to help Newmans start up the mill there at the turn of the 19th century. The seventh lock provided access to a section of canal that ran alongside the northern bank of the Boyne to Rathnally. Here another lock, known locally as Brennan's Lock, provided access to the river a short distance downstream of the long gone railway bridge at Tribley. This section of canal bypassed the fishing weir at Iffernock and another located downstream of Scurlockstown, which I believe was known as Dunganny Weir. The 1837 OS map shows details of the old canal and the weirs on the river – in the 1840s, however, the O.P.W. commenced a drainage scheme that led to the destruction of many old weirs. In the 1970s, the same far-seeing public body completed the destruction by obliterating most traces of the weirs and the canal locks. This included filling in the section of canal isolating the piece of land known as Magee's Island, which explains why the single crumbling stone arch stands forlornly at the bottom of the Porch Field – high and dry alongside the ever flowing Boyne and providing access to nowhere in particular. More details of the old canal system are included later in the chapter in the section dealing with Rathnally.

The bridge at Newtown (formerly Peter's Town) is one of the oldest Boyne crossings still in use today – whilst unsure of its exact age, I believe it was built sometime in the 14th century. At the time of writing, surrounding the bridge and on both sides of the river are the ruins of an ancient monastery: as an indicator of progress and present day appreciation of the once beautiful landscape, a modern sewage treatment plant graces the western bank. Here, in 1206, Simon de Rockfort founded an Abbey of Canons Regular of the Order of Saint Victor; in doing so he transferred the *See of Clonard* to this beautiful spot by the River Boyne. The monastic settlement was named the Abbey of Saint Peter and Saint Paul, it flourished and supposedly became one of the wealthiest institutions in the land: in 1486 its Prior, Thomas Scurlock, became the order's treasurer for all of Ireland. The monastery was suppressed by King Henry VIII around 1540 and subsequently fell into ruins. In my opinion, the construction of the sewage works in such an historic and beautiful place is a testament to official attitudes towards our heritage.

Further on towards Scurlockstown, on the right hand side of the road in a place named Teagucstown, Larkin's Map of 1812-1817 shows an oval shaped track which it names as a racecourse. Next we come to a little bridge spanning the Knightsbrook River or the Glearnog – the smaller river falls into the Boyne to the left of the road just before Scurlockstown crossroads. From where it rises close to Kilmore, near *The Hatchet* (an ancient Inn on the road between Summerhill and Dunboyne), the stream had several names, both in times past and at present. These include the Moynalvey River, the Clonymeath River and the Dangan River, finally becoming the Knightsbrook as it meanders through that district. This multi-naming of rivers was a common enough feature in the rural landscape of old, especially when the benefits of satellite photography weren't available. It has been the source of much contention from time to time and given rise to many a heated discussion around firesides in olden times; possibly being the cause of an occasional faction fight in the days when such sports were popular.

The ruined mill, where the Scurlockstown Olympiad was held in recent years, was a thriving local industry at one time – this was one of the few watermills on the Boyne catchment system powered by an overshot wheel. Larkin's Map shows the headrace for this mill running alongside the river from about a half mile upstream beside 'the Rock Road', where it's taken from the main river course. The 1837 OS map also shows the long headrace, together with a weir, artificial lakes and a complex series of water channels close to Knightsbrook House, these would appear to be part of the water supply to the nearby mills. A bridge is shown on the OS map at the easternmost end of the lake system– this bridge is nowadays known as the Knightsbrook Bridge and consists of seven stone built arches, which mostly span dry land. It's a very unusual structure, with the arches varying in size and of tricentred construction. The old bridge is approximately five feet wide and has a parapet wall on the downstream side, which reduces its passage width to just over three feet. Some suggest that it was either a footbridge or perhaps a bridge for packhorses, though the narrowness of the passage would seem to be unsuitable for the latter purpose. Its origin is uncertain, but legend says that it was once part of an ancient right of way leading into the town of Trim. Like many such structures in Ireland, the bridge is in poor condition, if measures are not taken to preserve this relic of the past, pretty soon it too will become another pile of rocks lying in a field or end its days with the stones adorning some modern progressive development!

The elevated headrace explains how the water head was obtained to power the overshot wheel. The mill is set well back from the old turnpike road and is accessed by a laneway leading off the road to Laracor – of Dean Swift fame (the Rock Road). The 1837 OS map indicates that this lane ran on and joined the turnpike road at a crossroads near Newtown. A study of Griffith's valuation of 1854 shows two separate mills in operation at Iffernock in that year. One was a corn mill worked by John Shiel, this mill being part of a property of just over nine acres, the rateable valuation of which was £63 per annum. The other was a flourmill that stood on a little over two acres and was operated by Richard Keefe; this enterprise had an annual rateable valuation of £80. The valuation report doesn't indicate which mill was located where, except that both were in Iffernock. The 1837 OS map names the mills at this location as 'The Knock Mills' and shows the buildings, together with a mill dam.

On the Boyne nearby, Larkin's Map of 1812 shows one mill, while the OS map of 1837 indicates two mills at the same location. These were sited to the left of the old turnpike road, opposite the racecourse and on the riverbank downstream of Newtown Bridge at the former site of the previously mentioned Keeley's Weir. Both mills were accessed by a laneway leading from the main road. On the OS map one mill is named a corn mill and the other a tuck mill (*see description of tuck, or fulling mills, in chapter thirteen*).

At Scurlockstown crossroads another small stream flows under the road and eastwards into the Boyne close by the road to Bective. This watercourse is known as the Boycetown River, it rises to the southeast over near Culmullin (the corner of the mill J.O.D 1836) and on its route to Scurlockstown is named the Derrypatrick River for some distance along its meandering course. After passing under the road at the crossroads the stream flows on by the ancient church and motte then into the bigger river. Close to its confluence with the Boyne stood a corn mill, which was driven by the waters of the smaller river – this was known as Scurlockstown mill. Griffith's valuation shows that in 1854 Thomas Cassidy operated the mill. The premises consisted of a house, a corn mill, a kiln, offices and 15 acres 2 roods 26 perches of land, with a rateable valuation of £27. Local folklore says that there were two millwheels at this mill – perhaps an explanation can be found for the legend on the 1837 OS map, which shows two sets of buildings on the site and marks the location as Corn Mills.

While researching and writing his famous book *The Beauties of the Boyne and Blackwater*, Sir William Wilde travelled along this section of road in the 1840s. In the book, Sir William mentions another motte in this nook of the Boyne Valley and states that it was dug out for *manuring* the local fields – with the remains of the central chamber or Kisvaen being the only reminder of its former presence. In earlier days, manuring was done by using limestone gravel, the main building material used in many of these ancient mottes or forts. Unfortunately, throughout the years a great number of the ancient Raths all over the countryside were destroyed in this manner; especially on the nearby Hill of Tara.

The ruined church and graveyard in the nook by the bend in the Boyne are very old. Reputedly Walter de Lacy, a relative of Hugh de Lacy, built the church in the 12th century on the site of a more ancient church. Later it was granted to Saint Thomas's Abbey in Dublin in the early 13th century. During his travels Sir William Wilde remarks on the ruins and notes the circular chancel arches and the remains of a very ancient stone cross, which at the time was used as a headstone in the cemetery.

At the crossroads stands a hostelry, which in older days I seem to recall was thatched. It was later owned by the famous Meath footballer, Jack Quinn – many people refer to the place as Jack Quinn's Cross. Turning left here and heading eastwards towards Bective we come upon the place where the dark bulk of Scurlockstown castle once towered above the road. Because I have been unable to find much information readily available I'm reliant on Sir William Wilde's description of this old towerhouse, or *watchtower of the Pale* and its condition when he travelled the road in 1849. Larkin's Map, the OS map of 1837 and the sketch map in Sir William's book all show the site of the castle to the right of the road, about halfway between the crossroads and the place where the railway line from Kilmessan ran in later years. This was opposite the little laneway leading down to the previously mentioned corn mill(s) (Cassidy's mill), which stood close to the Boyne on the Boycetown River. Not a trace of the castle remains today and I can't discover what happened to the structure or when it was demolished; it would seem to have vanished into thin air. History records its construction in 1180 by William de Scallog, an Anglo-Norman Fief of Meath, but it does not show who removed the old building or why. Sir William mentioned that the eastern wall was cracked from top to bottom and that this was supposedly caused by 'the balls of Cromwell', whose army, legends say, met stiff resistance here on their way to deal with Trim in the wars following the rebellion of 1641. I notice that he didn't mention anything about cannons, but assume 'the balls' referred to are cannon balls. He states that the castle was a Donjon, or square keep, with round towers on the diagonal corners and that many of the stone floors (barrel vaulted) were in good repair. The accompanying woodcut engraving would seem to suggest that the castle was build diagonally to the road.

The 1650s Down Survey Barony of Lower Deece map depicts some interesting features in the vicinity of Scurlockstown. The Knightsbrook River appears to be named Druels Brooke, perhaps this was the name of the Knight after whom the district was named – a mill and castle are indicated in the approximate area of Scurlockstown Castle and Cassidy's Mill. The name of the River Skane, which forms much of the boundary with the adjoining Barony of Screen (Skreen), is spelled Skeine or Skeene and fords are shown on this river at Kilmessan and Athronan (further details about the derivation of this river's name are noted in chapter 10). The Boycetown River's source is shown as a bog in a place named

*Galtrim and Boystown* – two fords and a castle are also indicated on this stretch of river. But the most interesting feature, vis a vis the subject of ancient roads, is a double row of dotted lines running from Trim through Scurlockstown and Kiltale then on to Knockmark (Drumree or Drumry) towards the edge of the Barony near Dunboyne. I would suggest that these lines represent the path of an ancient road – the turnpike road from the Black Bull to Trim appears to have been built upon the same line, which is almost the exact line of the present day road. As a further point of interest, the Taylor and Skinner map of 1778 indicates that the turnpike from the Black Bull to Trim was part of the main route from Dublin to Granard and Sligo via Athboy and Finae (Finnae).

About a quarter mile past the former site of the castle, we come to where the railway bridge once crossed both the river and the road – this was known as Tribley (Trubley) Bridge and I remember it well. It was of latticed cast iron construction, resting on stone abutments on the riverbanks and stone piers in the river. In my youth I helped my father and my brother Tom drive cattle home from the market in Trim, on the way we passed under the old railway bridge: then drove them along the road and over through Bective to Lismullin. At the time, the narrow road descended a hill to the river's edge under the bridge – there it rounded the big stone abutment which formed a sharp blind corner, it then curved to the right again and climbed up to the higher ground. The River Boyne flowed under the bridge in close proximity to the low wall by the roadside. Reaching over this wall we could touch the water as it rolled lazily by. The passing traffic had to almost stop to round the blind corner and a few collisions occurred here over the years; I can only imagine what it would be like nowadays in the mad hustle and bustle of the present day. Nonetheless it was a peaceful little place, with the combination of the rippling river, the dappling shade of the overhanging trees and the ever-present birdsong providing very pleasant surroundings in which to spend a few moments of our boyhood years. Upon the railway closing down in the early 1960s, the bridge was dismantled and sold for scrap. The so-called visionaries of the time couldn't see any need for railways in the future: according to these 'experts', railways were an anachronism and surplus to requirements, road transport was definitely the way to go in the future.

Nowadays, with the evolving nightmare of traffic-clogged roads and cities, similarly dim sighted 'visionaries' preach that construction of motorways will provide the panacea for our travelling woes; the solution to all our transport problems. Should we believe these Guru's of transport planning whose predecessors called it so wrong in the past? I'm told that during the destruction of the railway a great number of old disused railway carriages were stored on the section of track between Kilmessan and Trim. These, being scrapped later at the railway yards in Kilmessan, were to be seen in many cottage gardens thereafter – being used as sheds or garages for the increasingly popular motorcars of the era. The road was diverted onto its present route, which runs a short distance up from the abutment on the southern bank: most likely it was the original route before the coming of the railway one hundred years earlier. How things go around and around and finish up in the same place.

If one wishes to see some of the stones that once formed part of the old Tribley railway bridge, a trip should be taken along the road from Dunderry towards Navan to a forked junction a short distance out from Dunderry village. To the left of the roadside stands a stone wall beside a house entrance, this wall is built from stones first crafted by long dead stonemasons to build the pillars and abutments of Tribley Bridge. They were *rescued* a few years after the bridge was demolished and put to good use, a fine memento of times past. For those who are not old enough to recall the location of Tribley railway bridge, at time of writing a quaint looking model house with red doors and windows stands by the roadside

*Tribley Railway Bridge (Upstream elevation)*

35

marking the place where the old line of road swung down towards the Boyne. This house was constructed by a local woman named Annie Kelly.

Nearby and downriver from the spot where the railway bridge crossed the Boyne lies an area known as Grange or Grangeboyne. In times past a Grange was a granary or storehouse (barn), a place where corn was handled in harvest time – these were generally located on farms associated with the monastic establishments of the area. In some places the entire monastic farm was known as a Grange. The Grange near Scurlockstown is believed to have been part of the nearby religious establishments in Trim, the yellow steeple, supposedly so named because of the colour of the stonework during sunset. Another place named Grange is situated close by, this was part of the Cistercian Abbey at Bective and is known as Grange Bective. Throughout the countryside are many places with this name, either as a stand-alone name or part of another longer title for a townland or district.

In olden times one of the earliest bridges to span the River Boyne was supposedly built at the Grange near Scurlockstown. Not a trace remains of this ancient bridge nor has there been such for many years – the Down Survey County and Barony Maps of the 1640s/1650s and Petry's map of 1685 indicate the bridge, but because of the poor scaling it's difficult to be precise about the location. None of the other old maps show this structure, but there's a clue in the road network in the area. Should the 1837 OS map and the latest Discovery maps be studied carefully, it can be observed that the road from Trim to Rathnally on the northside of the river has a 'T' junction near Littlerath, one leg of the 'T' ends in a cul de sac. This truncated leg of the road leads in the direction of the Boyne and towards the supposed location of the ancient bridge. Beyond the Grange and on the other side of the river, a couple of cul de sac roads lead off the road from Kilmessan to Pike Corner and pass through Curtistown and Creroge towards the Boyne at Grange. Perhaps these were once connecting links to the ancient bridge – or maybe the said bridge only linked the Scurlockstown/Bective road to Rathnally and Trim. Larkin's Map shows a cluster of buildings on the banks of the Boyne close to the location where the southern end of the bridge may once have been.

Though there is now no trace of the old structure, an official written record remains to show it did exist – this was found in the calendar of state papers for Ireland which referenced events supposed to have taken place during the 'nine year war'. The reference was discovered in a very detailed report from a spy to his paymaster, outlining a proposed invasion of the Pale by the armies of O'Neill and O'Donnell; the report was dated October 1599. It clearly stated that O'Neill's foot soldiers were to cross into the Pale at the bridges of Slane and Kilcarn and O'Donnell's men were to cross the bridge at the Grange, whilst the horses were to use the various fords should they be passable. As history records, the proposed invasion of the Pale never took place at that time – in 1600, O'Neill, with an army of 3000 departed south in an attempt to unite the warring chieftains in Munster, where he was defeated at the Battle of Kinsale in 1601. The record is a very useful marker, identifying as it does the three ungarrisoned Boyne Bridges between Trim and Drogheda and the reference to the horses using the fords would seem to confirm the narrowness of the bridges at the time.

On this stretch of the road there's a steep hill, known colloquially as Cromwell's Hill – local legends say that during the Cromwellian wars, an engagement took place here between some of the defenders of Trim and a detachment of Cromwell's army. The 'butcher of Drogheda' reputedly sent his men along this road to suppress the town of Trim.

From very early times a famous flourmill stood on the riverbank at Rathnally, across the Boyne from Tribley – I'm told that a record exists indicating the presence of a mill on this site since the 14th century. The

*Rathnally Mill, 2009;* left: *The Eastern section,* right: *The Western millwheel*

Master of the Rolls, Sir Thomas Carter, owned the Rathnally estate and mill in times past. The mill and the estate employed a great number of local people and a settlement developed in the area to house the many workers. In the late 18th century an act of Parliament was passed which subsidised the land transport of grain and flour to Dublin: hence a great number of horse drawn wagons plied the roads in the area.

In 2009 I visited the remains of Rathnally Mill, accompanied on this little trip down memory lane by Mickey Morris from Bective, who worked in Rathnally in days of yore. We walked along the Boyne Meadows following the line of the old headrace, but little remains except a small stone arched footbridge that once gave access for the mill workers to operate the sluices. The mill building is mostly intact, but the roof is gone and it's now an empty shell held together with the all-embracing ivy. Both millwheels were undershot, or breastshot, and are still in position but only the metal frames are intact. The main wheel is about twelve feet in diameter and approximately eight feet in width – it's located underneath the easternmost building, with the shaft and part of the broken main crown wheel gearing still in position. The second wheel seems to be of a newer vintage and is approximately fourteen feet in diameter and four feet wide; it's constructed from several 'V' shaped cast iron sections. This wheel is located on the western end wall and is of an overhung design and supported by a thick stone buttress wall, which carried a tail-bearing assembly. None of the gearing is on site for this unit, just a large hexagonal iron shaft about one foot in diameter – I suspect that this wheel was once used to drive a flax scutching mill.

The miller's house is restored and is presently occupied: this house was once the residence of McCannes, the famous family of millers who worked *The Big Mill* at Lower Kilcarn and several other mills in the county. The building that housed the kilns and grain store are still intact but unused at present. The famous walled garden of Rathnally can still be seen, it's located across the road from the mill buildings, but I'm unsure if it is being used. Rathnally House stands in spacious grounds just east of the mill – though it's still in use, I'm unaware of the present owner's name.

Rathnally lies in the heart of a beautiful and pastoral landscape alongside the River Boyne and, as previously stated, the mill was once the epicentre of a thriving community. Legend says that almost two hundred people were employed at the mill, the gardens and the manor house – additionally, hundreds of horses were stabled there, being used at harvesting, equestrian work and as draught animals to haul flour and grain to Dublin. As Mickey and I departed the now deserted scene, I was reminded of Oliver Goldsmith's poem *The Deserted Village*. Which poem decries the depopulation of the English countryside and the village of Auburn – but that was in England of the 1770s and not Rathnally in the new Millennium, one might wonder once again where progress is taking us?

In times past, a skewed weir directed water to the mill via a complex series of sluices – this weir caused the river to be non-navigable, so here again we encounter a section of the unfinished Boyne Navigation Canal. At this location the canal was cut on the Tribley, or south side of the river, to bypass Rathnally weir. This section of the navigation isolated a portion of land (2.348 acres), access to which was provided by a stone arched bridge built over the canal; a lock was located near the eastern end of the cut. The possible intention was to use the Rathnally canal and lock for barges, enroute from the mill at Bective to Navan, to traverse the weir, then cross the river and travel onwards to Trim via Brennan's Lock and the previously described section of the canal to Newtown. All this is now history, the weir, the locks and most remaining traces of the navigation were dug out and buried during the arterial drainage scheme of the 1970s. The only parts of the southside Rathnally lock system now to be readily seen are three coping-stones from the old canal bridge which are sitting in front of Joe Maguire's house in nearby Knocktown. Joe rescued the stones during the destruction of the lock by the O.P.W. and took them up to his house on a Fordson Major tractor. In recent times, while discussing the old canal locks with Joe, he told me that he couldn't drive forward up the steep banks because the stones kept sliding off the buckrake, so he reversed the old tractor up the hill. Joe did a great service for posterity by preserving a piece of our heritage – though but a small gesture in the greater scheme of things, it was more than what the so-called guardians of the landscape did to preserve any memento of a much cherished local place for swimming and recreation in days of yore.

*Ladies on the Boyne - boating at the shallows near Navan circa 1880/1900* (Courtesy D. Halpin)

As a footnote to the Boyne's previous beauty and a requiem to its passing, the devastation caused by the O.P.W's blinkered approach to the Boyne catchment drainage scheme beggars belief. Amongst many other ill effects it deprived local people of recreation facilities from which they benefited for many generations. The once beautiful, island-dotted and salmon-rich-river, tumbling over weirs and meandering through a pastoral landscape was transformed into a canal-like watercourse with fewer fish and much less aesthetic appeal. Many of the tributary rivers are clogged with mud and vegetation and some resemble mere drains. The massive expenditure of money was supposedly to prevent flooding and increase farmable land along the riverbanks. Nowadays our European masters limit by decree the amount of output Irish farmers can produce, and in many cases pay them *not* to farm certain land – flooding will continue until greedy developers and road builders are prevented from building on the floodplains of rivers, so what was it all for?

The onward extension of the Boyne Navigation Canal, from Navan to Trim, was abandoned during the first half of the 19th century. In addition to the previously described sections of the navigation at Rathnally and Trim, in bygone days other traces of the unfinished waterway could be found in Navan, Curraghtown and Robinstown, but these have mostly been removed from the landscape by developments in recent years. I'm told that a field near Robinstown is still named *The Lock Field*. Two stone arched

*Constructing a canal barge at Navan Lightering Yard* (Courtesy D. Halpin)

bridges were built in Navan, one in Bridge Street and the other at Railway Street close by the old Forester's Hall and the Leighsbrook. If my memory serves me well, the unused bridge on Bridge Street had two arches, which were lined with brick, but some people say that there was but a single arch. Local legends tell of the famous sculptor, Thomas Curry, working under these arches whilst sculpting the ornamental stonework for Saint Mary's Chapel in Navan, these carvings included the Celtic Cross dated 1864, now standing in the church grounds. The famous statue of Saint Patrick, which stands on the Hill of Tara, was supposedly constructed here, it was moulded from concrete and immersed in the Boyne for a period; then transported to Tara. Perhaps this lends a somewhat different and more poignant perspective to the old song *Underneath the Arches*. But *Official Ireland* saw no historical value in this ancient landmark. Like many other items of interest it was officially vandalised – the eye(s) of the former bridge, located on the old Navan to Dublin turnpike road, were filled with numerous tons of concrete and buried during the construction of the inner relief road in the 1970s. The bridge at the Leighsbrook was built up years ago. Some time ago, while work was being carried out on the Circular Road in Navan, a brick-lined section of the canal was unearthed close by the old Spa Fountain; it was reburied following an archaeological examination.

During the heyday of the inland waterways, from the early 18th to the

*Rowley's Lock - Boyne navigation during heavy snow about 1900* (Courtesy D. Halpin)

middle years of the 19th centuries, several plans were drawn up for the onward development of the canal network in Ireland. J. Taylor's engraved *County of Meath* map (1802) shows some of the proposed routes, including: from Dublin to Navan via Johnstown and Kilmoon, Navan to Trim via Robinstown and Navan to Kells, then onwards to Lough Ramour. I believe that the proposed summit level of the Kells section was near *The White Quarry* at Ardbracken. According to J. Taylor's map, the extension to Trim was intended to bypass the town and rejoin the Boyne to the west, near its confluence with the Trimblestown River (Tremblestown). It would seem, therefore, that the partly completed sections, from Trim to Rathnally, may have been intended to provide a water transport link between Bective and Navan, through Trim, possibly joining up with the main canal at Trimblestown. However, it's difficult to visualise how the narrow reach of the river through the town of Trim could have been made navigable, so perhaps the Rathnally section was intended to link with the main canal near Newtown or Peterstown.

The next place of note is Trubley, or Tribley, as we knew it in our youth. This was both a parish and a townland and supposedly named after a family that came here during the early Norman settlements. In his writings of 1836, John O'Donavan refers to the name as follows: *Trubley, a family name of English origin – they came from Glamorganshire to trouble ye Bregians of old* (sic). In pre-Norman Ireland, Brega (Bregia) was an area in the north east of Meath, Ua Cellaig country, which also encompassed some of Louth and much of the Boyne Valley and parts of several bordering counties. Other versions of the Trubley name existed, including Tubberville and Turburvyle. In olden times the turf cutting rights on some bogs were known as 'Turburys', one wonders if this title is connected to the last mentioned name? At one time a castle and church were located here, standing on the high ground above the River Boyne, on the southern side of the river across from Rathnally. The Down Survey Barony Maps show that in the 1650s, a mill was located near Trubly on the riverbank downstream of the castle, but like many other places, not much remains today. Local anecdotes mention that Oliver Cromwell spent a night here while his forces were en route to attack the town of Trim – some historians cast doubts upon these legends and conclude that he was never near Trim, but sent his minions to do his work. The 1837 OS map shows the ruins of the castle and the old church. During his travels in the area, Sir William Wilde concluded that this castle was yet another *watchtower of the Pale* and was similar to Sculockstown and other such castles – in his time the remains of two circular towers were visible together with a well-built dovecote (pigeon house).

Slightly east of Tribley, to the right of the road a laneway leads off to a farmhouse and outbuildings located near the townland of Ballynavaddog (the town of the plovers). At time of writing a family named Bagnall own this farm, but in times past the laneway was called Mackey's Lane. I'm told that located on this property was a small corn mill, known as Harvey's Mill, which mill was powered by the waters of several small streams, possibly collected in a millpond. I cannot find any record of this mill, either on the maps or from other written sources – the only reference to be found being in the folklore of the district. From the descriptions given it would seem that this wasn't a commercial mill, perhaps it produced

*Harvey's Mill on Bagnall's Farm near Bective - 2009*

flour and meal from crops grown by the owners of the large holding; many such local mills existed in times past. On a recent visit to the site I saw the old stone building that housed the mill, though it's in good condition, not a trace remains of the machinery or the millwheel and sluice systems of former days. The stone built structure stands close to a raised embankment, located on its southern side – where a large arched doorway is built on the upper floor level. The aforementioned Joe Maguire said that the mill ceased operation long before his time and added that his father never remembered it as a working mill. Upon bidding farewell to the hospitable Bagnall family, my final thoughts on the location near Ballynavaddog were somewhat in the abstract – I wondered would local folklore ever refer to the old mill laneway as Bagnall's Lane?

At the eastern end of the townland of Trubley we come to an area known as Ballina or Ballyna – this is the western boundary of the area more generally named Bective.

# 4

# Bective and District

Bective Abbey and Clady – Bective or Begteach, The Little Palace – Ballyna; Bridgeend, The Street – Two fairdays, The Fair Green and Spalpins – Horan's Limekiln – Reilly's Pub and the Widow Donegan – Bective Mills and the Turrey Gardens – the Boyne Bridge – The Corpse at Clady Gate and Bolton the Tyrant – Balbradagh, a thievish town and Scab Forges – the Farrier Foley and Eddie McKeever.

As children we visited Bective Abbey on many occasions. This old Cistercian Monastery is situated on the banks of the Boyne over towards Trim and about three miles distant from our house at Dowdstown. The edifice is very old, being built around 1150 and in our childhood days it was pretty ramshackle and run down. Anecdotes said that the roof was removed and many of the stones taken away to build the King's Mills and to reinforce the walls of Trim, then later to construct Bective House. The stones were supposedly taken to Trim during and after the dissolution of the monastery in the sixteenth century (1535) – while the construction of Bective House took place in the early part of the 19th century (around 1830). In the 1960s during our teenage years the abbey was partially restored.

The ancient site being so far away and me so young I was totally

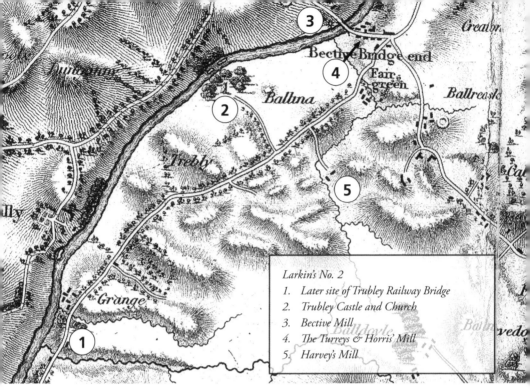

Larkin's No. 2
1. Later site of Trubley Railway Bridge
2. Trubley Castle and Church
3. Bective Mill
4. The Turreys & Horris' Mill
5. Harvey's Mill

dependent on somebody else to carry me along the country road. Sometimes we travelled by pony and trap or by bike and occasionally by shank's mare. If an elder sibling carried me on a bike my usual seat was on the back carrier but while with Dad I mostly rode on the crossbar of his bike. I travelled a lot on Dad's crossbar in those days and learned early on to keep my feet clear of the front wheel spokes.

On our way to Bective we headed over past Bellinter House then passed under the railway bridge at Asigh (Assey) and on by Balsoon and Craystown to Bective village. Turning right at Tutty's (Lynch's) shop and pub, which was thatched then, we went down the steep hill towards the Boyne Bridge. The village supposedly contained over thirty houses in olden times, with the area down towards the bridge known locally as 'the street', the southside of the bridge was also called Bridgend in times past. The old thatched pub was once owned by *The Widow Donegan*, a local legend, and may have been built during the middle years of the eighteenth century.

Having crossed the long narrow bridge over the Boyne and passed the old Bective Mill on the left (still a working mill then) we went on up to the abbey field and entered through a small wicket, set in the old iron gate. The abbey itself is located behind a low boundary wall, with a set of stone steps providing access to the buildings. The old pile commands the grassy slopes high above the Boyne – a beautiful spot with a wonderful view over the surrounding countryside. We spent many happy hours exploring the ruined buildings and climbing the towers, from which eminences our youthful eyes enjoyed the pastoral setting along the Boyne Valley. Below our vantagepoint, traces of the medieval sunken roadway could be seen, heading from the direction of the bridge across the fields towards Mary Lavin's house. To the east we could see Bective House and the old Clady (Claidy) churchyard nearby. Off to the southwest the roof of the mill peeked above the treetops, whilst the ancient Fort or Rath in the higher fields above the valley cast a lengthening shadow in the afternoon sunshine. Later, we crept through the deserted cells of the long gone monks – some of these darkened passageways gave us the creeps and we continually glanced over our shoulders until we emerged back into the sunlight once more. The ancient legend of the burial of Hugh De Lacey's corpse close by was oftentimes recounted around the firesides of old. Of how he was killed at Durrow Castle by having his head chopped off, supposedly by a young man of Teffia named Gillagan O'Megey, in revenge for his despoilation of so many churches. Then the row between the clerics as to where he should be buried, which was reputedly solved in true Irish tradition by burying his torso at Bective and his head at the Abbey of Saint Thomas in Dublin. The story I heard said that because of this separation of head and body, the famous (but very ugly) knight was forevermore destined to wander the darkened corridors and cells of the ancient abbey in search of his missing head. Hence we were scared stiff lest we met his headless corpse treading the gloomy passages. This was but one of many ghostly stories to be heard in the flickering lamplight during the long dark winter nights of yesteryear ere the advent of rural electrification dispelled many ghosts from darkened corners.

When older we walked along the riverbank to Clady Graveyard, an old burial place nestling on the Boyne's green banks at its confluence with the smaller River Clady: Clady or Cladach meaning a river with muddy banks. Close by the ruined church were the remains of several semi-subterranean stone beehive-like structures, supposedly dating back to pagan times. The entrances to these resembled empty eye sockets in a skull and though we sometimes gazed into the darkened spaces beyond the threshold, we dared not enter because these places gave us the creeps. Local legends told of how these ancient crypts connected to the abbey through subterranean corridors, some of which also ran beneath the Boyne to Balsoon Churchyard on the southside of the river. To the east of Clady Churchyard stands an ancient twin arched stone bridge with different sized arches spanning the small river. It's supposedly the oldest stone bridge in Ireland and I'm told it was part of an old public right of way known to some as the circular walk whilst others knew it as the bow walk. The structure is a footbridge approximately four feet wide, with a span of about forty feet across the river. We played around here for a while, running over and back across the narrow grass covered crossing and clambering amongst the ruins, Then returned to the abbey by walking along Bective House avenue to the main gates and around by Connell's Cross.

Some more frolicking ensued beneath the shade of the beech trees growing by the grey walls of the abbey and then it was time to go home – in the gloaming we travelled back over the almost car free road to Dowdstown. Sometimes, upon hearing the rattle and hum of an approaching car, we stopped on the roadside, expectantly awaiting the

*A woodcut of Clady Bridge from William Wilde's book* The Beauties of the Boyne and Blackwater *(1849)*

48

arrival of the rare motorcar. If perchance it was Neddy Quinn in his big maroon coloured *Model A Ford* he usually stopped to give us a lift. We loved the spins in this old car, even though it was shake, rattle and roll all the way home. Yes they were great days then and though our horizons were somewhat limited we enjoyed those short trips then just as much as longer journeys in later days.

The foregoing was based on my youthful memories of visits made to the old abbey, which were exciting and eagerly awaited occasions, scarce enough in days of yore.

Legends say that the name Bective derives from Begteach, which means The Little Palace. Supposedly, the High King's household was transferred to here following the priest's cursing of Tara, 'Teachmor' or the big palace, in the middle years of the sixth century A.D.. Local anecdotes tell of the name deriving from the small beehive structures near the Clady Churchyard. However the name evolved, it has several variations to both its spelling and meaning – amongst these are Bectiff, Begty, Beigthigh and Ballyna (Ballina). It's generally accepted that Ballyna (Ballina) translates to Beal an Atha in Gaelic, which means *the mouth of the ford*. Another name proposed by John O'Donovan during the 1836 ordnance survey is Mainistir an Aonaigh, or the monastery of the fair – some historians refer to the area as 'the place of the crosses', while several of the old maps also name it as Bridgeend. So there are many names and anecdotes from which to choose, but as I make no claims to be an historian, I will leave exact definitions to those who are more knowledgeable.

Continuing our journey along the road from Tribley (Trubley), upon entering the village we pass between Ballyna (Ballina) on the left and the townland of Ballynavaddog on the right – the latter name translates to 'the town of the plovers'. Larkin's Map and the 1837 OS map show the Fair Green near the corner of this townland, on these maps the Green is indicated as occupying the southwestern sector at the crossroads and several buildings are shown along its perimeter. Local history tells of how two fairs were held here annually – on May 16th a fair for dry cows and heifers and on November 1st a fair for cattle and pigs. I have also heard it said that in the earlier fairs in May the practice of hiring Spalpins (Spalpeens) was widespread. Spalpins were also known as 'penny a day men' and I'm told that the name derives from this expression – Speal means a scythe and Pin supposedly being a shortened version of Pingin or Penny. Hence, it would seem that Spalpins were hired for mowing the meadows and corn, but in some places the name became synonymous with migrant labourers and was used as such for many years.

The crossroads at Bective was formed by the intersection of the main road from Dunshaughlin to Athboy and the old road from Trim to Drogheda. As stated, the pub on the corner was thatched during the days of my youth when we travelled over to the abbey across the Boyne. At the time of the ordnance survey of 1836, between thirty and forty houses stood in the village and a population of about one hundred and forty people resided there.

To visit more of the ancient parish of Bective, let's depart the road to Duleek for a short spell and turn left to proceed down the hill towards the river. This is the area known to some in bygone days as *The Street* and to others by the nickname *Duck Street*. The old maps indicate a number of houses on both sides of the road, hence the name The Street, but I'm unsure of how it acquired the sobriquet Duck Street – perhaps this title reflected the number of ducks frequenting the River Boyne at its lower end? There was a small quarry to the right just above the riverbank, with a limekiln being operated by the Horan family until relatively recent times.

A mill once stood on the south bank of the Boyne about halfway down the hill and to the left of the road – local legends name this

ancient mill as Horris's Mill, perhaps it was named after a well-known local family of that name.

I have recollections of a watercourse in the swampy bottoms alongside the river in the time prior to the Boyne arterial drainage scheme of the 1970s. Mickey Creighton, a native of Bective and a good friend of mine during my cycling days, told me his grandmother said there was a mill here and that it was driven by the waters of the little stream flowing from Ballynavaddog. This small river was reputedly named the Versheen and the mill supposedly powered by a small horizontal water wheel. According to his grandmother, the millrace, or pond for this mill was known as *The Turreys* (Turrys) and the field in the Boyne meadows through which it flowed was named the Turrey Gardens. Having found no written references to either the stream or the old millrace, I'm unsure of the correct spelling of either name – but a local anecdote says that the stream was named after a long dead Norman Knight. Research shows that the story of the mill is indeed true and a close perusal of the 1837 OS map indicates the little stream flowing into a clearly marked millrace, then on past a building close by the southern end of the bridge. The building shown on the map was presumably the old mill and, if my memory serves me correctly, some traces of it remained on the site during my younger days. Recently, upon searching the fields by the roadside I found the small stone arched bridge that once took the tailrace of this lost mill under the Bective to Robinstown road and into the Boyne downstream of Horan's quarry. Though completely overgrown on the Trubley side of the road, the top

Facing page: *Boyne Bridge, Bective, downstream aspect - 2008.* This page, left: *The overgrown Clady footbridge,* right: *Top of arch, buried Tailrace Bridge at Horris's Mill, Bective*

51

of the arch is visible from Horan's field on the downstream side, situated about one hundred yards from the village end of the Boyne Bridge. As it was possible to see but a small portion of the arch at time of writing in 2008, the exact size of the bridge is difficult to determine, but I would hazard a guess that it was approximately four or five feet in river width.

It's possible that the aforementioned mill, shown sited to the east of Trubley Castle on the Down Survey Map of the 1650s, may have represented a mill on this site. Before the advent of the larger industrial mills in the 18th century, many of the more ancient mills were built on small rivers; hence this may have been the location of the original monastic mill for Bective Abbey.

Near the top of the hill below Lynch's old public house at the crossroads, now a modern shop and pub, I'm told that a house standing there was once used as a pub and formed part of the old street of Bective. Local legends say that the reason for the two pubs was to provide a form of class segregation, or apartheid as it might be known in more recent times. Seemingly, the Toffs frequenting the pub at the crossroads disliked mixing with commoners, hence the plebes supposedly frequented the humbler hostelry lower down the hillside.

The bridge spanning the Boyne here is a twelve arched stone structure with battlemented walls and a road width of about eighteen feet. Because the river was narrowed during the drainage scheme several of the arches are high and dry on the riverbank nowadays. The arch on the abbey side is narrower than the others and once carried the tailrace of the big mill into the Boyne downstream of the bridge, though at time of writing it's mostly closed up because the millrace is long gone. Nobody seems sure when Bective Bridge was built and apparently no record can be found. Peter O'Keefe, a renowned expert on stone bridges, concluded it was built towards the turn of the 17th century or early in the 18th century – possibly between 1690 and 1720. None of the early maps, including Moll's Map of 1714, Petty's Map of 1683 or Pratt's Map shows a bridge at Bective, though there's a clue in Pratt's Map of 1702. This map clearly marks the road from Killeen to Bective, but significantly, it indicates that the river cuts the road at Bective, whereas it shows the bridges at Trim and Kilcarn cutting the river. Thus it would seem that there was no bridge at Bective in

Larkin's No. 3
1. Reilly's Pub
2. The Tinker's Garden
3. Ripperstwon/Balsoon Castle
4. Asigh (Assey) Church and Castle
5. Asigh Railway Viaduct
6. The Mullaghcrewy
7. Bonfield
8. The Butler's Bridge
9. The Lost Village
10. Arnold's Mill
11. Bective/Connel's Cross
12. Clady

1702, or when Pratt's Map was surveyed. If one is to believe the definition of the name Ballyna as meaning 'the mouth of the ford', there must have been such a ford for crossing the river here in earlier times.

In the area of the present day Bective village, immediately adjacent to the Boyne and in the parish of Balsoone, the Down Survey Map of the Barony of Deece shows a townland named *Bridgent*. To the east, in the approximate location of the present day Craystown, was another small parcel of land named *Bridgent plo*, possibly meaning a plowland (ploughland)? These names might suggest that a bridge across the Boyne existed at Bective previous to the 1650s: perhaps this provides a clue to the derivation of the later name Bridgeend?

Another interesting point about Bective Bridge – during the Boyne drainage scheme in the 1970s, the pillars and abutments were underpinned to compensate for the deepening of the river. While this work was in progress it was discovered that the pillars were built on wood. I spoke to an engineer from the Board of Works, who told me that this was a common enough feature on old bridges especially in boggy terrain. He said that whilst working on a road bridge spanning the River Inny over in Westmeath, it was found to be build upon a foundation of Greenheart timbers. Which explains why the locals referred to it as *the floating bridge.*

On the northern side of Bective Bridge a little laneway leads off to the left and upstream along the riverbank in the direction of Rathnally – the lane is the entrance to Bective Mill, which was once powered by a waterwheel driven by the waters of the Boyne. But nowadays this is rather difficult to believe because the remains of the old mill stand high and dry on the green grassy banks of the river and not a trace of water is to be seen within stone throwing distance. The crumbling building stands forlornly near the edge of the Boyne, commanding a magnificent view of the lovely valley. The stonework of the old bridge in the foreground and the ancient abbey downstream form a mediaeval-like backdrop to the scene: though the rotting and rusting remains of its big undershot waterwheel provides a stark reminder of the ravages that progress sometimes brings to ancient settings.

During my boyhood things were very different, in those times the mill was still a working sawmill and corn mill, I remember it well. Dad was a keen hurler in his younger days and won some County Championship medals whilst playing for Kilmessan and Skryne. My older brother Tom followed in his footsteps and took up hurling while attending the De La Salle Brother's school in Navan. It was very difficult to obtain good hurling sticks even in those times when ash timber was plentiful in

*The Boyne Bridge at Bective - upstream elevation. The mill tailrace passed through an arch, now almost buried, out of picture to the left*

the countryside. So Dad decided we would make our own – thus the relevance of the sudden introduction of hurling to the story of the old mill at Bective.

We searched the woods in Dowdstown until several suitable ash trees from which to fashion 'the Camans' were found. A good hurling stick (hurley) requires certain built-in characteristics – the most important of these being a fine spring so that it can be bent almost into a hoop, a nice curved grain at the boss end and to be light of weight. Having found three or four small ash trees with curved roots, we cut these about five feet above the ground and dug up the roots. Loading them onto the pony cart and with Dad driving we set off over the road on the long trek to Bective and the sawmill at the far end of the bridge.

Wheeling in at the gateway we drove on up the mill lane, which ran on a rampart alongside the millrace and close to the Boyne – the tailrace was like a small fast flowing river that disappeared into the dark eye of the smaller arch on the great bridge. Upon our arrival at the big stone building we could see the huge waterwheel turning and hear the rush and gurgle of the turbulent water passing through the headrace. A sluice diverted some of the river's flow to the eel traps, while the other branch flowed down through the big undershot wheel. It was a very exciting experience for Tom and I because we were very young at that time in the early 1950s, Tom being aged about eight years and I was seven, neither of us had been to a working mill before. The owner, a man named Bill Smith, came out and questioned Dad about the origins of our ash trees. I remember distinctly that he wanted to know whether we obtained them from a wood or off a ditch, but I didn't realise then why he was so curious about such seemingly trivial matters. When Dad convinced him that we had indeed obtained the trees from a wood, he and his assistant, Bill Gargan, unloaded the stumps and took them into the mill. Bill Gargan was a well-known character around Bective who for some reason was named Billy Mac.

With great interest our young eyes watched the sections of trees being placed upon the big sawbench, which was then trolleyed along on rails to move the logs into the reciprocating saw. The bench dwarfed our relatively tiny ash stumps because it could handle much larger trees, probably up to four feet or more in diameter. As we gazed upon the scene in awe, the big horizontal crosscut saw cut into the log, converting it into thick slices or boards – the crisp rasping of the crosscut and zinging of the nearby bandsaw rang out loud and clear, almost drowning the other sounds of the mill. The crosscut saw was about eight feet long and driven by a crank, which in turn was powered by a wheel driven by a belt from a layshaft: the primary source of power being the waterwheel thumping and splashing away outside. The saw could be swivelled and used in the vertical position, just as a conventional crosscut was used to cut logs. When the planks were cut into timber slices known as roughcuts, Dad marked them out using a hurling stick he brought along as a template. Then, using the bandsaw, one of the millers fashioned each one in the shape of a hurley. We obtained about a dozen good playing sticks from the stumps taken to the mill on the day, but back home we still had a lot of hard work to do, using spokeshave, broken glass and finally sandpaper, ere the finished products could be called hurling sticks or Camans. It was only later, when older and a little bit wiser, that I discovered the significance of why Bill Smith asked Dad so many questions concerning the source of the trees. He was worried lest we had dug them from a ditch or hedgerow, there might be embedded in the timber some gate hangers, spikes or sneibles, which could have caused grievous damage to his pride and joy, the big crosscut saw. On subsequent occasions during those *too few* boyhood years we visited the mill – sometimes having more hurleys cut out and occasionally bringing oak or elm tree trunks to be sliced into boards. I have fond, but dimming memories of those times when we travelled the road to Bective Mill.

The Boyne drainage scheme of the 1970s, in addition to ruining the salmon spawning redds and the river's natural environment, which took millennia to develop, wiped out many other items of both historical and general interest along the river. The said scheme also eliminated the prospects of Bective and many such mills being restored to their former use as water-powered mills. The weir upstream towards Rathnally was demolished thus ending an ancient tradition whereby local people came to swim and cool themselves in the clear waters of the Boyne during the hot summers of yesteryear. The place where once the merry laughter of adults and the clamour of happy children resonated between the grassy banks is no more – it's gone forever and many of the older folks mourn its passing. The headrace and eel traps, the tailrace and the little kesh, all these have vanished, being filled in and buried, such that now there is little trace of their former presence on the riverbank.

I'm uncertain about the history of Bective Mill, legends say that a corn mill and eel weir existed there during the heyday of the nearby abbey – possibly the ancient mill was on this very site. In 1854 Griffith's valuation shows that the corn mill at Bective, together with 36 acres of land and a

*The Big Mill at Bective - 2007*

*Bective Mill lane and Mill - 2008*

house were leased from Richard Bolton at an annual rateable valuation of £40. 0s. 0d., the lessee was named as Thomas Byrne. During my youth, in addition to being a sawmill it was still being used as a corn-mill – oftentimes, during our visits we saw local people bringing corn, such as wheat and oats, to be ground into meal on the old millstones. Perhaps the little mill on the small stream across the Boyne stood on what was once the site of the original monastic mill at Bective. But it's unlikely that we will ever know for sure – because of the rate at which the relentless march of progress is devouring the landscape of County Meath and elsewhere at the present time, soon all traces will be eliminated. And in the future perhaps some generations will wonder what was there – but their greatest wonderment of all may be why our generation allowed it to be destroyed and wiped from the landscape?

I won't dwell upon the former magnificence of the ancient abbey at Bective: scholars and historians have written tomes about this famous place so there's nothing I can add to the fount' of knowledge. At time of writing, another archaeological investigation is in progress; perhaps more historical information will be gleaned from this?

Going on by the abbey we pass the entrance to the home of the famous writer, Mary Lavin, then come to a crossroads known as Connell's Cross, which takes the Athboy road across the "new" Trim to Navan road. Nowadays this area is going through great change due to the realignment of the main road, so in years to come it may be known by some other name on future maps? Referring to the 'new line' of the Navan to Trim road, while researching the Grand Jury presentment books I came across several references to this section of road. The 'new line' runs from Navan through Balreask to Balgil – where it joined the route from Trim to Kilcarn via Rathnally, Grange Bective and Cannistown, known to some as 'the road to the mill' (possibly because it led to The Big Mill at lower Kilcarn). At Dunganny it joins the old Trim to Navan road that ran through the Commons and Robinstown. The Grand Jury books, between the years 1812 and 1816, contain several entries regarding the building of roadside walls at Clady and arches (bridges) on the 'new line' at Balgil (Balgyl) – this would seem to set a marker for the cutting of this new road between these dates.

Larkin's Map does not show Bective House, but indicates the old church at Clady close by the confluence of the Clady River with the Boyne: perhaps the house had not been built at the time the map was surveyed. The OS map of 1837, however, shows the house, together with a single entrance avenue and a lodge located at what later became the middle-avenue. No other entry is shown leading to the house – to the east of the lodge a laneway is indicated leading to a quarry and some buildings close to the banks of the Boyne. A separate entrance leading to the old Clady Church and graveyard is indicated on the OS map: this lane led off the roadway from a point just to the east of the present day lodge gate near Connell's Cross. The lodge and large stone-pillared entrance gateway and avenue must have been constructed post 1837 and prior to 1862 – the avenue cut across the older laneway to the Clady, thus making the new gateway the main entrance to the Clady Churchyard. We know the later date because of an occurrence at the gate in 1862, which has remained alive in the psyche of local people to the present day. The incident is remembered in a poem/recitation entitled *The Corpse at Clady Gate*.

The poem names the owner of Bective House as *Bolton the Tyrant* and describes him as the spawn of a Cromwellian cur and other such less than complimentary sobriquets. Supposedly, he was a noted bigot and to prove this he locked the gates leading to the ancient cemetery at the Clady: thereby denying local people their inalienable and long cherished right to bury the dead and visit their graves. The poem goes on to recount how, in 1862, a funeral arrived at the gates and found them locked with *a ponderous chain.* And the response of local Blacksmith Sean O'Reilly, an offspring of *Myles the Slasher of Finae,* to the bigot's bullying actions. Sean addressed the crowd of mourners who were about to quit and depart the scene – then, following an impassioned speech, which included many of the uncomplimentary names mentioned earlier, he returned home to his forge and fetched a crowbar and sledgehammer. With these tools he smashed Bolton's lock and led the cortege to Clady, where the corpse was interred with full religious honours. The tyrant was none too pleased and supposedly persecuted O'Reilly thereafter: but he survived and lived to the ripe old age of 84 and passed away in 1917.

Bolton died in 1868, he broke his neck in a fall, ere some of the local populace could do it for him, and was interred in a vault at Bective Church (the Black Church). But his spirit is alive and well around the Clady yet – *his lock has returned to the Clady gate.* The stone stile, part of an ancient right of way from the abbey to the churchyard, has been fenced off and the big ornamental gates securely fastened with lock and chain, thereby denying access to the Clady Graveyard once more. This gate was an older version of the Celtic Tiger F.U. electronic gates, nowadays guarding the entrances to many of the *nouveau riche* residences in the Irish countryside; proving yet again the wisdom of the old adage 'put a beggar on horseback' … Well we might wonder, what the so-called guardians of our ancient

The Tyrant's *locked gate to Clady Graveyward - 2008*

heritage are doing to prevent such blockading of old established rights of way that deny the public access to national monuments like the Clady. Perhaps it's time for post Celtic Tiger Ireland to produce another Sean O'Reilly to sunder the *ponderous chain on Clady's gate*!

Proceeding onwards we cross the Clady River and arrive in Robinstown, once known as Robinstown Crosses, here the Athboy road crosses the previously mentioned old Navan to Trim road.

Two Smithies, or forges, existed in the village in olden times, one near where the school stands at time of writing and the other to the right of the road in a yard close by the old crossroads (at the old RIC barracks). I'm unsure if both forges were in operation during the same period, but maybe the following little anecdote may throw some light on the matter and perhaps explain the presence of two forges in one small village.

The story I heard concerns a widow, a parcel of land and a broken promise and goes as follows: Many years ago a widow who lived in Trim had her eye on a small farm of about thirty acres or so. This farm, which had a fine two-storey residence, nestled on the banks of the Boyne close by the mill and Bective Abbey. The property was coming up for auction and the widow was very keen to buy it, but in those enlightened days it wasn't considered seemly for a woman to bid at auctions, hence she was caught upon the horns of a dilemma. She therefore made an agreement with the owner of the forge in Robinstown to bid for the farm and to cede possession to her afterwards. The tale also relates that although the forge was then a thriving business, its owner also possessed a bull, which serviced many cows in the area, thus enhancing the Blacksmith's income. The auction was held and the Blacksmith duly bought the farm, supposedly in proxy for the widow – but, as the story goes, he fell more in love with the farm than the widow, so reneged on his agreement and declined to sign over the property. Upon hearing the tale, the local populace boycotted the Blacksmith, refusing to use his forge or take their cows to his bull. Furthermore, they started up a forge of their own and procured a bull, thus making the boycott complete. I have no idea as to the veracity of the yarn or what happened to the second bull of Robinstown, but this old anecdote might go some way towards explaining the existence of two forges in the village long ago.

Griffith's valuation of 1854 indicates that one forge existed in the village at the time. It shows that Richard Bolton leased a house and forge, together with 3 roods and 20 perches of land to Joseph Reilly at an annual rateable valuation of £2. 0s. 0d. – the valuation report also shows a national schoolhouse and garden for females in the area during that period. Another possible explanation for the second forge in the village is that one may have been what was colloquially known as a *Scab Forge*. These forges originated during World War I in response to the Blacksmith's Association raising their tariffs because of the increase in the price of raw materials such as coal and iron. Many farmers and businesses refused to pay the inflated prices and started up their own Smithies, which became known derisively amongst the Blacksmith's fraternity by the previously mentioned name. I'm told that when regular Blacksmiths forged horseshoes, they used a special stamp to mark the shoes fitted at association-affiliated forges. Should a horse, previously shod at a 'scab forge', lose a shoe and be taken to an association run Smithy and the remaining shoes found to be unstamped, the Blacksmith refused to re-shoe the animal at less than double the normal price. So it seems that very little new exists under the sun!

*The 1933 Kilmessan Senior Hurling Team; Back row L-R; Bill Donnelly, Tom Madden, Anthony Holten, Paddy Touhy, Billy Smith, T. Loughran, Tom Costello, Ickey 'Ike' Madden, Jimmy Maguire. Front row L-R; Kevin Farrell, Jack O'Neill, Pat Donnelly, J. Loughran, Mick O'Brien, Tony Donnelly, Toss Fagan.* (Courtesy M O'Brien)

The old name for the townland in which Robinstown is located was Ballybradah, variously spelled Balbradagh/Balbratha/Balbradach, which townland was part of Bective Parish. John O'Donovan's OS field notes of 1836 state that in 'The Boundary Sketch' of 1829, the place was named Baile Bradach *the thievish town*. As no mention is made of a Robin (*an Spideog as Gaeilge),* perhaps it might be more historically correct had the name evolved as Robberstown or Robbingtown. Fortunately this didn't happen, as such an address might not have been the flavour of the month on a job application form or in an entrepreneur's address book during the inflated ego times of the so-called Celtic Tiger. Larkin's Map names the crossroads Balbratha, while the OS map of 1837 names it Robinstown – possibly this is one of the many Anglicisation's of place names that took place during this survey. Nowadays the Discovery series of OS maps names the place Robinstown in English and Baile Roibin in Gaelic – I can find no meaning for the latter name in Collins Irish Dictionary. Perhaps there's a further clue in O'Donovan's writings about the same place in 1836 – which stated that the police barracks was occupied by a staff of six policemen, consisting of one senior and five junior constables. By present day standards this would seem an enormous staffing level for a small country village, so maybe in those days it was indeed a 'thievish town'?

But I'm digressing far off my chosen path; therefore, let's return to the crossroads at Bective. On the northeastern sector of the village stands the old pub which legend says started as a *Sibin* sometime in the early 1700s – then in the 1750s it became a licensed premises, which was owned by the O'Reilly family and remained in that family's possession until 1945. Anecdotes say that *The Widow Donegan* ran it for a time during the 19th century. The widow, a relative of the O'Reilly family, is mentioned frequently in O'Donovan's writings during the times of the 1836 ordnance survey: seemingly she was very involved in farming and had several parcels of land leased in the area, including a farm in Ballynavaddog. There's a plot in the nearby Balsoon Cemetery bearing the name Donegan – perhaps this is the final resting-place of the famous widow. The Tutty family took over the pub after the O'Reilly's left in 1945 and, if my memory serves me well, it was they who owned or ran the shop and pub during our early childhood. My strongest recollections are of the Lynch family who owned it from the late 1950s or early 1960s and that it had a thatched roof during that period. I remember getting my first ever ice cream from here when I was very young, if I recall correctly it was around 1950 or 1951. Rural electrification came to Kilmessan and Bective about 1949, a year or so prior to this seemingly magical event occurring in Dowdstown and lighting up our lives – quite literally. Hence, Cathy Robinson, who ran the shop at Garlow Cross, didn't stock ice cream then because she had no electricity to power a fridge. One day, a cousin of mine rode on his bike over to the shop in Bective to fetch a block of the magic elixir and some wafers. As it transpired we didn't need the wafers, being such a hot day the ice cream melted during the return journey and we drank the surviving cream from mugs.

Across the road and on the southeastern corner of the crossroads stood an old thatched house: this was the home of the McKeever family, which was built around 1820. During my lifetime the late Edward McKeever, known as Eddie, lived there with his family and was renowned locally as a historian. The people of Bective and Kilmessan owe Eddie a debt of gratitude for his work in researching local history. He penned the fruits of this research and his local knowledge into several books – these provide very interesting reading and lend great colour to the landscape, as they are filled with the customs, personalities and characters of former years. I recall the thatched house very well, during my youth it stood there at the crossroads commanding the junction, but in later years it was demolished and replaced by a modern bungalow.

In former days two buildings stood on the Kilmessan road corner of the Fair Green. One of these was a stone structure standing on the very apex of the crossroads; hence it became a major source of aggravation to motorists because it obstructed their view. Nobody seems to know the origins of this building and many anecdotes were related about its past usage – some of these said it was a hospice or rest house for the monks from the monastery; others that it was perhaps a brothel for the long departed brethren of the abbey. I doubt the veracity of these stories, as despite its age, it seems unlikely to have survived in that location from the times when the abbey was still in use. Other legends say it was a coachouse, which seems a likelier explanation. I believe Meath County Council demolished it with explosives in the 1940s – supposedly a stone crusher was brought in and the stones from the building were crushed and used for road building.

On the Kilmessan side of this old building stood the famous old Bective Smithy, which was started up in the 1920s by Jack Twomey

*Bective Pub - an artists impression*
(Courtesy Anne and John Sherlock)

– who came to Bective to work for John Watson, a famous horseman resident in the nearby Bective House. Jack set up the forge beside the crossroads and became renowned in the locality as a farrier and for his general prowess on the anvil. A man from Kilmessan, named Michael Foley, was trained by Jack as a farrier: in later times he took over the Smithy and for ever after was known as *The Farrier Foley*. In recent years the old forge was demolished and not a trace of it remains today. But one memento of former days adorned the crossroads at Bective for a time – on the spot where the ancient stone building once stood at the corner of the Fair Green lay a circular 'shoeing stone'. I'm told that this stone has disappeared in recent times, to where nobody seems to know; perhaps it was spirited away by aliens to repair wagon wheels on some distant planet. The stone had a hole in its centre for recessing the hubs of the cartwheels of old whilst the Blacksmith shaped the iron tyre, or shoeing, before welding and shrinking it onto the wooden felloes (felly) of the wheel. This particular *stone* was made from concrete, yet I have seen many that were constructed from real stone, some being old millstones originally used to grind corn. Unfortunately, though it survived many years in the nearby Smithy, it failed to endure the ravages of the Celtic Tiger's greed feast, perhaps its very disappearance is another reflection on the modern progressive Ireland?

# 5

# From Bective To Bonfield (Droimlagh)

Balsoon Castle and Craystown – The Tinker's Garden – Bothar Na Mhuillin – Asigh (Assey) Castle and Churchyard – the Dublin Navan Railway – The Ford of Sidhe – The New Road and the Mullaghcrewy – The Five Roads of Tara – Bonfield or Droimlag.

Leaving the village of Bective we carry on eastwards towards Bellinter and Dowdstown. Here the road winds between the hill of Craystown to the right and the ancient parish church of Balsoon on the left. About a half mile to the east of the village we come upon the little cul de sac road to the right leading to Craystown, which at time of writing is the home of George Briscoe, owner of the Bellinter estate during my younger days. Some say this old road was once part of an ancient *Slighe,* perhaps *An Slighe Mor (Mhor).* To the south of Craystown in Balreask (the town or place of the morass or mire), the 1837 OS map shows a castle which was accessed by a laneway leading off the Bective to Kilmessan road, local people tell me that this was the ruins of Elliot's castle. A castle is shown at this location on the Down Survey Barony map of Lower Deece in the 1650s.

According to John O'Donovan, Balsoon translates to *the place or town of Samhan,* which he concluded meant the town of the Sorrel. The word

*Bective Forge*

Sorrel means inter alia a tree or a red tinted salad plant of the dock leaf family. Sorrel is a North American tree, sometimes known as Sourwood and a horse of a reddish brown hue is called a Sorrel – the connection between the various definitions eludes me. Whatever its meaning and however it is derived, I found the name Balsoon had a certain attraction and ring to it, somehow it seemed to add colour to the area during our childhood days when we travelled the road to Bective. A much less attractive name by which the area was known in the past is Ripperstown; a name that might suggest the place was occupied by rather shady folk at one time.

The old Church of Ireland Parish lies within a big loop in the River Boyne and was once noted for its old castle and churchyard: some historians say that in ancient times it was connected to the King's household on the nearby Hill of Tara. A famous Norman family named Ussher owned Balsoon from about 1300 to 1713 – Prestons' of Bellinter came into possession of the estate circa 1720. Archbishop Ussher built the castle in the 1590s; a member of this family became the first Assistant Provost of Trinity College in Dublin. It's said that in 1643 Owen Roe O'Neil captured the stronghold, supposedly a *towerhouse of the Pale*, in one of his raids during those turbulent times. The castle was demolished

*Tara Village*

about 1830, with the stones being used to build the new residence – the only remains of the castle are part of the late medieval barrel-vaulted structure. If I recall correctly, during the 1960s the well-known writer J.P. Dunleavy, author of *The Ginger Man* and other works, lived in Balsoon. The track of an old road can be discerned running northeastward from the avenue towards the Boyne at the Assey end of the parish – this is known as Bothar Na Mhuillin or the road to the mill. In 1836 John O'Donovan notes that the Civil Survey of 1654/56 states there was a corn mill in Assey at that time, perhaps this explains the name of the old road in Balsoon. As mentioned, I have also heard the road leading from Bective to Cannistown and Kilcarn referred to as the road to the mill.

Eddie McKeever concluded that the old road in Balsoon was once part of an ancient *Slighe* running from Tara towards the northwest. If one follows its path back towards Tara it could have led through Craystown and Cardiffstown then up the western slopes of the hill; some historians conclude that this was the approximate direction of *An Slighe Mor*.

Travelling along the road towards Duleek again, we come to a lane leading to the right, which is located about three hundred yards beyond the entrance to Craystown. Nowadays the lane is merely an entry to some fields, but Larkin's Map shows a little hamlet of about twelve houses occupied a site at the southern end of the laneway. This section of the road was a favourite spot for what we knew as Tinker encampments during the days of my youth. These were so prolific at times that the area became known colloquially as *The Tinker's Garden*. This map also indicates many dwellings in Balsoon near the old churchyard and castle. The presence of these two hamlets in the area at that time might explain why the name Ripperstown was applied and also why such a large population, over 300 in 1836, resided in the district in times past.

A short distance further to the east we top a small knoll from which we catch a glimpse of the Hill of Tara, then descend to the site of the ancient church and castle at Asigh (Assey - Assy). In my youth a railway bridge spanned the road here, this carried the now defunct Dublin to Navan railway line across the line of the Trim to Drogheda road. Similar to the location of the former Tribley railway bridge, the road dipped into a wooded hollow to pass beneath the bridge, which, unlike Tribley Bridge, was of stone arched construction. It was a very tricky and dangerous corner and I believe a relative of my mother was killed here in an accident in the 1940s.

Having passed under it during my boyhood on pony and trap, on shank's mare, riding my bike and by various forms of motor transport, I have many recollections of Asigh railway bridge. I even crossed it on steamtrains whilst travelling on football specials to Croke Park – *sinn sceal eile,* a story for another day. My most abiding memory of the bridge is during the great flood on the 8th of December 1954, the Marion Year. That evening we sat by the fireside in Dowdstown, in the midst of the inundated Skein valley. Things were pretty grim because the floodwaters were lapping the back doorstep and it looked like we might have to retreat upstairs, then a loud knock on the front door distracted our attention and dispelled this pensive and gloomy mood. Upon the door being opened we beheld a priest from the nearby Dalgan Park standing there. He was clad all in black except for his legs, which in the dim light looked like two whitened pegs protruding from the darker clothing. The reason for the

*Bective Station closed down in the 1950's - it is now a private dwelling*

strange attire being, that despite the freezing cold, his trousers were rolled up above the knees to enable him to walk through the floods on the road. I didn't laugh at the funny sight he presented because people didn't laugh at priests in those times. He called to us on that dark night long ago, as he was unsure of how to reach the college because the road at Dowdstown Bridge was flooded, so he asked Dad to guide him up to Dalgan Park. Dad did so and on his return told us that the priest had driven his car into a flood lurking in the dark hollow beneath Asigh railway bridge: fortunately, the water being only about three feet deep, he scrambled out and walked to our house. Next day we went to Asigh with Dad on the pony cart and helped tow the old Morris Minor from the hollow and down to the lane at Bonfield. Though a rather short-lived experience, the excitement it caused in my young life was such that the memory lingered on through the years.

To the left of the road a little stream passed under a small stone bridge and beneath the railway embankment. This stream rose nearby in Balgeeth and in the swampy bottom fields known as the Skane Meadows, Upper Skane and Harry's Hill to the west of the Cluide Wood, passed through Bonfield, then under the road and railway, it fell into the Boyne near Edward McNamee's farm. The McNamee's house, farmyard and orchard were located on the banks of the Boyne west of the railway, while the larger

*Asigh railway vaduct on the old Dublin/Navan railway line - downstream elevaion*

part of the holding lay to the east between the trackbed and Bellinter estate. This farm was acquired by the Bird family of Bective House in the late 1950s and has been used as a stud farm since. Long before the advent of electronically controlled FU gates the entrance to Bird's farm had a set of unusual lever operated gates, which could be opened by horse riders without the need to dismount. The old farmyard and house is now overgrown and one would scarcely know it ever existed. The railway crossed the Boyne on a stone viaduct and ran on to the station over at Grange Bective where we once boarded the football specials for Dublin. The railway bridge, spanning the Trim/Drogheda road in Asigh, was built in the early 1850s and demolished in the 1970s during road realignment work. The Bonfield River stone arched railway bridge, a structure well worth viewing, survived the railway's destruction in the 1960s. The entrance laneway to the stud farm runs from the rerouted road, crosses over the ruins of the railway road-bridge and the Bonfield River, and continues along the trackbed that once carried the trains from Navan to Dublin. The line spanned the Boyne on a stone arched viaduct, which still enhances the beauty of the Boyne at time of writing. But the beautiful bridge barely survived the ravaging lion of progress in the 1960s, being spared an ignominious fate by George Briscoe, who bought the structure from CIE for £60, prior to this far-seeing public body blasting it from the landscape with explosives. The remnants of the railway in Asigh are yet another stark reminder of the shortsighted vision, or innate stupidity, that allowed the destruction of such vital infrastructure in bygone days. The enormous cost of former bad planning will once again be borne by Irish taxpayers for its future reconstruction, should such an event ever occur?

Assey or Asigh is a place of myth and legend that some historians linked to the High Kings of Tara. Sir William Wilde maintained that the legendary long lost House of Cletty, one of the reputed abodes of infirm High Kings, could have been located in Clady across the ancient ford and on the northern bank of the Boyne. The place derives its name from the Gaelic *Ath Sidhe* The ford of Sidhe. According to The Annals of the Four Masters, Sidhe, the son of King Dian, was killed here in a battle in 524 AD and the place named after him. The remains of a very old church and attendant graveyard lie to the west of the defunct railway line – attached to this was a glebe of about three and a half acres. In times past the glebe was part of the townland of Assey and owned by Lord Trimblestown (Tremblestown) but in more recent years it has been in the possession of the Crinion family, whose residence is located close to the old churchyard. The former parish of Assey consisted of the townlands of Assey (with the glebe), Ballinter and Balgeeth. Beside the house and close to the Boyne

*Asigh (Assey) Graveyard and Church ruins - 2009*

stood the remains of another *watchtower of the Pale*, Assey Castle. I'm told that the remains of this former landmark were demolished in recent years by the O.P.W. because of the dangerous state of the structure – the stones being used as filling for an access road to Warrenstown College. Yet another reflection on the official mindset towards preservation of our uniquely historic landscape! In his book, Sir William Wilde gives a description of this castle as seen in 1849 and concluded that it was similar to the castles in Trubley and Scurlockstown, being a square keep with towers on the eastern and western corners. Though the date of its construction is uncertain or who resided therein, it's reasonable to propose that the castle was erected in or around the late 12th century. Some historians conjecture that it may have been in the possession of the Plunkett family for a time, as their coat of arms is to be found carved on some stonework in the adjacent graveyard. A skewed weir was located on the Boyne upstream of Assey and below Bective House; the weir can be seen on the 1837 OS map so it dates back to at least then. The Down Survey Barony map of Lower Deece shows a church, a towerhouse and a mill close by the River Boyne in Assy, on a direct line with the aforementioned Road to the Mill in Balsoon. Unlike elsewhere in the Barony, this mill is displayed in text, rather than shown as a depiction of a water wheel.

A narrow road leads off to the southeast from the site of the former Asigh railway bridge, this little road was known as *the new road* and links the Trim/Drogheda and the Kilmessan/Navan roads. At its eastern end in Riverstown stands another *watchtower of the Pale,* known as Riverstown Castle; it was once the abode of the Dillon family – more about this castle in the next chapter. The byroad winds its way through Balgeeth, which O'Donovan interprets as Baile an Gaoithe, *the town or place of the wind*, and passes several old played out gravel pits, one of which was located at a place known locally as the Mullaghcrewy. I cannot find a definition for this name as spelled, but a slight alteration of the spelling, to Mullachcrua, would mean *the hardy summit* – Mullach meaning top or summit and Crua meaning hard or hardy. This definition suits the place admirably, because the little hilltop is indeed a hardy place; on a March day, the cold east wind scything across the open countryside is fit to shave off the hardiest of beards. I oftentimes traversed this windswept hillside during my cycling days, but it had its compensations, in my opinion the most splendid vista of the Hill of Tara can be obtained from the bare summit of the little ridge. A local legend says that during the Irish War of Independence, 1918 to 1922, Sinn Fein courts were held in the Mullaghcrewy: supposedly, the presiding judges were named Horan and Plunkett.

I wondered why the little road was called 'the new road' and asked many questions about it over the years, but never received a definitive answer. Researching the maps has shown there was no through road until relatively recent times. All the old maps, Larkin's Map, the OS maps of 1837, 1882 and 1911 show a short length of road at each end. The 1911 map also indicates a dotted line, which I presumed to be a path or right of way, running in a circuitous route between the two lengths of road. All the OS maps depict a river ford on the Skane at Riverstown where the concrete bridge is now located. I also heard a local anecdote about there being a small kesh or footbridge located here – for a period this consisted of an old iron girder and some of the local lads rode their motorbikes across it for fun. In one of Eddie McKeever's books I came upon a mention

*Bonfield river railway bridge - on the closed Dublin/Navan railway in Asigh*

of how, in the late 1920s, R.J. Murray and some locals pushed hard and 'persuaded' Meath County Council to build the bridge linking the two ends of the road. So, thanks to Eddie's writings, the mystery of 'the new road' was finally solved for me. Further mention of the construction of this road is made in chapter seven.

Though the foregoing answers the questions of how and when the road of the present day came into being, yet this little road may hold some further mysteries and have a greater significance in the context of the much fabled five ancient roads of Tara. Larkin's Map shows the road continuing eastwards across the Kilmessan road and up towards the western slopes of Tara, near Cardiffstown. This, and the fact that the road linked the famous hill to one of the ancient fords on the Boyne, might suggest a possible connection to *An Slighe Mor* which reputedly ran to the northwest from a starting point at the Great Banqueting Hall on the hilltop.

Over many years there has been much divergence of opinion amongst the great scholars as to whether these ancient roads actually converged on Tara or on Dublin. But, whether the five roads first appeared in a dream on the night of the birth of 'Conn of the hundred battles' in AD 123, as stated in The Annals of the Four Masters – or if they were purpose built to help repel a threatened Roman invasion, as believed by others, matters not a whit to my story of the local roads. Being born and reared in the locality and brought up on the ancient legends of Tara I would tend towards the belief that the fabled five *Slighte* once converged on Tara. Indeed there could be an element of truth in both schools of thought, as the roads of the myth could have been epicentral to either location at different epochs in our history. Whatever the truth of the matter, we will never know for sure now as too much time has elapsed since those days. This is another reason why I believe we should record what we do know whilst it can be verified.

Leaving the place of the ancient Ford of Assey, we carry on eastwards towards the edge of the Bellinter (Ballinter) estate, which was part of Assey Parish in olden times. This is a lovely section of the route and it's where we get our first sustained view of the Hill of Tara in the near distance to our right. Before we come to Bellinter we first pass the little laneway to

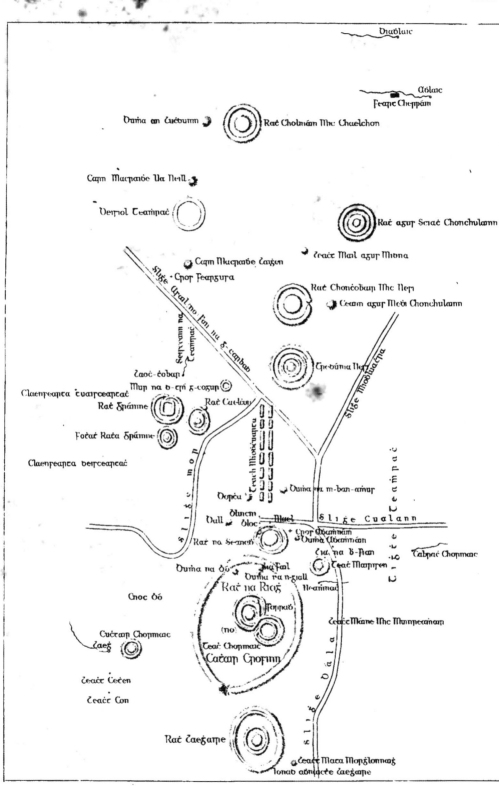

MONUMENTS OF TARA HILL RESTORED FROM ANCIENT DOCUMENTS.

the right leading to Bonfield, "a pretty name", as so described in some old writings I read. The name may have derived from the Scottish word Bonny, often used colloquially to describe something nice – Bonfield was also a common enough surname amongst Huguenots (French Protestants) and was fairly prevalent in County Clare at one time. The townland is small, consisting of just 33 acres and 4 perches, it was known in times past as Droimlag (Droimlaige). The name may translate to 'the back of the small ridges' – in Gaelic one meaning for Droim is 'the back side of a low hill or ridge' and Lag can mean something slight or weak. This old name would seem particularly apt for the location, as gravel ridges (eskers) form the higher ground above the valley; hence the profusion of local gravel pits in bygone days. This area is shown on Larkin's Map as Dromna. In times past the townland was a detached portion of the old parish of Balsoon and in 1836 formed part of Preston's estate in Bellinter. Several dwellings were adjacent to the laneway leading up to Farrelly's big gravel pit located to the west of the Cluide Wood. In our youth we often went there with the pony cart to bring back gravel to our home in Dowdstown – but this pit is now played out and the land returned to agricultural usage.

Facing page:
Monuments of Tara Hill Restored From Ancient Documents *From George Petrie's paper* On the History and Antiquities of Tara Hill *((1837). This shows the route and names of Tara's legendary five roads - as gleaned from ancient manuscripts - the five wells are also shown*

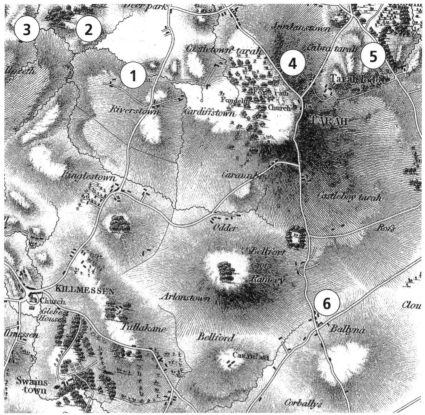

Larkin's No. 4

1. Riverstown Castle
2. The Cluide Wood
3. Harry's Hill
4. Slope of the Chariots
5. Newhall/Tara Hall
6. Ballyna Crossroads

Riverstown castle - 2008

# 6

# Riverstown Castle

This ancient *Towerhouse of the Pale* is located to the west of the Hill of Tara and less than two miles from its summit (see author's note on the Pale at the back of the book). It stands in a farmyard a short distance down along the line of the previously described 'new road', a few hundred yards from its junction with the Kilmessan/Navan road. The castle is set in a pastoral landscape, which at time of writing is becoming a somewhat scarce commodity in this part of County Meath. To set the scene for this brief description of the castle's history it's well worth quoting from Sir William Wilde's writings on the place, from his book *The Beauties of the Boyne and the Blackwater* published in 1849:

> *Turning southward from Bellinter Bridge, as we begin to ascend the hill towards Tara, the castle of Riverstown, about a mile and a half from the Boyne's brink, will be found well worthy of inspection. This was one of the best built castles upon the Boyne; and the remains which still exist, in the perfection of their masonry, and the sharpness and beauty of their lines, still bear witness to the fact. The ruins of this beautiful building show it to have been of the same type as most other castles of the Pale which we have examined, consisting of two portions, an ancient and a modern. The*

*former is a massive square tower, entirely built of cut or hammered stone, with three square turrets at the corners, which batter very much towards the foundations, and at the top rise several feet above the principal part of the building. The eastern turret was principally a pigeon-house, and that on the west side contained a spiral staircase which led to a parapet at top. These turrets were lighted by small square windows and loop-holes, and were, as well as the central tower, divided into four floors and an attic. In the wall of each of these turrets we find one of these chimney-like, concealed flues, or upright passages, common in some of the ancient castles, and popularly known among the people as "murder holes." This part of the castle was inhabited within the last eighty years, and portions of the plaster still remain upon the interior of the walls. The more modern portion abutted against the western wall of the tower, and show, by two gable-grooves, which are still visible in the latter, that it was erected or re-edified at different periods; and this conjecture is further supported by the fact of the existence of a large stone arched keep, still remaining on the north-western side. Portions of the wall of the bawn can still be traced in the surrounding farmyard.*

*By whom, or at what precise time, the original castle of Riverstown was built, we have no means of ascertaining, but we know that in the sixteenth century it was in the possession of the Dillons. In the churchyard of Tara may be seen the monument of Robert Dillion of Riverstown, who died in 1595.*

End of quotation from Sir William Wilde's book.

From the foregoing extract it's obvious that, though Sir William was unaware of the exact date of the construction of the castle, he was greatly impressed by the magnificence of its structure. It seems likely that the older part was built shortly after the Norman invasion of Meath, in the latter half of the 12th century or perhaps in the early part of the 13th century. Adam de Feypo (Pheypo), of the Norman Barony or Fiefdom of Skryne (Skreen), one of Hugh de Lacy's leading knights, granted the lands of Riverstown to the de Wivella family (Wile) shortly after the Norman settlement of Meath. The granting of the land included an obligation of building a castle to defend against the disgruntled Gaels – this possibly sets a marker for the building of Riverstown castle in the early part of the

13th century. The castle became one of the many *towerhouses of the Pale* and was resided in by a feudal lord.

The following are some snippets gleaned from various historical references: The Dillon family first came to Ireland during the time of the Norman invasion and settled in County Westmeath. At the time, the family name was *de Lion*. They spread throughout the Pale and became prominent in the Norman/English administration of Ireland, with many members holding high-level positions in government. Over the years they diverged and their loyalties split, both in politics and in religious beliefs, with a few embracing the new religion. Some left the Irish shores as members of the Wild Geese, they fought on opposing sides in the rebellion of 1641 and later in the Battle of the Boyne, with some being dispossessed of their lands after both conflicts.

The arrival of the family in Riverstown seems to have been brought about by the marriage of Sir Richard Dillon, descendant of the Dillon's of Drumranney in County Westmeath, to the heiress Jean de Wile (formerly de Wivella); who inherited the lands of Riverstown. I'm uncertain as to the date of the marriage. In the intervening years the descendants of this union included many prominent people, such as a chief Baron of the exchequer, an Attorney General to Henry VIII and Sir Lucas Dillon, who with his wife are interred at the Dillon Monument in Newtown church ruins (near Trim), the date of this monument is 1586. Local legends name this as "the tomb of the jealous man and woman", I have no idea why it is called such an odd name. As mentioned by Sir William Wilde, a Dillon who once owned Riverstown castle is interred in a crypt in Tara church. His name was Sir Robert Dillon and he died in 1595 – the memorial being erected by his wife, Katherine Sarsfield. I note that some historians speculate that she may have been related to Patrick Sarsfield of 'Siege of Limerick' fame. As a point of interest, supposedly, Patrick Sarsfield's sister Anna was married to a Jackobite named Cheevers (Chevers) and lived in the nearby castle at Castletown crossroads on the old Dublin to Navan turnpike road. Legend says that Patrick stayed with her at Castletown Tara prior to the Battle of the Boyne in 1690. I have also heard these claims being made in respect to Macetown Castle over near Rathfeigh.

The Dillon family was associated with the castle in Riverstown until sometime in the 18th century. Some say they acquired the estate in Lismullin (formerly one of the Nangle properties) at that time but I have seen other references showing they were in possession of Lismullin one hundred years earlier and may have acquired this estate during the land confiscations following the rebellion of 1641. An Arthur Dillon supposedly owned Lismullin Manor and the associated mill (reputedly the King's Mill of legend) in 1656. The Civil Survey of 1654/56 notes the following about Riverstown: under the heading of "Propriators in 1640 and their qualifications; Andrew Dillon of Riverstown Irish Papist" (sic). And under the heading 'Observations', it further notes: "On the premises a ruinated castle" (sic). Some historical references state that Sir Robert Dillon constructed Riverstown castle during the middle years of the 16th century. These references possibly apply to the construction of the newer part on the western side. Other references state that Sir William Fitzwilliams, the Lord Deputy, was a friend of the family and stayed at Riverstown for a time – also that the Irish antiquarian and classical scholar, Robert Wood, was born in the newer part of the castle in 1717.

I will conclude the historical references with the story of the alleged feud between the Dillon family of Riverstown and the Nugent family of nearby Kilcarn, who were also of Norman descent but at the time in question were of the Catholic religion. The story goes that in the 1570s Sir Robert was competing with Nicholas Nugent of Kilcarn for the position of Master of the Rolls, a very prestigious position. The power struggle resulted in Nicholas Nugent being arrested and tried on a trumped up charge of treason. On being convicted, he was hanged in Trim. Reputedly, after the trial, Robert Dillon stood on the bridge in Trim and shouted back towards where Nugent was incarcerated: "Ha friend Nugent, methinks I am even with thee now". The feud lasted for several years thereafter, culminating in the trial of Sir Robert Dillon, also for treason – the reference does not record his fate, but as he was buried in Tara in 1595 perhaps he had a similar end to his 'friend Nugent'.

In May 2008 I visited Riverstown castle. I will not attempt to describe the castle and its former splendour, after all, what modern day scribe could come close to matching, much less surpassing, the eloquence of the description given by Sir William Wilde in 1849. So I will content myself with an account of its condition in the recent past. Over the years since 1849 the castle deteriorated and, to copy a quote from the Civil Survey of 1654/56, was most definitely in a 'ruinated' state. On the older part, the towerhouse, most of the cut and hammered stonework from around the doors, windows and embrasures, together with the outside corners and cornices so well described by Sir William, was removed during the passage of time and the surrounding walls were crumbling. This gave a very dilapidated appearance to the once splendid structure, with the ragged holes giving the impression of empty eye sockets gazing blindly over the surrounding plains of Royal Meath and the gently sloping Hill of Tara to the east. The internal floors were no more, the spiral staircase in the southwestern tower had collapsed and many of the square flat stones had been removed from the pigeonholes of the dovecote on the top northeastern corner turret. Additionally, parts of the turrets were gone, as were the upper parapets and the walkway around the topmost part of the towerblock, where in days of yore sentinels prowled, their eyes ceaselessly scanning the surroundings lands of the Pale for signs of the invading armies of O'Neil and O'Donnell. Most of the newer section, formerly attached to the western side of the tower, had disappeared. The largest portion of this being a magnificent barrel-vaulted structure at ground level which was used for housing farm animals for many years and until quite recent times. Altogether, the once impressive castle of Riverstown presented a less than inspiring spectacle in the surrounding pastoral landscape of County Meath.

The following is a brief description of the castle's lay out. The main entry is at ground level on the south-facing wall. This leads into a dark bottom chamber with no fireplace, I'm told that most of the cooking was performed in open fires in a nearby gravel hole just outside the bawn. The exit from this chamber is through a small opening in the western wall which leads through the small porch-like lobby of the murder hole and out to the large barrel vaulted structure to the west. The murder hole is so called because it is a very small chamber, which provided the only access to the spiral staircase leading to all the upper floors. Supposedly, if the castle was under attack and its defences were breached, the occupants retreated to the floors above. Should the attackers have attempted to storm the higher levels, they had to pass through the murder hole and try to break down the strong door blocking the stairs. While carrying out this assault they were confined to the small hallway and exposed to a rain of missiles, stones, arrows, the inevitable boiling oil and water and God knows what else being hurtled through the corbeled aperture in the roof of the tiny space, hence the name 'murder hole'.

The only entry to the feudal lord's treasure chamber (or secret room) was from the first floor bedchamber. The spiral staircase leads to all the upper levels and ascends from the 'murder hole's' tiny chamber or porch and up to the top or open air attic, as described by Sir William.

Each floor is a self-contained apartment, a surprisingly modern concept for the time. In addition to having its own fireplace, every 'apartment' contained a small separate bedchamber with niches built into the stone walls as storage space. For those who think an 'ensuite toilet' is a modern idea, it's time to think again, as each level contains a small antechamber with provision for a toilet. The toilet was rather crude, being only a hole in the floor connected to one of the vertical flues, or upright passages mentioned by Sir William. One wonders what types of toilet bowls, if any, were used in those days – perhaps they were of the 'squatting pan' variety, one of which could be seen until recent years in the little public toilet on the fair green in Navan. The small vertical flue, or passage, led to an outside midden (cesspit) at the bottom of the southeastern tower. Each of the chambers is laid out in a similar fashion, with the interior dimensions of the main room being about fifteen feet square.

I could go on indefinitely extolling the virtues of this ancient ruin but space does not permit such latitude so I will conclude with a brief mention of the immediate surroundings and one question. Not much trace remains of the ancient bawn or courtyard mentioned by Sir William, just the remnants of some stone walls here and there, whose date of construction is uncertain. My question is two pronged: Who installed the stone Gargoyle-like facial image high up on the eastern wall of the tower and why is it set in that place, gazing eternally towards the east and the gently rolling slopes of Tara?

# An Ode to the Valley

I ofttimes dream of sights once seen,
where in youth we wandered keen.
'Neath summer skies, through woody glen,
past brookside bank and meadow's fen.
To deep dark pool where rivers met,
close by Clooneen in watery tryst.

Where stone arch bridges o'er
bright mingled rippling waters.
Tarry whilst on plains once green
see rustic fields of fair Tara's scene.
On Gabhra's banks roam by Sally spinney,
to Dillon's Bridge school and Smithy.

Then return by Skein's fair sweeps,
and ramble past Boyne's dark wet deeps.
Hear rail and coot their wild bird's call,
while we lie on grass 'neath waterfall.
Past St. Brigid's well and limekiln go
home again to fire's warm glow.

by Anthony Holten

Larkin's No. 5

1. Bellinter Bridge (1813)
2. Dowdstown House
3. Dowdstown Church (ruined)
4. The conjoined Rivers Skane
   and Gabhra
5. Old Line of Turnpike across
   the River Field

6. Bellinter Crossroad
7. The Clooneen Wood
8. The Clooneen Junction
9. Ambrose Bridge (1814)
10. The Limekiln Hill
11. Old Line of Summerhill
    /Navan Road

# 7

# Bellinter to Dowdstown

The Dead Hole – Bellinter and the Prestons – pink Thunderbirds and Migrants – The Skane Meadows and Harry's Hill – a lost hamlet and the White Gates of Balgeeth – tales of Croppies and the Cluide Wood – the Decoy of Bellinter and The Butler's hole – joyrides on Airplanes and a tale of Faith, Hope and Charity – Bellinter Cross.

Back on the road again we continue on from Bonfield and enter the townland of Bellinter. In our younger days this was a beautiful stretch of roadway with many oak, beech and elm trees overhanging the highway and a great view to the southeast towards Tara. On the left and close by the edge of the roadway was a small dark pond which locals called 'The Dead Hole', or 'The Pool of the Babies'. Because of the ivy covered trees overhanging the gloomy looking greenish water, we as children considered it to be a creepy and sinister place – in some ways it rather spoiled the otherwise peaceful scene. I noticed that when passing the spot most of the older folk tended to bless themselves and murmur a prayer. Anecdotes were told about the little pond, some of which said that over the years the bodies of several babies were found floating in the pool. One such yarn told of how, back in the 1920s, a doctor's car was seen there just before the body of a baby was found in the water. There were dark whispers about the portents of this, most of which flew over our heads in those days of true innocence. As children we didn't tarry when passing by on our many trips to Bective Abbey, but hurried past this place, the occasional furtive glance we cast over our shoulders indicating our fear of what we might see in the shadowy woods. A local farmer drained and filled the hole in recent years and the legends have died out long since.

In the woods just behind the dark pool stood the walled-in garden of Bellinter House, this was once famed for its great vegetables and the many greenhouses wherein grew all sorts of exotic plants. A couple of old dwellings stood here which in my youth housed people working on the estate. In later years most of these buildings and the garden were flattened during the bulldozing of the woods – but part of the high wall survived and is still standing at time of writing. Further on we come to the entrance to Bellinter House, this was known as the Bective Gate – at one time there were three entrances to the demesne, the Bective Gate, the Decoy Gate and the Kennel Gate. Much has been written about Bellinter and its history so I will give but a brief account here.

John O'Donovan interpreted Ballinter as meaning 'Baile an tSaoir', or 'the town of the carpenter'. The Down Survey Barony map shows that Bellinter, from the River Skeine (Skeene) to the River Boyne, was located in the Barony of Lower Deece and named Ballniteeran in those times. In the 1650s, John Preston, a son of Hugh Preston of Bolton in Lancashire, came into possession of many tracts of land in Counties Meath and Laois, totalling almost eight thousand acres. Supposedly he acquired most of this land from mercenary soldiers and adventurers who campaigned with Cromwell and received confiscated land as payment for their services to the Parliamentarian Army – many of these people were not interested in settling in Ireland then. Much of this land was seized from the Nangle family, one of the prominent former Norman families in County Meath at the time (AKA De La Corner – see chapter 13 for further details of this family name). Preston assigned a sizeable portion of this land in trust to schools in both counties. His admirers say this was a magnanimous gesture, whilst his detractors take the opposite view and contend that it was but a clever ruse to prevent the rightful owners reclaiming their property in the future. Whatever the truth of the matter, John Preston was confirmed as owner of most of these lands when the acts of settlement were passed following the restoration of King Charles II. Preston had four sons who inherited his property and later owned estates in Bellinter, Balsoon, Swainstown and Ardsallagh – thus forming a dynasty that became dominant in the county for many years. In the 1890s the Briscoe family came into possession of the estate after a disputed will was contested in the courts. The original vast estates were greatly diminished following the enactment of the Wyndham act in 1903, whereby tenants were allowed to purchase their holdings from the estate owners at a fixed price. This act went some way towards redressing the injustice of the land confiscations put into effect during the Cromwellian and Williamite periods. The Bellinter estate was reduced to just over 800 acres, including the deerpark, part of which became the Bellinter Park Golf Club in the 1920s. There were also some smaller properties elsewhere.

A Yorkshire man named William Holdsworth bough the estate in 1955: I recall the Holdsworths driving past Dowdstown in a large pink American open topped car, which, if my memory serves me well, was either a Chevy or a Thunderbird. In the early 1960s the property was taken over by the Land Commission and divided into small holdings, then followed an influx of migrants from the west of Ireland and elsewhere to take possession of the new farms. In 1966 the Sisters' of Sion started a retreat centre in the house and became famous for both their cultivated flowers and their seminars – they remained there until very recent times. At time of writing, Bellinter House has been turned into an exclusive country club and now, instead of Holdsworth's pink Thunderbird, pink hued stretch limousines travel down the road from Garlow Cross and helicopters spoil the once tranquil scene with their discordant clattering.

A short way to the east of Bellinter's Bective Gates there's a gateway on the opposite side of the road, which was once known as the Skane Meadow's Gate. In my boyhood, Dad leased some land here and grazed a few cattle on the meadows by the River Skane. Several times during those years our family travelled over on sunny Sunday afternoons and had picnics by the river at the spot where it curved around the Cluide Wood in the area of the fields known as the Upper Skane and Harry's Hill. We paddled in the clear waters and ran some childish races on the grassy banks. At the time it seemed an almost idyllic spot and I still retain some fond memories of those days when the chestnut and beech trees of the dark Cluide hung down over the clear waters at the big sweeping bend in the river.

I have another fleeting memory of the place near the long gone wood, of the old laneway leading from the roadside gate and winding across the meadows by the Skane. On its way it crossed over some little keshs (bridges) spanning the stream, which rose in the bottomlands here and in Balgeeth, then flowed into the Boyne in Asigh. Very few traces of any of this remains today, the Cluide Wood fell to the axe and bulldozer many years since and the green meadows reverted to swampy bottoms for a time – the little lane became just another cowpass onto part of a small farm. Travelling along the road nowadays, I sometimes wonder if these times of childhood were real – or were they just another of those tantalising partly recalled times of yesteryear which come flitting out of some buried recess of our mind's eye to haunt us from time to time. While doing research, my siblings confirmed the picnics by the Skane and our mini sports days on its grassy banks, but none of them could recall a great deal about the old laneway. Then, whilst talking to Brendan Farrelly, a local man from Lismullin who once lived in Bonfield, I mentioned my vague recollections of the old lane – his response was: "sure that's the old laneway that was once a right of way up to Balgeeth".

He went on to tell of the Skane Meadow's Gate and how in his youth, when walking home he sometimes took a shortcut along the lane and crossed over the fields to his home in Bonfield. And how from time to time, the famous R. J. Murray took his threshing mill along the lane to his farmyard in Balgeeth. Brendan informed me that a man named Anderson, a relative of the Briscoes, operated a small cement block making business in the Skane Meadows sometime in the early 1950s. This site was in the field known as Harry's Hill and located at a gravel ridge over near Bonfield, it was accessed via the lane – several men from around Garlow Cross worked there for a time. I believe some of these were named Hubert Smith, Tommy Kennedy, Starchy Fay and Pasie Kennedy: It being a manual operation, all the blocks were made by hand in individual moulds. My brother Tom reminded me that circa 1952, cement blocks manufactured at Harry's Hill were used to rebuild the Palace Cinema in Navan, which was burned down in 1949.

Extensive scrutiny of the old ordnance survey maps revealed that in times past a laneway ran through the fields named the Skane Meadows and Harry's Hill and linked the road from Bellinter to Balgeeth. The first edition of the 1837 OS map indicates the lane winding its way through the big woods (variously known as the deal, dale or larch wood) to the west of the Cluide and on towards Balgeeth, but it doesn't show it continuing on to the Bellinter road. The second edition of the 1882 OS map indicates the said laneway running from the Bellinter road through a gap in the woods and on towards Balgeeth, whilst the map of 1911 shows only the various little bridges across the small streams. So our youthful memories proved to be accurate enough, there was indeed a laneway between Bellinter and Balgeeth in times past. This probably dated back to the time when Balgeeth was part of the Bellinter estate in the days long before the 'new road' had been joined up by the construction of the bridge at Riverstown.

The rediscovery of this old laneway helped to solve another little riddle, which had been puzzling me for some time. The late Ita Maguire, nee Fleming, who was born and reared on the Bellinter estate, told me that there was a village in front of Bellinter House in olden times. She heard of this mystery village long ago, when as a child she sat by the fireside in their home near the gardens on the estate and listened to the old folk telling tales of the ancient hamlet. Searching the maps revealed nothing of this long lost village with no trace of it to be found in the fields and woods to the north of the road. Then, shown on Larkin's Map, I found a small

*White Gates, Balgeeth*

cluster of buildings to the south of the road near the River Skane and west of the Cluide Wood – I wondered could this be the little hamlet referred to in the fireside stories of yesteryear? I wasn't too sure as there was no sign of any road or pathway linking the houses to an access road. Now that I'm certain about the existence of the laneway to Balgeeth, which would have passed through this hamlet, I'm convinced that this was the village Ita told me about whilst chatting to me by her own fireside many years after she first heard the stories!

Richard Farrelly of Balgeeth confirmed the stories about the laneway and the old extinct hamlet. He told me that the lane once led to Michael Murphy's house, later Mrs McCabe's – supposedly this was at one time the herd's house for Preston's of Bellinter. He showed me some old photos of R. J. Murray, his grandfather, a few of which depicted the old threshing mills being hauled across the new concrete bridge over the Skane at Riverstown when it was but partly constructed. He told me that his mother, Maude Farrelly, nee Maude Murray, had maintained the right of way on the old lane even after the division of Bellinter by the Land Commission in the 1960s. She achieved this by driving her old grey 1954 Ford Popular along the route from time to time until the said Commission came to a settlement. Richard took me down through the fields and I saw some of the old route and the site of the long gone village of which there's now no trace. He said that over the years, many domestic artefacts were found here. At the spot where Murray's land had a mearing with the old Bellinter estate the laneway was closed off by a set of iron gates known as the *White Gates*. These gates are still there, hanging on stone pillars and all in good condition, but they're no longer white. The ancient hamlet once occupied the field to the northeast of these gates.

More recently, Richard discovered some documents pertaining to the construction of the previously described new road from Asigh to Riverstown. These were old records kept by his Grandfather, R.J. Murray of Balgeeth, who was a contractor on the job. The paperwork consisted inter alia of orders for materials such as fence posts, wire and staples, and included some time sheets submitted for the various gangs of workmen fencing off and doing general work on the new road. These old papers provided a glimpse into the past, to times that are long gone when men worked for 3s. 4d. per day (three and fourpence) and received the princely sum of £1 for a six day week – and when 460 oak posts could be sawed at Farrell's sawmill in Kentstown for the sum of £15 at the rate of 8s. an hour. It was fascinating to browse through these old papers so generously loaned to me by Richard – these records indicate that work on the new road was in progress in late 1929 and in early 1930. One time sheet shows that the following men were working on the Asigh section of the road in February 1930: Joe Smith, James Boyle, Frank Smith, Patrick Lynam, Joseph Mulligan, John Flynn, Tom Moran, W.m. Keegan, W.m. Smith, James O'Neil, W.m. O'Neil, Dan Costello, M. Montague, P. Ward, and B.&T. Horris. The total earnings of the men for one week were £5 7s. 8d., with the price of three insurance stamps shown as 1s. – I note with interest that no mention is made of either income tax or V.A.T.!

Now to relate the story of the oft' mentioned Cluide Wood. This was a vast wood of over fifty acres, which ran from the Kilmessan to Navan road at Castletown Tara, and all the way down to the big sweeping bend on the River Skane near Harry's Hill. I would contend that the names of both the wood and river derived from the big curve in the stream – but more about this presently. At its eastern end near the road the great wood was quite narrow but at its western extremity it widened into an extensive area of woodland. It was an odd shape; viewed on the old OS maps from the southerly aspect it's shaped rather like a lightening flash with a zigzag in the middle. Between the zigzag and its wider section to the west was a large field – the field being bounded on three sides by woodland and to the north the Skane formed the fourth boundary; this field was known as The White Field. The big wood presented a dark gloomy image to us as children and we shunned the place, mostly because of the stories with which we were regaled around the fireside at night. These tales, told in whispers during my childhood years, were the horror stories of yesteryear ere we visited the cinemas and became acquainted with Count Dracula and the Mummy. In places like Kilmessan, Bective, Dowdstown, Bellinter and Garlow Cross, prior to the advent of rural electrification, fables were related to a hushed circle of listeners sitting in dancing shadows cast by flickering wood and turf fires. Mostly they consisted of the commonly recounted tales of headless horsemen, red eyed black dogs, stray sods, the hungry grass, the dreaded 'lone bush' and suchlike, but the legends most firmly rooted in my memory are of the dark deeds that supposedly took place in the Cluide Wood following the battle of Tara in 1798.

The yeomen and militias of the times, though fully armed, were oftentimes poorly trained and not subject to full military discipline. History attests to the indiscipline and rapine of the yeomen in particular, who were led mostly by local gentry and often considered as their private armies. One story says that these forces of the crown ruthlessly pursued the defeated Croppies. Reputedly the yeoman cavalry chased the terrified survivors of the battle – some of this cavalry being the same people who, in more normal times, hunted the equally terrified foxes as their chosen sport. We were told that a number of rebels were shot out of hand, some died of their wounds received in the battle, but several were captured and dragged into the dark recesses of the Cluide Wood to be dealt with. Supposedly about a dozen men were 'lynched', strung up without trial at a place known thereafter as *the hanging tree* and their bodies buried in the wood. One of the stories I heard said that the tree, a great oak or elm, never sprouted leaves again, yet it never died: legends said it was still there in the wood to the west of the white field, a stark reminder of those terrible times. The same legend went on to say that a local stonemason carved a stone and placed it in the wood near where the bodies were buried; this custom being common enough near the many Croppy graves scattered throughout County Meath, with plain marker stones hidden in the nearby hedges. Sometimes these stones were kept whitewashed by local people, which practice was maintained over many years but in later days it died out. When I was in my early teens and had overcome my fears of the headless horseman and fiery-eyed dogs of yesteryear I often wandered through the wood and searched for the hanging tree; the big oak with no leaves. I never found it or the marker stone, nor did the aforementioned Brendan Farrelly who knew every inch of the great wood, but some local people tell me that they saw the stone in the wood many years ago.

A new sanitised version of the ancient legend emerged in more recent times, long after the green sward of the golf course covered most of the area where the Cluide Wood once towered above the River Skane. Revisionism at work again I suspect. This story suggested that it was the local gentry who supposedly erected a headstone in the Cluide to commemorate the dead Croppies of 1798. I would give this version of the story less credence than nowadays I give to the fable of the headless horseman of former days. After all it's scarcely credible that the gentry of the period erected a monument, bearing testament to the cruel deeds perpetrated by their forebears in bygone times. In my humble opinion, it's more likely that this edition of the story emanated from the 19th hole of the golf club rather than from the depths of local folklore.

There are many legends about Croppy graves throughout County Meath – these tales abound from Curragha to Navan and Nobber, to Trim and Kilmessan, from Dunshaughlin to Timoole and the Deenes. Old scores were settled during those terrible times, so no doubt some of these stories are true: supposedly up to seven thousand rebels gathered at Tara on the day of the battle, 26th May 1798. Reputedly nearly five hundred of these were killed in the battle, some being buried on the hilltop, but many more were spirited away by friends and relatives and their bodies buried elsewhere. Many of the Croppy graves in the county derived from the Wexford insurgent column that marched through Meath in July 1798 and fought skirmishes with the military; further mention is made of this in chapters fifteen and sixteen.

Leaving the area of the Skane Meadows, we travel eastward along the road for about a half-mile until we come to the Decoy Gate, once the grand entrance to Bellinter House. Here lies another mystery from the past in the form of *The Bellinter Arches* or *Butler's Bridge.* This is the name given

Left: *Fr Keegan of Johnstown unveiling the Croppy monument - Hill of Tara - 1948*
Right: *The decoy gates of Belinter*

by the old natives of the area to a little twin arched bridge that nowadays stands in a field on dry land – but more about this mystery bridge later, first I'll describe the Decoy Gate and its immediate environs.

This old gateway must have been the original main entry to Bellinter long before the entrance from Bellinter Bridge via the Kennel Avenue became the principal access to Bellinter House. The explanation for this is quite simple, there was no bridge on the Boyne or even a road to provide access – the building of the bridge and the new road will be covered in succeeding chapters. Throughout my childhood years I heard this gateway being called the Decoy Gate and I sometimes wondered at the origins of the name. Research shows that the name Decoy is most likely used in the context of the common practice of the time, namely the decoying, or luring of wild ducks and their capture. This was to provide sustenance at the tables of the big country houses, sometimes also supplying the markets in the nearby towns and cities. The decoy usually consisted of small lakes or ponds upon which the wild ducks were enticed to alight; whereupon they were captured with nets or by other means. Oftentimes the lures used were other ducks with clipped wings, or various mock-up devices. The 1882 OS map indicates the possible presence of such a lake or pond in a small wood between the road and the River Skane. This map shows that the avenue ran across the Trim to Drogheda road, through a field named the Lower Park and over the Skane; then crossed a field named the Upper Park, now part of the Royal Tara Golf Course, to the Kilmessan road at Castletown Tara. This location was once known as *The Green Gate of Bellinter* and nowadays provides the main entrance to the golf club; which in my youth was called the Bellinter Park Golf Course. The area now the golf course was once Bellinter Deerpark and is shown as such on Larkin's Map. This route would have provided a splendid drive through the former parkland.

The Butler's Bridge, or Butler's Hole as it was known to some, is a name buried deep in local folklore: supposedly, in the distant past a butler drowned here. At time of writing the crumbling remains of the small bridge stands high and dry and is part of a boundary ditch in the middle of a field between the Skane and the road. As the butler of legend was unlikely to have drowned on dry land one wonders where was the water in which he supposedly met his watery end? Since early times when I frequently travelled the road, I wondered why the double arched bridge was there and came to know it as *The Bellinter Arches*. In recent times I did some research and found no records of the place – but old natives of the area like Ita Maguire and Brendan Farrelly provided the name out of their extensive well of local knowledge. A close examination of the bridge yielded some interesting information – it consists of two well-constructed arches of rough-hewn stone. Each arch spanned about five or six feet and was approximately the same in height, a three-foot wide stone pillar separated the two arches. The bridge is four feet or so in passage width and has no sidewalls or parapets, meaning that it could have been used only as a footbridge and it's about the same girth as the well-known Clady Bridge. But what stream did it span? The bridge was erected at approximately right angles to the nearby road, yet the arches were built askew within the structure; this meant that whatever stream once ran beneath didn't flow parallel to the road. If one followed the line provided by the skewed arches, it ran slightly to the southwest towards the big curve in the River Skane over towards the Cluide Wood.

It seemed strange that the River Skane ran in a dead straight line from the big sweeping bend all the way to Ambrose Bridge on the Kilmessan road. Somehow it was uncharacteristic that the Skane, which had hitherto wound its way in a meandering course from its source in Dunshaughlin along the alluvial plain to the Cluide Wood, should suddenly run on a course resembling a canal. John O'Donovan in his letters of 1836 concludes that the word Cluide translates to 'the corner' or nook – this seems particularly apt, as the wood once grew on a salient of land, almost a peninsula, around which the river flowed in a great curve. A study of the old maps revealed some interesting facts that might explain when the straight canal-like section of river came into being – but not the reason for the realignment of the stream. After the great curve, Larkin's Map shows the Skane's circuitous route continuing on eastwards and towards the bridge. It appears to have run close to the road at the Decoy Gate and on towards Bellinter Cross, then swung back to the southeast towards Ambrose Bridge and onwards into Dowdstown. This line may have taken it under the small stone footbridge at *the Butler's Hole*. The 1837 OS

*Bramble covered Bellinter arches located at Decoy gate.*

map shows the river running on the straightened course from the Cluide to the bridge. But interestingly, this map indicates the union, or parish boundary, running wide around the Cluide Wood and probably on much the same erratic line as the Skane takes on Larkin's Map of earlier years. The boundary can be seen clearly, it follows a winding course between the river and the Bective road, then rejoins the new path of the river at Ambrose Bridge and follows the line of the river to Dowdstown Bridge. The old boundary was most likely based upon the former border between the Barony of Lower Deece and the Barony of Skreen, which followed the course of the river, as can be seen on the Down Survey Maps of the 1650s. Further upstream, another such, but much shorter divergence of river and boundary is shown to the south of the ford at Riverstown. This section is marked on the 1837 OS map as *the new cut of river*.

I would suggest that the information gleaned from the maps tends to imply that the line of the River Skane was altered to its present straight course sometime between 1812 and 1836. The reason for this seems unclear but perhaps it was connected with the construction of the new line of road from Castletown to Cannistown between 1808 and 1815 and the consequent building of Ambrose Bridge? Or possibly it was realigned to reclaim the land between the river and the Bective road – more information, obtained from further research on the Grand Jury Books, is provided about the Skane and Ambrose Bridge in succeeding chapters. The purpose of the foregoing long explanation is to show that it's likely the River Skane once flowed beneath the arches of the old stone footbridge standing in Nealon's field of the present day. And that, whilst crossing the ancient stone arches, it was into the waters of this river the fabled butler fell and drowned. Though not conclusive, there are some indications on the OS maps that a footpath may once have run from Castletown through the Cluide Wood and across the Skane to Bellinter – the logical crossing point of the Skane would have been via the old stone bridge. The wooden bridge across the new line of the Skane is shown on the 1837 OS map but no sign of the avenue through the Deerpark is evident until it appears on the 1882 OS map – hence the old stone bridge would have been redundant after this date. It's logical, therefore, to suggest that the stone arches predate that era – so they would appear to be very old indeed, perhaps dating from the 17th century during the early days of the Prestons?

During my early years a prolific number of woodlands graced this area, with many copses and spinneys adding great charm to the landscape. A large wood surrounded the Decoy gate on the Bellinter House side of the road and a long wood ran all the way to Bellinter crossroads. Bridle paths and cart tracks meandered everywhere through the trees, making the area a pleasant place for woodland walks in the summertime and a veritable heaven for children's birdnesting adventures in the springtime. Following the change of ownership in the 1950s, progress suddenly came to this once peaceful part of our world, its disharmonious arrival being announced by the loud roar of diesel engines as bulldozers demolished the woods of Bellinter.

I remember when aeroplane joyrides were held at Bellinter in the early 1950s. These events took place during summer weekends and the flights operated from the front lawn to the south of the big house and alongside the avenue from the Decoy Gate. But this 'lawn' being 111 acres in extent wasn't typical of the green sward surrounding the average modern bungalow. Captain Darby Kennedy was the main operator of the joyrides and I believe the plane used was a De Havilland Dragon. I recall the big silver Biplane landing and taking off in those far off days when air travel was very rare indeed and the sight or sound of a plane in the blue sky caused much excitement for us children. The joyrides were held for several summers but I never became airborne at the time because I was considered too young – the tariff was five shillings (five Bob) and I'm told that the flight path was over Navan and around Proudstown racecourse then back to Bellinter. Looking on as 'a too young' but nonetheless very interested spectator, I noticed that most of the passengers were much paler of visage descending from the plane on their return to terrafirma; perhaps they reckoned that flying wasn't all it was cracked up to be? The air joyrides took place several times during those early years of boyhood – then they ceased forever, leaving a void in our lives at the time but providing me with some very happy recollections of times past. The old Dragon flew again in the skies above County Meath however, I'm told that to commemorate their early days of flying, Aer Lingus restored the old plane and at the start of the new millennium flew several sorties from the airfield at Dunganny near Trim.

In earlier years, during World War II, some different air activity took place at Bellinter. In those years the Irish Army sometimes carried out manoeuvres in the area and frequently bivouacked in the woods – from time to time the Air Corp accompanied them. The Corp had three old Biplanes stationed there and these were reputedly christened Faith, Hope and Charity: perhaps these names reflected the sentiments of the pilots flying the ancient kites? One of the pilots involved in air operations at Bellinter in those times was named Des Johnson, but I'm unsure as to which plane he flew.

The road runs eastwards along the Skane valley for about half a mile from the Decoy Gates, until its intersection with the Kilmesan to Navan road at Bellinter Cross. In my youth a long wood formed the northern boundary of the road all the way to the crossroads – the overhanging trees enhancing the beauty of the rustic setting, especially in the evenings when the westering sun cast giant tree-shadows on the roadside. Looking over the low wall towards the south, in the foreground could be seen the dark eye of the stone arched Ambrose Bridge – whilst the Hill of Tara, peeking over the remaining trees of the Clooneen Wood, provided a perfect backdrop to the most beautiful pastoral scene imaginable. Then came prosperity and with it many changes: first the woods were cleared and the land bulldozed, then the estate divided into small farms. Bungalow bliss followed and across the Skane the golf course expanded, but despite all these great changes the area retained much of its pastoral aesthetics. Now,

Clockwise from left: *Bivouacking in Bellinter woods 1941 - 'The Glads' under camouflage at Bellinter House, Constance Briscoe with Faith, Hope or Charity and Des Johnson, astride motorbike, collecting payroll at 1st Brigade H.Q., Ratoath House.* (Courtesy Annette Peard)

at time of writing, the greatest change of all is coming. A new road is to be built from the top of the valley near Philpotstown Cross to carry the Trim to Drogheda road across the M3 motorway at Dowdstown. This road will rejoin the Bective road close by the spot where the butler was supposedly drowned in the middle of a dry field all those years ago. The last vestige of the Clooneen Wood has disappeared and been replaced by a large sewerage plant – built to handle the burgeoning effluent from Dunshaughlin and to facilitate the redevelopment of a country demesne into an exclusive golf course. So the Skane valley has almost literally been transformed into an enormous sewer. Somehow I doubt that the area will retain its pastoral excellence following these latest changes and many more that will undoubtedly follow the relentless marching feet of progress – I wonder if the Bellinter arches will survive for much longer?

Larkin's No. 6
1. 1796/1798 Line of Turnpike
2. 1814 Line of Turnpike
3. The Cuille and Conlon's Field
4. The Deepark Lane
5. The Decoy
6. Jocks Cross
7. The Gabhra Island and Mill
8. Dillon's Bridge
9. The River Gabhra
10. Billy's Road
11. Rathmiles
12. Castletwon Crossroads
13. Old Summerhill/Drogheda Road
14. Site of R.I.C. Barracks
15. Tara Cross
16. The Nith Stream
17. Tandragee Wood
18. Baronstown/Meaghers Crossroad

# 8

# Dowdstown and Philpotstown

Chronology of road evolution – the ancient route from Tara towards Teltown – the old road from Bective and Trim through Dowdstown – the first turnpike 1729 – Realignment of Turnpike from Dunshaughlin to Dowdstown - New road from Bellinter to Philpotstown – construction of Dowdstown Bridge.

Our road now takes us to the once beautiful valley of Dowdstown, enclosed between the northwestern slopes of Tara and the big-bend on the River Boyne at Ardsallagh. The valley is home to the confluence of three historic rivers, the Gabhra, Skane and Boyne: long ago it was the meeting point for three of County Meath's ancient Baronies, Skreen, Lower Deece and Upper Navan. Historically, this area was epicentral to many roads, with the main road from Dublin taking at least four distinct lines through the area in different eras. At time of writing, the M3 motorway is the fifth, and hopefully the last, such route to cut through this once beautiful area. As can be visualised, the profusion of old roads, together with river confluences provides a complex backdrop against which to portray the evolution of the road network. As a starting point, let's begin at the mearing (mereing) between Dowdstown and Bellinter – the former boundary between the Baronies of Skreen and Lower Deece.

Currently, Bellinter crossroads is formed by the intersection of the Trim to Drogheda road and the Kilmessan to Navan road – the latter road runs south to north alongside part of the said Barony boundary, from the River Skane to the Boyne. Unlike the Trim/Drogheda road, which is much older, the section of the Kilmessan road cutting it at this crossroads is relatively new; being formed between 1809 and 1815. This is the first major alteration to the old route we encounter on our journey, the first of many changes made between 1796 and 1817. These were to alter the landscape around Tara and much of the surrounding district for many years into the future.

*The following chronology will provide assistance in understanding these complex changes:*

Pre 1730: An existing road ran through Dowdstown from the Hill of Tara to Kilcarn Bridge and Navan – anecdotes tell of this road being built over part of *An Slighe Asail*, the ancient route from Tara to Teltown of the Tailteann games. Close by the ruined church in Dowdstown, the old line of the road from Trim linked with both this ancient route and the Dublin to Navan road via Ratoath and Skryne – this junction was the precursor of the present day Philpotstown crossroads (now known as Garlow Cross).

1729 to 1796/98: Ancient road from Tara through Dowdstown became part of the Dublin to Navan turnpike road in 1730 and operated as a tollroad on this route between these dates.

1796 to 1802: Turnpike realigned from Dunshaughlin to Dowdstown.

1801 to 1804: A new line of the Trim/Drogheda road was cut from Bellinter through Dowdstown to Garlagh Cross (old Garlow) and a new bridge built across the coalesced Rivers Skane and Gabhra at Dowdstown.

1808 to 1815: A new line of the Summerhill to Navan road built from Castletown Tara to Cannistown – including the construction of Bellinter and Ambrose bridges.

**1814 to 1817: Turnpike road realigned from Dowstown to Kilcarn – formation of Philpotstown crossroads (Garlow Cross).**

# The Ancient Road From Tara

Following the chronology, let's start with the ancient road from Tara through Dowdstown and onwards towards Kilcarn. Initially, when studying the old road network in Dowdstown on the 1837 OS map, I noted that a big 'S', the first letter of the name Skreen, obscured this particular area, including the artificial lake which in times past was located to the north of Dowdstown Bridge. Then I noticed that the 'S' itself provided some clues – a wavy line, I thought was a crease in the old map, turned out to be the line of an old road or pathway. Closer examination indicated it was a road, as the drafters of the map had intentionally cut it through the 'S' and it stood out boldly.

Currently, it is my opinion that the line running through the 'S' on the OS map provides an indicator of the course of the road prior to it becoming a turnpike in 1729. This was probably the path of the more ancient road running from Tara towards Navan and beyond. The northern end of a short section of older road was discovered recently (circa 2005) during an archaeological dig and caused some head scratching amongst the learned experts. The buried roadway was about fifteen feet wide and built of stone – it had the same location and orientation as the line through the 'S' on the map. To the south, and on the same map, a wooden bridge is shown crossing the River Gabhra, in line with the section of old road. This seems to be confirmation that the ancient road from Tara, pre 1730, skirted to the east of the swampy valley of the Skane at Dowdstown. It rejoined the later line of the turnpike just to the south of the old church on Dowdstown Hill and possibly followed this line to Kilcarn Bridge.

This old line made sense during those earlier times, as the route probably crossed the smaller River Gabhra at the site of the wooden bridge, thus avoiding two crossings of the larger river Skane. Additionally, it followed the tradition of the ancient roads by traversing the hillside to the east of the valley. No trace of this old route was evident to the south of the Gabhra during my youth. It's unlikely that anything of historical note will be discovered in future years, because the great swathe of the M3 was cut through this area, tearing up and destroying everything in its path. The turnpike road, built over parts of this ancient road in 1730, ran straight across the valley on a raised embankment from the southern ridge at the old Clooneen Wood to the northern ridge at Dowdstown Hill

## The Old Road from Bective and Trim

There is evidence to suggest that in times past, the road from Bective and Trim followed its modern line to the place where Bellinter crossroads is now located – but what was its onward route from there? As stated, Bellinter crossroads, Dowdstown Bridge, Philpotstown Cross (Garlow Cross) didn't exist and the present day linking road hadn't yet been built – I would suggest, therefore, that the road from Bective once crossed the old stone bridge in Dowdstown, which was destroyed many tears later in the 1954 floods. The original route from Bective ran on the higher ground above the flood plain, about midway between the present day locations of Bellinter crossroads and Dowdstown Bridge (built in 1802), the route swung northeastwards to cross the river via the aforementioned stone bridge. Following the river crossing, it joined the previously mentioned older line of the road from Tara (as shown cut through the 'S' on the 1837 map) near its junction with the Dublin, Ratoath and Skryne road close by the ruined church.

Long ago, a gate was located on each side of Dowdstown Avenue at the site of the long gone crossroads. This area was known as the cross gates and we thought the name derived because of the gates being located on opposite sides of the avenue, but perhaps the name originally meant *the gates at the crossroads*? During childhood Dad told us that a crossroads existed here in earlier times – but did not mention anything about the other roads and from whence they came or how he knew about the junction. My research proves that he was correct, as the junction is shown on Beaufort's Map of 1797, J Taylor's engraved map of 1802, the OS map of 1837 and the Longfield Map of Dowdstown dated 1822. This little tale shows how folklore can provide vital clues and the way in which it passes down through the generations. The reason for this road junction's omission from Larkin's Map will be explained in the section covering realignment of the turnpike in the 1790s.

This was a logical line for the road to take during those early times, with the medieval church being central to a hub of activity – a place where main routes converged on Kilcarn Bridge; the only dry crossing point of the Boyne between Trim and Navan. People who ploughed the nearby fields, both in older and more recent days, told me that from time to time they unearthed parts of an old stone built road in this area and wondered about it. The buried road ran from the Bective/Trim road towards the concrete bridge presently carrying Dowdstown back-avenue over the Skane.

It's necessary to revisit my early memories once more, to explain how I know about the old stone bridge. About 1952, my brother Tom and I sometimes stood on a stone arched bridge carrying the avenue across the River Skane in Dowdstown. This bridge, which is still there at time of writing, is protected by iron handrails and has no parapet walls. We knew it then as *the swimming pool bridge*, because in those days it overlooked an outdoor swimming pool. The pool was built on the west side of the avenue during the 1940s, to provide swimming facilities for the students in Dalgan Park seminary – the location is about three hundred yards to the south of the old church. From upstream, the Skane passed through some serpentine-like bends and underneath the bridge where we stood, then its waters flowed over a moss and lichen covered waterfall, or weir, through the pool and onwards to the Boyne. Three boyscouts were drowned at the waterfall a few years earlier in 1948, which event cast a dark shadow over our childhood and we dreaded the spot thereafter.

Our main interest at the time, however, was not in the soft murmuring of the Skane tumbling over the waterfall or the beautiful pastoral setting – our boyhood attention being absorbed by gangs of workmen digging out a diversion to the river nearby. Two groups were at work, one on each side of the avenue, hand digging a new course for the river, to take it under the other stone bridge further south along the avenue towards the lodge at the Trim road gate.

We watched with great interest as the workmen dug out the oozy, muddy path of the new riverbed. This new cut caused the river to flow on a different course and under the older stone arched bridge, before rejoining

*The Swimming Pool Bridge built circa 1810/1820 looks north towards Churchill. The back avenue in Dowdstown follows the line of the turnpike - the long gone crossroads was situated where the avenue turns the corner on the hill*

the original path of the Skane just downstream from the swimming pool – until that time in 1952 we were unaware of the existence of the other stone bridge. A small side stream remained on the former riverbed to keep the pool supplied with fresh water. In later years I discovered that the reason for diverting the river was to prevent the swimming pool being filled with mud and detritus during the winter floods.

Both my brother Tom and I recall the more ancient bridge because we witnessed the diversion of the river back then. The older stone bridge is no longer there, most of it being swept away by the great flood on the 8th of December 1954. We saw the remains of the broken arch soon after the bridge was wrecked – the entire downstream side of the structure, about three metres in width, was carried away by the raging floodwaters. We wondered why the remaining stonework was so regular, with no jagged edges; it was like a separate small bridge. A couple of spruce tree trunks were placed across the yawning chasm, these, together with the remaining few feet of the stone arch became the avenue bridge for a year or more. We drove the pony and cart many times over this makeshift crossing; hence I remember it very well indeed. A short time later, if I recall correctly 1956, the remains of the stone bridge were dug out and replaced by a concrete bridge, which nowadays carries Dowdstown Avenue across the Skane.

The manner of the destruction of the old stone bridge at Dowdstown

*Concrete avenue Bridge in Dowdstown on the site of an ancient stone arched bridge that was swept away in the floods of 1954*

in 1954 suggests to me that it was once a much narrower bridge; probably about ten feet in road width. The small remaining and clean profiled section, that survived the flood, would indicate the widening of the structure in earlier days, possibly in 1729 to carry the turnpike road. Further details of this bridge are included in the section covering the development of the turnpike road through this area. If my theory is correct, the destroyed stone bridge in Dowdstown must have been very old indeed. Had it been widened in 1729 during the road's conversion to a turnpike, the old structure obviously predated that time and was possibly built in medieval times – but like many other things in the area, we shall never know for sure. I note Peter O'Keefe mentions in his book that when he first inspected Dowdstown Bridge (the stone arched bridge of 1802) in the 1980s, he was surprised to find a modern bridge and not one from more ancient times. Perhaps the old stone bridge on the avenue was the one he was expecting to find, but it was long gone by then and now exists only in the memories of some ageing codgers like myself.

From the old stone bridge, the lost section of road from Trim ran northwards for about one hundred metres and linked up with the old line of the road from Tara. The joined roads ran on to their meeting with the Ratoath/Skryne road beside the ruined church. At this junction, the older route of the Trim/Drogheda road turned eastwards and ran along the line of the Skryne road to Garlagh Cross (Old Garlow). A presentment, which covers the closure of this portion of the old route in 1802, is included in the section dealing with the realignment of the turnpike road during the 1790s.

The following Grand Jury presentment proves the existence of the older road from Bective. Recorded under the Barony of Skreen (Query Book) lent assizes of 1801 and reads: *Item 543 Wher £18,, 8,, &18,, 5 wag' be raised off Barony Skreen & Acc for by Lord Tara Th's Williams Ja's King Jo'n & Will Dignan to rep' 92 Per's from Trim to Drogheda betw' Bellinter & bridge of Dowdstown @ 4,, p* (sic). The distance presented for equates to 644 yards or 0.36 of a statute mile, which matches the suggested old line between Bellinter crossroads and the previously described former stone bridge in Dowdstown. As the survey of the new line from Bellinter to Philpotstown was not presented for until the summer assizes later the same year (1801) and the new bridge on this line wasn't built until 1802, it's unlikely that the presentment was made for repairs to a non-existent road.

## The Old Route of the Turnpike Road Through Dowdstown in 1729

As my previous book (entitled *Where Toll Roads Meet*) covers the routing and history of this road, I will give but a synopsised account here; which includes some new data discovered during further research of the Grand Jury records.

The Dublin to Navan turnpike road was part of the much longer main route from Dublin to Ballyshannon in County Donegal. Part of the route, from the city to the Blackbull, was also a section of another main route, the Dublin to Granard road via Finae. The road from the Blackbull through Trim and Athboy was run as a tollroad from its inauguration in 1731 until becoming a *free road* in 1752 – this was the first turnpike road in Ireland to cease being a tollroad.

The Navan turnpike road ran from the number 1 milestone at the

*The lodge at Dowdstown gates on the Trim/Drogheda road - the avenue in the foreground was built upon the line of the 1729 turnpike road*

tollhouse in Stoneybatter to the number 23 (formerly number 24) milestone at Canon (Cannon) Row in Navan – from there it continued onwards as the Kells turnpike. The old coachroads were measured from the gates at Dublin Castle in Irish miles (2240 yds or 1.27 statute mile), hence the number one stone's location at Stoneybatter; later day mail coach roads were measured from the G P O. On a point of interest, the milestone in Stoneybatter being the number one stone for several other routes, perhaps this provides a clue to the derivation of the placename, which translates to *The Stony Road.* The turnpike to Navan was routed as follows: From Stoneybatter to Blackhorse Lane, Castleknock, Abbotstown (Blanchardstown), Mulhuddart (Malahidert) and on to Clonee. It bypassed Dunboyne and ran through *The Sheaf of Wheat* to the Blackbull Inn. From there it passed through *The Ten Mile Bush* (now The Black Bush) village and ran through Dunshaughlin to Killeen, Belper (Ballyna), the Hill of Tara, Castletown Tara to Dowdstown. It crossed Kilcarn Bridge and continued on via *The Old Road* in Balreask, passed by *The Swan Inn* to Ludlow Street and through Trimgate Street to Canon Row in Navan.

In this section I will concentrate on the route from the Hill of Tara through Dowdstown and its immediate environs.

Starting at the road's summit by the church gates, we follow the old route down the northwestern slopes of Tara. Some historians know this section as *The Slope of the Chariots*, or *Slighe Fan na gCarpad*; because the warriors of the High Kings supposedly raced their chariots here in days of yore. John O'Donovan's field notes and sketches of 1836 mark this part as an ancient road and include therein the name *Slighe Cualann;* other scholars conclude that it was part of *An Slighe Asail.*

Near the bottom of the hill we come to Castletown Tara crossroads, where the turnpike intersected the former line of the Summerhill to Drogheda road. At time of writing, this road links the Kilmessan to Navan road, from the gates at the Royal Tara Golf Club to the N3 at *Soldier's Hill* – more details about this road are included later in this chapter. To the northwest of the crossroads stood the castle from which the townland derived its name; some ruins of this *tower house of the pale* still stand on the site. Note the other references to this castle in chapter six. Daniel Augustus Beaufort's map of County Meath (1797) shows buildings immediately adjacent to the crossroads and a rectory in the townland, perhaps at the site of the castle. The crossroads and castle ruins are shown on both Larkin's Map and the 1837 OS map. Though the castle is not marked as such on the Taylor and Skinner map of 1778, a building is shown on each corner of the crossroads. The road running westwards is marked as the Trim road: this was correct at that time, because it linked with the Summerhill, Kilmessan to Navan road, which in turn joined the Trim to Blackbull turnpike at Pike Corner.

The old line of the turnpike running northwards from Castletown crossroads can still be driven upon today, as it forms a cul de sac road leading to a dead end on the edge of the valley at Dowdstown. Travelling downhill for about a half-mile along the old roadway, we come to a right-angled corner, where the turnpike road abruptly changed direction and ran due west for a short distance. Perhaps this is the place where the more ancient road from Tara towards Navan and beyond, carried straight on – then crossed the Gabhra and ran east of the swamp in Dowdstown, to join the Dublin to Ratoath and Skryne road near the ancient church on the hill, as described previously.

At time of writing, should we follow the muddy laneway leading westwards from the sharp corner, we come to a rusty iron made gate blocking our path. This partly overgrown track, once the old line of the turnpike, is the last vestige of the ancient road that can be directly linked to the northside of the Hill of Tara in the topography of contemporary times. From here, through Dowdstown to Kilcarn Bridge, I could trace

Left: *The 1729 line of the turnpike, marked in black, crossed* The River Field - *The Hill of Tara is in the background. This area is now under the M3 motorway. Right: The clumpwood in the river field, Dowdstown 1970*

the route of the turnpike because my childhood memories of Dowdstown aided me to decipher the clues found on the old maps.

About midway between the sharp corner and the old gate, the route crosses a little river that rises over near Cardiffstown on the western slopes of Tara. Beside the stone kesh carrying the road across the stream, Larkin's Map indicates a laneway leading northwards to a watermill on the nearby river Gabhra. This lost mill is discussed further in Chapter 13 titled *The Mills of Gabhra.*

To the west of the old gate, the traceable remains of the turnpike comes to an abrupt end near a scarred field, once the site of the oft' mentioned Clooneen Wood – which name translates to *the wood of the little meadow.* In my youth, this was a charming and almost idyllic spot, though many of the trees were felled for firewood during the fuel shortages of World War II, the place still contained plenty of elm, lime, beech and pink blossomed chestnut trees. The spring blossoms and autumn tints of the old wood were a sight to behold from our home across the valley – but this place too has been decimated by progress. As mentioned previously, the beautiful woodland of yesteryear is now home to a huge sewage plant; constructed to aid greedy developers in further despoiling the landscape of County Meath.

In this once lovely place now ravaged by development, the turnpike linked with the old line of the Summerhill to Navan road – which intersection I now refer to as the Clooneen Junction. Larkin's Map shows the old line of this road running from just north of the current location of the Royal Tara Golf Club gates and linking with the old turnpike to the east of the Clooneen Wood. The 1837 OS map does not show the junction, because, around 1814, the old route was superseded by the new line of the Summerhill, Kilmessan to Navan road, from Castletown to Cannistown; this road is discussed in another section. In the small remaining portion of the Clooneen Wood, at time of writing, part of the old line can be found where it angles up the steep hillside to the edge of Swanton's (formerly Holmes's) field. This follows the same line and is on a similar location to that shown on Larkin's Map. The junction can be found on the Taylor and Skinner map, on which map the lesser road is truncated and marked as the Trim road.

Two presentments made to the Grand Jury in 1806 and 1807 show that this road was still in use during those times, because, as stated, the new road from Castletown to Cannistown was not cut and opened before 1814. The first is in the Query Book of 1806 under the Barony of Skreen and reads: *Item 274 Wher £9 be raised to widen 62 per's of road to 32ft Summerhill to Navan from Ringlestown to Dowdstown.* This presentment is not quoted verbatim as the original text was in poor condition. The second relevant presentment is in the summer assizes Query Book of 1807, under the Barony of Skreen, it reads: *Item 423 Wher £14,, 3,, 6 be raised & Acc for by Nath'l Preston Tho's Swan & Barth'w Cooney to rep' 63 p from Summerhill to Navan betw'n Ringlestown & Dowdstown @ 4s 6d* (sic). These presentments may be for the same section of road.

At the forked Clooneen Junction, the turnpike turned sharply northwards to run across the flat plain towards the banks of the River Skane in Dowdstown. It ran on a raised embankment or causeway, straight as an arrow shaft across the river bottoms to the banks of the Skane, this suggests that the route was newly cut in 1729 during conversion of the old road to a turnpike. The causeway passed through an area known to us long ago as *the river field*. The elevated line of the defunct roadway was plain to see during my early years and we took many a shortcut along its raised banks on our way to the Hill of Tara; it disappeared sometime after 1971 during farm redevelopment work. This part of the turnpike is discussed extensively in *Where Toll Roads Meet*.

Long ago, *the river field* was comprised entirely of a portion of land named Dowdstown and marked such on the 1837 OS map. This was a small area of 22 acres, 2 roods and 3 perches, bordered to the south and east by the townland of Castletown Tara and to the north and west by the rivers Gabhra and Skane. The area was separate from the old parish of Dowdstown. In John O'Donovan's 1836 field notes on Dowdstown Parish, I cannot find a reference to this portion of land being a townland or why two Dowdstowns are shown. The field was located in the then parish of Tara, as indicated on the 1837 OS map and discussed in O'Donovan's field notes under that parish heading and amongst its other townlands. All the aforementioned maps show the turnpike crossing the Skane close by its confluence with the Gabhra in Dowdstown. The river crossing was obviously a bridge, because the road is shown cutting the river – but what type of structure was used? During my lifetime no trace of this bridge was apparent, nor can I find anyone who recalls such; but I suspect it was a stone arched structure constructed in or around 1729.

Following the first crossing of the Skane, the turnpike ran through Dowstown, linked with the old line of the Bective/Trim road, then crossed the combined rivers at the previously mentioned widened stone arched bridge; the joined roads ran on to the former crossroads beside the ruined church. Nowadays this is the line of Dowdstown back-avenue, which I conclude was built over the old turnpike road. The Taylor and Skinner Map, Larkin's Map and the 1837 OS map, all clearly indicate the line from the Clooneen, across the causeway and the two river crossings to the old church. The Longfield Map of Dowdstown (1822) shows the road from the Clooneen through Dowdstown and marks it as *the old road to Dublin*. The Taylor and Skinner map depicts the junction of the old line of the Bective/Trim road with the turnpike – it's shown as an unmarked 'T' junction between the two river crossings. Beaufort's *Map of the diocese of Meath* (1797) and J. Taylor's *engraved Map of County Meath* (1802), both show the road from Bective/Trim joining the old turnpike beside the River Skane, but the definition is poor. Traces of this old forked junction were still evident in the now long gone gravel pit wood in Dowdstown during our childhood, but we never realised its significance then.

From the ruined church, the turnpike followed the line of the avenue, winding over Dowdstown Hill and passing between the old walled garden and the rear of Dowdstown House. It then followed the current line of the farmyard avenue alongside the old stone-built stables – to the north of the farmyard the route swung northwestwards through the woods of the present day and disappeared for several hundred yards. It can be traced through the field to the west of the avenue, which forks near the edge of the old woods. Nowadays the old line runs northwestwards through the field and is used as a cowpass. Re-entering the woods near the mearing between Dowdstown and Kilcarn, the old route crossed an ancient stone bridge, known to us as *Brian Boru's Bridge*, and ran onwards to the mill at Upper Kilcarn. Running past the miller's house, it continued on alongside the River Boyne and past *the Big Mill* at Lower Kilcarn and ran across the old bridge at Kilcarn, then continued onwards to Navan.

A presentment, made for repairs to the aforementioned Brian Boru's Bridge, is listed in the Grand Jury summer assizes Query Book of 1808 and reads: *Item706 Wher £19,, 1,, 3 be raised & Acc for by Chal's D Dillon A Lynch to repair & cope a bridge on the lands of Dowdstown & Kilcarn road from Navan to Dublin* (not quoted verbatim). Two stone bridges straddle the Follistown River, a small stream forming the mearing between Dowdstown and Kilcarn – one is the previously mentioned structure on the old turnpike, the other being located a few hundred yards to the northeast on the new line of the turnpike (now the N3). The latter bridge was not built until about 1814, as evidenced by a presentment for its construction, made to the Lent assizes of that year. It's most likely, therefore, that the 1808 presentment was made for repairs to the older bridge. Construction of the new bridge is covered in the section dealing with the realignment of the turnpike between Philpotstown and Kilcarn. The 1808 repairs to the bridge is an important clue to the evolution of the turnpike road, being proof that this road was still in use several years after the opening of the new line from Dunshaughlin to Dowdstown.

# Realignment of the Turnpike from Dunshaughlin to Dowdstown

The new line of the Dublin to Navan turnpike road, from Dunshaughlin to Philpotstown, was cut during the 1790s, and probably opened prior to the rebellion of 1798 – Grand Jury records show development work continuing on this route in 1801. The Postmaster General was taking many main routes in charge during that era, upgrading them to post office standards by realigning or widening roads and bridges, shortening distances and levelling gradients, thereby reducing travel time for mail coaches. The old route across the Hill of Tara, therefore, no longer suited the changing expectations of the times. The narrow winding route through Killeen and across Tara was not a great deal longer, as evidenced by the differences in the milestones, yet the steep ascent increased the time taken to cover the journey. Consequently, the route across the ancient hill was a prime target for change and the new line was approved by Parliament in the early to mid 1790s.

This realignment made a vast difference to the route – bypassing the Hill of Tara removed the turnpike from the path of an ancient *Slighe,* thus opening a new road through virgin countryside. The new road, though merely six Irish miles in length, nevertheless had a profound impact on the surroundings, possibly disproportionate to its actual distance. From Dunshaughlin it cut through parishes and townlands, bisecting some in the process. The following route was chosen: From Dunshaughlin to Cooksland, enroute skirting the western fringes of a famous bogland, known as *The Great Red Bog* – many interesting artefacts were found when this bog was drained in a later period. From Cooksland, the new line passed through Roestown (Rosetown), Smithstown and the Glebe, then through Clowanstown, Ross and Baronstown to Cabragh. Running alongside the mearing of Lismullin, it cut through Jordanstown and Blundelstown to link with the Dublin to Skryne and Navan road at Philpotstown. These areas, together with others not mentioned, were affected by its passage, place names were born and a new route opened, which has remained until the present day.

As the route is covered in *Where Toll Roads Meet*, this description is limited to the district immediately adjacent to Tara and Dowdstown. The new line made a sharp change in direction near the boundary of Cabragh and Lismullin, taking it in a more northwesterly direction to a place colloquially known as *Soldiers Hill*, where it reverted to its original line running almost due north. Crossing the River Gabhra at Dillon's Bridge in Blundelstown, it continued on to a new forked junction in Philpotstown.

The sharp course alteration near Cabragh mearing prevented the turnpike from running through Lismullin Park Demesne. The reason for this can be deduced from the following reference in Peter O'Keefe's book *The Dublin to Navan Road and Kilcarn Bridge*. Though written in the context of the mail coach road from Ashbourne to Slane, it mentions the realignments of the turnpike road through Dowdstown during this period and reads:

> *Section 22 of the 1792 Post Road Act prescribed that no Grand Jury could present for any new road to be laid or any old road widened through or into any demesne or deer-park without the consent of the owner being first obtained in writing under his hand. This was mitigated somewhat by the 1805 act. The ink was scarcely dry on the print before an amendment was introduced in the following year, Section 9 of 46 G3, c. 134 making the prohibition more embracing than ever by adding any field enclosed within a wall of lime and stone or brick, on or through any planted lawn or avenue or orchard planted before 17 May 1805, without the owners consent. This explains the failure to find a better line through Slane and probably much of the mystery surrounding the improvements at Dowdstown including the abandonment of the old road from the Hill of Tara to the Old Mill upriver of Kilcarn Bridge* (sic).

It would seem that the above-mentioned act of Parliament bestowed upon landowners an absolute right to prevent the passage of roads through their domains and estates. The landlord of Lismullin, Charles Drake Dillon, was born in 1770 – he married the daughter of FD Hamilton, the reeve or sheriff of Navan, a reputed rogue who supposedly helped dispose of Navan Commons to his friends and acquaintances. Dillon was juror number six on the Meath Grand Jury list of 1803 and named in many presentments for road alterations in the area; including the realignments of the turnpike road. So it is less than surprising that the new line of the turnpike avoided passing through Lismullin Demesne.

The following is but one of many records indicating Dillon's involvement in the turnpike realignments and other road developments of the period – it also shows that work on the turnpike was ongoing in 1801. The entry is in the Query Book of 1801 under County at Large and reads: *Item 266 Wher £41,, 13,, & £4,, 8,, wag' Be raised as Before & Acc for by Cha' Drake Dillon Earl Fingall Mich' Mc Dermott Jo'n Lynch to build over a Water Course on the lands of Jordanstown New Road from Navan to Dunshaughlin & for sinking &c* (sic). It is likely that this presentment was for the construction of a bridge across the little River Nith, a tributary of the Gabhra – further mention is made of this stream in chapter 12. The bridge, which cost forty-six pounds and one shilling to build in 1801, nowadays carries the N3 over the small river flowing down from Tara. At time of writing, part of it collapsed due to heavy traffic: it's safe to say, however, that its reconstruction will greatly exceed the initial building costs all those years ago.

As some history of Lismullin and Dillon's Bridge is included in chapters 12 and 13, let us now examine the turnpike road's passage through Philpotstown and Dowdstown. Larkin's Map provides the only graphical record I can discover of the three different lines the turnpike took through this area. This map is confusing, because the three road lines are shown and appear to be the status quo in 1812, the date indicated on the map. This anomaly is explained in Peter O'Keefe's aforementioned book, in which he concludes that Larkin's Map wasn't published until 1817, when most of the new road alignments in the area were completed. Which explanation solves the puzzle and the map can be more easily interpreted. As the crossroads already existed prior to the survey, the 1837 OS map provides little assistance in deducing the series of road alterations that caused the evolution of the modern day Philpotstown Cross.

The new line from Dunshaughlin linked with the Skryne/Navan road at a forked junction in Philpotstown – the combined roads taking a new line from there through Dowstown to merge with the older route across Tara

*The Trim/Drogheda road at Dowdstown Bridge before the coming of the M3. The new line was cut from approximately 400 yards west of the bridge in 1801/02* (Courtesy Maria Bradley)

near Brian Boru's Bridge, as described previously. The turnpike followed the old route onwards and across Kilcarn Bridge to Navan.

This line is shown on Larkin's Map, with the new road passing through Dowdstown to the east of both the old church and Dowdstown House. The Longfield Map indicates both lines of the turnpike road, naming one *the new road from Navan to Dunshaughlin and Dublin,* the other as *the old road to Dublin.* These maps show that the turnpike was realigned through Dowdstown concurrent with the new line from Dunshaughlin. Beaufort's 1797 *Map of the diocese of Meath* and J. Taylor's *County of Meath* map of 1802 both confirm this road layout in Dowstown – with Taylor's map also indicating the new turnpike line from Dunshaughlin. The Longfield Map, though of poor definition, reveals details not shown on other maps. It indicates where the 1796 line intersected the Skryne-Navan route to the old turnpike at Dowdstown Church: the crossing point being just east of the Dowdstown/Philpotstown mearing in the field to the rear of the later day cottage resided in by Dan Norton.

In addition to the data gleaned from maps, the following Grand Jury presentment proves the existence of this long lost road and its link between the new line and the old turnpike beside Dowdstown Church. Recorded in the summer assizes Barony of Skreen Query Book of 1802, it reads: *Item 303 Wher 5s & 3s wag' be raised as before and Acc for by Char's Drake Dillon Esq. & Jo'n Read to stop up an old road betw'n the old church of Dowdstown & new Turnpike Road* (sic). The closing of this old road formed a forked junction, the forerunner of Philpotstown crossroads, which in later days was located about three hundred yards to the east. Larkin's Map marks a building close by the forked junction while the OS map of 1837 shows only the building. The 1796 turnpike road through Dowdstown seems to have disappeared entirely by 1837 as it's not indicated on the OS map, which shows only the 1815 line to Kilcarn. During my childhood years some traces remained on the topography within the estate, but these have vanished. In my opinion, this old line ran from the priest's (new) graveyard in Dalgan Park, across the sports fields and followed the cowpass alongside the handball alleys, then through the farmyard towards its junction with the old route, as described.

## The New Road from Bellinter to Philpotstown and the New Bridge at Dowdstown

This new section of the Trim/Drogheda road was mapped and surveyed in 1801, possibly with the intention of bypassing the circuitous route through Dowdstown. Other agendas influencing its construction will be discussed in the next chapter. The new road was opened and in use by 1802, as shown by the above record for stopping the old route.

The following presentment was recorded in the Grand Jury summer assizes Barony of Skreen Query Book of 1801, it reads: *Item 247 Wher £3,, 12,, 6 be raised as before & paid to Tho's Carberry for surveying & mapping 290 Per's of new road from Trim to Drogheda thro' the lands of Dowdstown & Philperstown @ 3s* (sic). The presented distance equates to 2030 yards or 1.15 statute miles, almost the exact distance between Bellinter and Philpotstown crossroads.

The development of this new road can be traced by several presentments recorded under the Barony of Skreen in the Grand Jury Query Books of 1801/1802, two of such read: Summer assizes 1801 – *Item 246 Wher £20,, 17,, £1,, 0,, 10d wages be raised off Barony of Skreen & Acc for by Lord Tarah Charl's Drake Dillon Esq. J Carthy & Tho's Carberry to ditch & fence 139 per' each side of the new road from Trim to Drogheda thro' the lands of Dowdstown & Philperstown @ 3s* (sic). Another reads: Summer assizes 1802 – *Item 522 Wher £58,, I,, 7 & £2,, 10,, 1d wages be raised a & Acc for by Lord Tarah Char's Drake Dillon Esq. F Swan F Gough to make 149 per' 32ft wide new road from Trim to Drogheda betw'n Lynch's house & new turnpike road @ 8,, I* (sic).

To the southwest of Dowdstown Bridge and within the Taylor estate, the 1822 Longfield Map shows a section with the name Lynch inscribed thereon. A house is shown on this property, which is marked number 15 (lease lot number) and located in the triangular shaped area between the River Skane and the new line of the road. The 1837 OS map shows a house on this location, but no name is indicated – perhaps this was the house referred to in the presentment as Lynch's house: my childhood home is located on the same site by the river.

Two presentments to the Grand Jury in 1802 record the construction of Dowdstown Bridge, which was obviously built in conjunction with the new road between Bellinter and Philpotstown. I experienced great difficulty in discovering these notations because of the poor quality text and the townland name being spelled incorrectly – instead of Dowdstown the name was inscribed *Doubtstown*. The first of these, listed in the Query Book Lent assizes under County at Large, reads: *Item 593 Wher £114,, 8s & £5,, 14,, 5 wag' be raised as before & Acc for by Charl's Drake Dillon Esq. Jo'n & Ambrose Lynch to build a bridge at Doubtst'n road from Trim to Drogheda* (sic). The second relevant entry is in the same book, listed in the summer assizes under County at Large and reads: *Item 377 Wher £44,, 7,, 6 & £4,, 4,, 4 ½ wag' be raised off CO' at Large & Acc for by Cha's Drake Dillon Esq. & Jo'n Lynch to finish the Bridge partly built on the lands of Doubtstown road from Trim to Drogheda* (sic). Later in the summer assizes of 1802 item 162 superseded 377 for the same sum of money. The two presentments indicate a total cost of £166 14s 9½d for the construction of the beautiful tri-centre stone arched bridge still

*Dowdstown Bridge - built 1802 at the confluence of the rivers Skein and Gabhra*

spanning the merged rivers Skane and Gabhra two hundred and seven years later. This seems pretty good value for money, but one might wonder what caused the addition of the extra halfpenny to the account?

The new line of the Trim/Drogheda road created a crossroads at Dowdstown Bridge – this crossing is shown clearly on Larkin's Map and the Longfield Map of 1822, but is less well defined on the 1837 OS map. Though the old turnpike line from Tara was open concurrently with the new road for some years, as evidenced by the two maps, little certainty exists as to when it was finally closed down. John O'Donovan's field notes of 1836 include the following entry, made in the context of the aforementioned small townland of Dowdstown in the parish of Tara: *A by road passes through it from N. to S.* Perhaps this suggests that the old line was still being used in 1836?

The last two road developments listed in the chronology, namely the new road from Castletown Tara to Cannistown and the new turnpike line from Philpotstown to Kilcarn, are discussed in the next chapter because they are relevant to other events covered therein.

# 9

# The New Road From Tara to Cannistown & an Ancient Feud

The road from Castletown Tara through Lismullin – the new road from Castletown to Cannistown – Ambrose Bridge – Bellinter Boyne Bridge – Turnpike realignment Philpotstown to Kilcarn 1814/1817. Brian Boru's Bridge – a Barony boundary, a double ditch and a feud – Progress!

At time of writing, Bellinter crossroads is formed by the intersection of the Trim to Drogheda road and the Kilmessan to Navan road. Unlike the former and much older route, the Kilmessan road crossing it here is relatively new, being cut in the period between 1809 and 1815. The previous route ran from the 'T' junction at Castletown Tara and joined the old line of the Dublin to Navan turnpike road near the eastern fringe of the long gone Clooneen Wood. Building the new road from Castletown to Cannistown included construction of two major bridges and cutting three miles of new roadway through virgin countryside.

Currently, the junction at Castletown Tara is formed by the Kilmessan to Navan road linking with a road running eastwards from the gates of Royal Tara Golf Club to soldier's hill on the N3. In former days this short stretch of road was part of the Summerhill to Drogheda road. Two entries in the Grand Jury books confirm the upgrading and repair of this road.

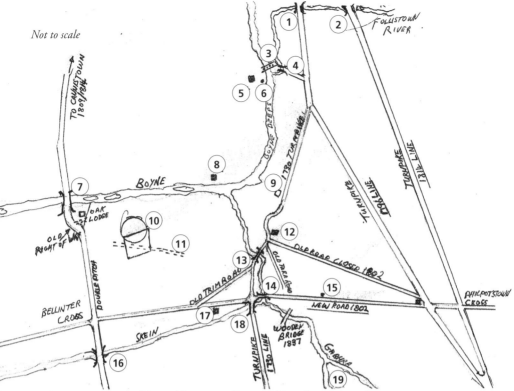

*Author's reconstruction of the road layout at Bellinter and Dowdstown c. 1814*

1. Brian Boru's Bridge
2. New Bridge on New Turnpike (1814)
3. Ford on Boyne – linking Ardsallagh to Old Turnpike
4. Connecting road from Ford to old Turnpike
5. Ardsallagh Castle/House
6. St. Brigid's Well
7. Bellinter Boyne Bridge
8. Mill at Ardsallagh
9. Dowdstown House
10. Site of the Motte and Bailey (discovered in 2006)
11. Ancient Paved Pathway
12. Ruins of Dowdstown Church (1180)
13. Old Stone Arched Bridge (destroyed by flood in 1954)
14. New Dowdstown Bridge (1802)
15. Tobar na Mias
16. Ambrose Bridge (1814)
17. Lynch's House (1802)
18. Long-gone Turnpike Bridge (1729)
19. Gabhra Island

The first is recorded in the Query Book of 1800 under Barony of Skreen, it reads: *Item 475 Wher £24,, 6,, & £,, 4,, 3 wag' be raised as before & Acc for by John Preston Esq. Rev' Arthur Preston & Tho's Holmes to build & fence 108 per's, 32ft wide from Summerhill to Drogheda betw'n the park wall of Bellinter & Castletown @ 4s* (sic). The second is in the 1801 Query Book under Barony of Skreen and reads: *Item 533 Wher £5 15s be paid to Arthur Preston C.D. Dillon T Carthy to repair 347 per's from Summerhill to Drogheda from green gate of Bellinter to New turnpike Road* (not quoted verbatim).

These two presentments are interesting from various aspects. They show inter alia that part of the road was widened to 32 feet, and that in 1800 the location of the present day golf club gates was known as the park wall of Bellinter and in 1801 as the green gate of Bellinter. It's interesting to note that the owner of Bellinter, John Preston, had not yet been granted his union peerage title of Lord Tarah. Further mention is made of this road in later chapters.

During research, I discovered a reference to a forge being sited at Castletown Tara in olden times. Griffith's 1854 valuation shows that Patrick Ward had a house and forge leased from George Harvey for an annual fee of 12.s 0d.. In more recent years, a man named Ward operated a forge sited between Ringlestown and Kilmessan, but this was not located in Castletown Tara. Further research revealed, to my great surprise, the most likely location for the old Smithy to be at the junction of the Summerhill/Navan and Summerhill/Drogheda roads of yesteryear. On the very site where I built a new bungalow in 1979 – which would explain the presence of so many stones found while digging the foundations, yes indeed, research can produce some surprises on life's canvas!

Starting at its southern end in Castletown, the following is a synopsis of the new route from there to Cannistown. The new line commenced opposite the current location of the Royal Tara Clubhouse, formerly known as the pavilion, then ran due north towards the River Skane. Descending *the limekiln hill* into the river valley, it crossed the Skane via Ambrose Bridge and ran alongside the Bellinter/Dowdstown mearing to intersect the Trim/Drogheda road at Bellinter crossroads. Continuing along the Dowdstown boundary, it ran to the edge of the River Boyne, which it crossed on the six-arched Bellinter Bridge. From the Boyne's northern bank it ran alongside the western boundary of Ardsallagh Demesne to Cannistown. Here it merged with the old road from Trim to Kilcarn and continued along this route to meet with the Dublin to Navan turnpike near Kilcarn Bridge.

The following descriptions cover some history of prominent features on the three-mile long section of this road, referred to in the Grand Jury books as the new Summerhill to Navan road. The Meath Grand Jury query books, covering road building in the Baronies from 1810 to 1816, were unavailable, therefore, information on the cutting of this road is difficult to obtain. The only data I could glean for this period being from the County Presentment Books, which cover the construction of main features such as bridges. Surprisingly, I found a reference to this new line in the Lent assizes Query Book of 1809 – listed under the Barony of Skreen it reads: *Item 243 Wher £27,, 3,, 6 be raised & Acc for by Andrew Warren & T Reilly to form, mould & fence 86 ½ per's of the new road from Summerhill to Navan betw'n the road leading from Navan to Dublin & from Trim to Drogheda @ 6s* (not quoted verbatim). Thought the exact location is unspecified, I consider the presentment refers to the new line between Bellinter Bridge and Bellinter crossroads. Perhaps this short section of new road was built earlier than the remainder of the route to provide access for the construction of the major bridge across the Boyne.

In regards to the previously mentioned limekiln hill, the following record probably referred to this section of road. I found the presentment in the Lent Assizes of 1814 for a sum of £44, to be paid to Lord Tara (John Preston) and C. Donnelly. Listed as item 98, it read: *to lower a hill and fill a hollow on the Summerhill Navan Road on the lands of Castletown Tara.* The date being coincidental with the cutting of the new line, it's likely this presentment was for work completed on a part of the road we knew as the limekiln hill. The hill is located about three hundred yards south of Ambrose Bridge, where the route ran through a cutting in the steep hillside and over a raised embankment towards the Skane. The name derives from a quarry and attendant limekiln to the west of the road, the quarry was evident in my younger days, but nowadays its top forms the tee box for the 11th hole of the extended golf course. In times past, a triangular shaped area between the hill and Ambrose Bridge was known as *The Pound Field.* Though I'm unsure of the name's origin, we could speculate that the place was once used as a pound for wayward animals. The field was entered via an old fashioned stone stile beside a gateway, which had two piers; each cut from a single stone and carved ornamentally. Another pair of similar piers was located at Daly's farm, near Dillon's Bridge, but I have never seen their likes elsewhere. They appear to be unique to the area and possibly fashioned by local stonemasons named Montague. Like many such things, the piers were uprooted by development work and not deemed worthy of preservation, even by record.

The bridge crossing the River Skane is named Ambrose Bridge on the OS maps, but whether this was a Christian or surname I had no idea. During my youth we knew the bridge as Anderson's Bridge, which title possibly derived from a colloquialism of Ambrose. The following record is entered in The County Presentment Books and covers the construction of the bridge, it reads: ***Item 63 We present £.141,, 13,, 8 to be raised as before, and paid to Rt. Hon'ble Lord Tara & Pat & Ambrose Lynch to build a bridge over the river Skeine ---------- On the lands of Ballinter ---------- Road from Summerhill to Navan --------- Wages £.7,, 1,, 9 Amount £.148,, 15,, 5***
***Certified at Lent Assizes 1814*** (sic).
This presentment appears in the Summer Assizes of 1813 as item 99, and includes the name of P. Barry – but it was traversed.

It would seem that the old bridge acquired its name from a man named Ambrose Lynch, but I cannot discover whom he was or how the bridge came to be called by his Christian name. Checking the genealogical records in Trim yielded no further information, so I suppose that this little secret from the past is destined to remain a mystery. The name

*Ambrose Bridge built in 1814.*

Ambrose Lynch was included in the Grand Jury records for construction of Dowdstown Bridge in 1802 and in a traversed presentment for the Boyne Bridge at Bellinter.

It's interesting to note that the spelling of the river's name in the presentment is Skeine or Skiene, it's difficult to determine which due to the quality of the script. This is further evidence of Anglicisation of names during the OS of 1836 – the first spelling of the name as Skane appears on the 1837 map. However, thanks to the presentment for Ambrose Bridge in 1814, we can produce an official record indicating that the name was spelled otherwise previous to the first OS being conducted. Further details on this river's name and its possible origins are included in a later chapter.

I knew that the construction of Bellinter Bridge across the River Boyne commenced in 1813 long before I learned of Grand Juries and presentment books. Because, in 1967, I saw this date on the foundation stone located on the southwestern abutment arch. Prior to the commencement of the Boyne arterial drainage scheme, the stone was removed from its original position and replaced on the western parapet wall, where it can be seen at time of writing. Engraving on the stone states that it was laid on July 1st 1813 by John Preston, Lord Baron Tara, the first and only holder of this title, one of the so-called union peerages bestowed prior to the Act of Union in 1801. The honour was awarded to Preston in 1800, supposedly for his leadership of the Navan Cavalry during the battle of Tara in 1798. The more cynical suggest these titles were handed out to many of the gentry for their support in the dissolution of the Irish Parliament.

Bellinter Bridge is a stone bridge with six arches and battlemented parapet walls – four arches span 35 feet and two span 28 feet. The width of the bridge is thirty feet, face to face and it's over two hundred feet long. Peter O'Keefe estimated that 1300 perches (1 perch equalling 24 cubic feet) of stonework were used to build the structure. Presentments for its construction were made to the Grand Jury prior to 1812, which were traversed, possibly because of the cost or perhaps due to political intrigue. A further presentment was made to the summer assizes of 1812 and certified by that sitting. This presentment is numbered item 60 and reads: *We present £.1,418,, 7,, 11 to be raised as before and paid to Lord Tara*

Clockwise from top: *Bellinter Boyne Bridge built in 1813. Bellinter crossroads, as it was in 2007 and the old line of the Turnpike at the ruins of Dowdstown Church*

*Joseph Maguire Rev'd Philip Barry Richard McGlew & Pat Springer To build a bridge over the River Boyne Wages £70,, 16,, 6 Amount £.1489,, 6,, 5*

*Certified at Summer 1812 (sic).*

The same presentment appears in the Lent assizes of 1813.

I note that, unlike many other presentments of the time, the townland, road name and location of the bridge are omitted. Whatever problems caused the traversing of the previous presentments were seemingly overcome by the addition of extra names to the summer of 1812 edition – the presented costs being also reduced from £1510 7s 6d to £1489 6s 5d. The apparent political conniving and possible objections to the earlier presentments are significant in light of anecdotes told and passed down through the generations – these concern an alleged feud between the Prestons of Bellinter and the Taylors (Taylours) of Dowdstown. The tale of this supposed feud and its possible causes is related presently.

Left: *Grinding corn at Martry Mill (Tallon's Mill), 2007* Right: *French Burr Runner millstone from the mill at Upper Kilcarn - now stored at Martry Mill*

# Turnpike Realignment from Philpotstown to Kilcarn and Navan

This new line of the turnpike was cut from the 19th milestone, near Dillon's Bridge, to the Big Mill south of Kilcarn Bridge, where it rejoined the old route running alongside the River Boyne. As stated, Larkin's Map indicates all three lines of the road through this area, thereby presenting a somewhat confusing picture, quite difficult to interpret. Approximately three hundred yards north of Dillon's Bridge, the new line diverged from the older route and ran northwards, cutting the line of the Dublin/Skryne road and forming Philpotstown crossroads (Garlow Cross). Continuing on a straight course through Philpotstown and Dowdstown, it crossed the Follistown River and cut the old line of the Drogheda road (now the Yellow walls Lane). Passing through Upper Kilcarn and bisecting Lower Kilcarn (Kilcarn Park), it rejoined the old route southeast of Kilcarn Bridge – the new route was just over two Irish miles long.

Because the Grand Jury Query Books of the period are unavailable, I could not discover an accurate date for the cutting of this road. The County Presentment Books, however, contain a record for building the single bridge on this line.

In 1814 a presentment was made to the Grand Jury Lent Assizes, which I consider refers to the bridge on the new line from Philpotstown to Kilcarn. Prior to discovering the aforementioned information on Dowdstown Bridge, I came upon references to this presentment several years ago whilst researching my previous book *Where toll Roads Meet*. In his book *The Dublin to Navan Road and Kilcarn Bridge*, Peter O'Keefe mentions this record in the context of Dowdstown Bridge. Listed as item 93, it reads: *We present £37,, 2,, 6 ------ to be raised as before, and paid to Phil Barry, Chris & Dan Montague   To build a bridge ------ On the lands of Dowdstown ----- Road from Kilcarn to Dublin ------- Wages £1,, 17,, 3d. Amount £38,, 19,, 9* (sic).

This entry puzzled me, as the presented costs seemed rather low for a large structure like Dowdstown Bridge. In 2009, while researching the subject further, I discovered a slightly different version of the above presentment in the 1814 summer assizes – marked as item 60, it reads: *We present £37,, 2,, 6 -------- to be raised as before, and paid to Phil Barry Christ' & Daniel Montague -------- to build a bridge & battlements &c -----------On lands of Dowdstown & Kilcarn ----- Road from Kilcarn to Dublin ------- Wages, £.I,, 17,, 3 ---------- Amount £.38,, 19,, 9 Certified at Lent Assizes 1814* (sic)

The significant differences in the second presentment being that it specified bridge battlements (sidewalls) and named its location on the lands of Dowdstown *and Kilcarn*. Which meant the bridge was to be built spanning the mearing of the townlands, formed hereabouts by a small stream known as the Follistown River. In this area there are two bridges matching this presentment – one, which we knew as Brian Boru's Bridge, is located on the old line of the turnpike. But this is a much older bridge, probably dating back to the start of the turnpike era in 1730, or possibly to earlier times. A close inspection of the structure shows that the bridge has been widened at least twice, with the centre section being built in an earlier period: Perhaps this span carried the more ancient road from Tara towards Kilcarn in times past. The other bridge is on the new line between Philpotstown and Kilcarn and is much smaller, about five feet in river width and the stone arch is scarcely four feet high. In my opinion, this is the bridge presented for and certified by the Grand Jury Lent Assizes of 1814. The record would suggest the new line from Philpotstown to Kilcarn being built in or about the year 1814.

Because of a dearth of information at the time, I hypothesised in previous writings that the new line from Kilcarn to Navan, via *the skelp*, was built during the same time period as the road from Philpotstown to Kilcarn. Further research has proven otherwise – two presentments to the

summer assizes of 1807 show that this road was cut during earlier times. Listed in the Query Book under County at Large, they read: *Item 430 to build an arch on New Line between Kilcarn & Navan £18,, 16,, 3.*
*Item 431 to build battlements on same £20,, 3,, 8½,* (not quoted verbatim). The names listed on both presentments, are: W'm Johnson, Chl's Montague and Ric'd McGlew. The only bridge on this section of road spans a small stream flowing down from Balreask and mingling with the Boyne on the Navan side of Kilcarn Bridge. This bridge has now been officially vandalised by persons employed by the N.R.A. - the stone arched structure was demolished on 27th March 2010, as part of the M3 motorway construction works, and replaced by concrete pipes!

The 1814 new line was the last major realignment of the turnpike between Dunshaughlin and Navan. It removed three choke points from the route between Dowdstown and Kilcarn, namely, Brian Boru's Bridge, the mill yard at Upper Kilcarn and the narrow section from near the Big Mill to Kilcarn Bridge. Perhaps the old road remained open for some time subsequently to provide access from Dowdstown to the cornmills at Upper and Lower Kilcarn. Ironically, the road continued to cross the greatest obstruction of all, Kilcarn Bridge, which remained on the route until a new bridge was opened in 1977, one hundred and sixty three years later. Which factor had a bearing on the construction of Bellinter

*The Miller's House on the old line of the turnpike. This old stone and mudwall house was formerly the Miller's house at Upper Kilcarn mill - later, in the 1880's, it was occupied by the Mongey family. James Mongey was captain of the Leinster Championship wining Dowdstown football team of !888.*

Left: *Old turnpike house at Kilcarn bridge circa turn of the century* (Courtesy D. Halpin)
Right: *Brian Boru's Bridge in Dowdstown probably predates 1730. east elevation.* (Courtesy G. Murray)

Bridge in 1813. The Dublin to Navan turnpike road ceased operating as a tollroad in 1856, when all such roads in Ireland were discontinued by act of Parliament.

Now let us revisit the anecdotes of the alleged feud between the owners of Bellinter and Dowdstown in times past. I first heard this fable being whispered around the fireside, perhaps during one of many visits to the O'Dowd family living in the herd's house in Bellinter farmyard – such being the way childhood tales were related in the days ere TV invaded our world. The story told of John Preston's request for the Taylors to contribute towards the construction costs of Bellinter Bridge and their refusal to do so causing a feud between the families. In retaliation Preston supposedly attempted to deny them access to the new road by cutting the route well back from the mearing with Dowdstown, thereby leaving a strip of Bellinter land running alongside the Dowdstown boundary. To consolidate the separation, a deep ditch was dug and a stone wall built from Ambrose Bridge to the Boyne – thus was born the fable of the double ditch between Bellinter and Dowdstown. The greater part of this wall, from Bellinter crossroads to the Boyne at Oak Lodge, remains in situ at time of writing. During my younger days most of the wall from the crossroads to Ambrose Bridge had gone, the deep ditch being filled in over the years. I recall that much of the wall was knocked by the roots

134

of trees growing in the Skane wood, which spinney has disappeared long since. The legend of the feud faded, but resurfaced in a strange way during later years when the estate was divided and new bungalows built along the Bellinter side of the road in the Boyne Field, the Middle Field and the Brick Field near the crossroads. The new owners discovering they had title to the strip of land on the Dowdstown side of the road, which caused the rebirth of the ancient anecdote in another generation.

While the tale of the double ditch made sense to us as wide-eyed children gathered around in the flickering firelight of yesteryear, yet it doesn't stand up to close scrutiny in the harsh spotlight of logic and research. As described, the Dublin to Navan turnpike road passed through Dowdstown and close by the rear entrance to Dowdstown House. The Taylor family, therefore, had full access towards Navan to the north and Dublin to the south; hence they had no urgent need to access Preston's new road or bridge. Had they so wished, they could have used Bellinter Bridge by means of the new line of the Trim/Drogheda road passing their rear entrance at Dowdstown Bridge. The presentments of 1812 and 1813 prove that Bellinter Bridge was financed by pubic money, so it was part of a public road to which Preston could not deny them access – which suggests the alleged feud wasn't caused by a disagreement over money. And the double ditch did not preclude all passage between the two properties; a public right of way ran from the new road through the parcel of land later to become the site of Oak Lodge. A small gateway formed an opening in the stone wall, possibly provided for hunting purposes and to access a well on the riverbank, known to us as *the mouth of the Boyne.*

The method of constructing the double ditch was similar to that used in building a haw-haw or sunken fence – with the steep face of the wall presented towards Bellinter. During our childhood we experienced great difficulty climbing up the wall into Dowdstown, whilst we had no problem dropping over the low wall from the Dowdstown side. I would suggest, therefore, that the boundary was to keep people from Bellinter out of Dowdstown, rather than to prevent the Dowdstown folk entering Bellinter.

Delving into the mysteries of the past reveals that the origins of the double ditch had nothing to do with a family feud in the early years of the

19th century. In my opinion, the ditch was part of the ancient boundary between the Baronies of Lower Deece and Skreen. Close perusal of the Down Survey (1650s) maps indicates the southern mearing between these two Baronies following the line of the River Skane, from southwest of Balgeeth to where Ambrose Bridge was built in later years. The northern boundary between Lower Deece and Upper Navan followed the Boyne from west of Bective to the Dowdstown mearing behind Oak Lodge and close by the later day site of Bellinter Bridge. These two natural divides were linked by a man made boundary running between the two rivers i.e. following the line of the double ditch – this line can be seen on the D.S. map, even the kink where the double ditch veers slightly eastwards towards the Boyne behind Oak Lodge. This boundary can be traced also on Beaufort's 1797 map. The salient of land enclosed within these three boundaries comprised most of the Bellinter estate prior to its division by the Land Commission in the 1960s.

I contend that the double ditch formed the aforementioned boundary; as such mearings were common enough in olden times. It's possible that the original ditch dates back to the 1600s or even earlier times. Perhaps the stone wall derived from a later date – maybe being built by John Preston, thus giving rise to the legend of the family feud.

Many such ancient anecdotes being based upon actual happenings in times past, I wondered what event caused the fabled rift between the two family estates. Research of the ancient road systems suggests a source for the legendary feud other than the supposed parsimony of the Taylors.

It is unlikely that John Preston (Lord Tara) awoke one morning and on a whim decided to build a bridge across the River Boyne, together with the new road from Castletown Tara to Cannistown. This scheme was well planned and advantageous to the owner of Bellinter in several ways, if the costs were borne by the public purse so much the better. The most obvious and immediate advantage accruing to the Prestons being that they could build a grand entrance from Bellinter House to the new road close by Bellinter Bridge. This avenue became famous for its scenic route alongside the river and through the woods of the demesne, in later years the entrance was known as the Kennel Gate. To journey to Navan, Preston now had his own bridge across the Boyne, thus avoiding the longer trip via

Dowdstown and Kilcarn Bridge or the even lengthier journey by Bective Bridge. Additionally, he had a new route to Dublin through Castletown Tara, to link up with the new line of the turnpike at soldier's hill.

From the smaller perspective all seemed rosy in the garden for the Prestons of Bellinter. But if such were the case what caused the supposed feud with the Taylors of Dowdstown? A possible explanation may be found in the unfolding scenario created by road developments in Dowdstown and its environs, the larger picture so to speak.

A name conspicuous by its absence from the Grand Jury presentments of the period is that of General Robert Taylor (1760 – 1839), the owner of Dowdstown. This name was not included in thousands of entries I reviewed while researching the period between 1798 and 1820, whereas names of local landowners such as John Preston, Charles Drake Dillon, Phillip and Charles Barry, Lord Fingal and Lord Dunsany appear frequently. It was as though General Taylor never existed or perhaps he didn't live in Dowdstown at this juncture? The Longfield Map of Dowdstown shows that in 1822 the estate was leased in numbered parcels to various named tenants, including inter alia: Nicholas Goff & Partners, Mahon, Lynch, King, Doolan, Boyd and Macking – perhaps this is an indicator that the Taylor family was not in residence.

During the time in question, General Robert Taylor was busy with military matters, most notably the Battle of Waterloo in 1815. The chronology shows many road developments taking place within Dowdstown during the periods 1796 to 1804 and 1812 to 1817 – Section 22 of the Post Road Act of 1792 decreed that the Grand Jury could not approve these without the written permission of the landowner, in this instance General Taylor.

As stated, much of the road redevelopment was initiated by the transition of turnpike roads to mail coach roads. Consequently, many routes were being taken in charge by the Postmaster General and upgraded, with gradients being lessened and road and bridge widths increased. Another factor influencing the routing of new roads was the increasing popularity of private demesnes, or wood embowered parklands surrounding the residences of landed gentry. Whereas in earlier times it was popular to have public roads passing close by the big houses, in this era the opposite approach held sway. It became a sign of prestige to have the said roads removed from private parklands and rebuilt somewhere else, oftentimes forming the domain boundaries as in Bellinter, Dowdstown, Lismullin, Sommerville and elsewhere in the county.

As shown by the relevant Grand Jury presentments, the main instigators of the road developments in the area close to Tara were John Preston (Lord Tara) of Bellinter and Charles Drake Dillon Esq. from Lismullin. These gentlemen owned the adjoining estates of Bellinter and Lismullin and, as evidenced by the official records, were prominent in the construction of the new roads through Dowdstown and the building of Dowdstown Bridge – but where did General Taylor feature in all this road building activity?

Most of what I have written so far is borne out by research and local knowledge, but now I must descend into the realms of speculation and conjecture. I would hypothesise, therefore, that Preston's master objective was to re-route the turnpike road from Philpotstown via Dowdstown Bridge, Bellinter crossroads and Bellinter Bridge, through Cannistown and Kilcarn to Navan. This route removed the previously mentioned choke points, including Kilcarn Bridge, but was over a half mile longer – the Grand Jury records show that Preston was ably assisted in this enterprise by Charles Drake Dillon. Yet he could not bring the plan to fruition without the active co-operation and connivance of General Taylor, because the aforementioned 1792 act of parliament empowered the incumbent landowners to prevent road passage through their estates. Alternatively, it's possible but very unlikely, that the road developments were completed without Taylor's knowledge or permission while he was away on active military service.

Although I can find no conclusive evidence thereof, it's likely that the development of Dowdstown Demesne took place during the period between 1822 and 1837. No traces of the ornamental lakes and extensive woodlands are evident on either Larkin's Map of 1812/1817 or the Longfield Map of 1822, whereas these features are shown on the OS map of 1837. I suspect that part of the advance planning for the demesne included rerouting various roads in the area, because the passage of the turnpike and other roads through the estate was a huge impediment to the planned demesne. After all, what self-respecting country gentleman of the time would wish to have a public road cutting through his swanky tree embowered domain, as would pertain with the turnpike route through Dowdstown. Though the major realignment in the 1790s had eased the situation somewhat, the tollroad remained close to Dowdstown house and passed through the heart of the intended demesne. The Trim to Drogheda road, via Bective, merged with the old route of the Skryne to Dublin road near the ancient churchyard and the road from Kilmessan to Navan still passed by his kitchen door. Were the demesne developed with the then prevailing road layout his private domain would be a very public place indeed.

It is stretching the bounds of credibility to suggest that the previously described major road realignments, instigated by Preston and Dillon, which provided a solution to most of Taylor's problems, occurred providentially or by coincidence. I would suggest, therefore, that sometime around 1800 General Taylor and Preston made a pact, or quid pro quo, concerning the mutually beneficial road alterations and construction of both Ambrose and Dowdstown Bridges. Which arrangement benefited Taylor by removing the main routes from the precincts of his proposed demesne and favoured Preston by enabling the re-routing of the turnpike road so that it passed over Bellinter Bridge. Because the turnpike or tollhouse at Kilcarn might be rendered obsolete by the new route, perhaps it was also intended to use the new bridge at the Boyne as a tollbridge – with the present day site of Oak Lodge being used to build a new tollhouse. This route would have become part of the Dublin to Navan turnpike or mail coach road, thereby greatly enhancing Lord Tara's prestige and power amongst his peers and within the wider community.

This hypothesis is supported by the following facts: The new road from Bellinter to Philpotstown was unusually broad for its time and usage and the new bridge at Dowdstown remarkably wide for the route and location. For instance, the width between its parapet walls is thirty two feet, approximately the same width as the new bridge across the Boyne at Bellinter. This was much broader than the old stone bridge at Kilcarn, which was circa twenty feet between the walls, though widened in earlier years to carry the turnpike road. Dowdstown Bridge was constructed as a tri-centred arch to minimise the hump on the road. Again, this was a rather unusual feature for a bridge on a country roadway, which would suggest that greater things were intended for its future. The three new bridges in the area, Dowdstown and Ambrose Bridges spanning the Skane and Bellinter Bridge across the Boyne complied with mail coach road specifications. The new line of road effectively formed the southern boundary of the planned new Dowdstown Demesne.

For one reason or another some of these events never came to pass and any agreement made seemed to have been broken. My view of what occurred can be expressed in the following quasi-military terms: The General of Dowdstown executed an outflanking manoeuvre on the Cavalry Captain from Bellinter by cutting a new line from Philpotstown to Kilcarn – or in modern parlance, he 'pulled a stroke' on Preston. Taylor opened his own grand entrance to his then modest cottage-style residence in Dowdstown from this section of new road - (Dowdstown front gates) – while Lord Tara's grand entrance to his Richard Castle designed Palladian-style mansion remained firmly rooted on a relatively minor country road. So, due mostly to John Preston's efforts and enterprise, all the public roads were removed from the environs of Taylor's private demesne, for which the new road network provided three boundaries, with the River Boyne forming most of the fourth. Ironically, the major choke point at Kilcarn Bridge remained on the route between Dublin and Navan for over one hundred and fifty years thereafter – a new bridge replaced it in 1977 but the old stone bridge is still used by pedestrians.

I suggest that this or a similar 'slight change' to the arrangement of the roads might have caused the legendary feud between the gentry of Bellinter and the General of Dowdstown.

Now, almost two hundred years later and somewhat ironically, part of John Preston's dream is about to be realised – the latest 'new' Dublin to Navan road, the M3 motorway, spans the Boyne a short distance downstream from his beautiful stone arched bridge. And there is even more irony, as it too is part of a tollroad. Unfortunately, this aesthetically less pleasing and graceless construction, a modern concrete and metal blue painted bridge, spoils the once lovely downstream vista from Bellinter Bridge.

One could travel the length and breadth of the land and not find a starker contrast to the beautiful landscape of yesteryear and the ravaged scene presented nowadays at Bellinter, Dowdstown and Ardsallagh. Though 'official Ireland', with its plethora of well heeled PR consultants and pet archaeologists would loudly disclaim this contention and state otherwise, the landscape of this once beautiful haven of tranquillity encompassing the big bend in the Boyne and the Skane confluence is ruined forever.

Conversely, in the times prior to computer-aided-design, pseudo public enquiries and environmental impact studies, John Preston's stone arched bridge across the Boyne at Bellinter enhanced the beauty of the place by adding rustic charm and aesthetic quality to the scene. Thus demonstrating that man's needs could be met in harmony with his natural surroundings without tearing the heart out of the countryside. During the 1840s, several years after the construction of the bridge, Sir William Wilde in his travels through the district waxed eloquently about the beauties of the Boyne hereabouts and the magnificence of the Ardsallagh Demesne.

In contrast, picture the scene at time of writing in 2009. As mentioned, in the late 1960s the O.P.W. inaugurated the drainage scheme at Bellinter Bridge, which led to the destruction of the river's much acclaimed fishing grounds and piled Aberfan-like heaps of spoil along the riverbanks. All the little islands, the old eel weirs and large sections of the riverbed were dug out and piled upon the banks – eventually the heaps were levelled, but by then the entire aspect of the river had changed. Now, as elsewhere along its course, it became a canal-like watercourse bearing little resemblance to the former place we knew as our beautiful Boyne. Meantime, Meath County Council and greedy developers, hiding beneath the mantle of progress, inflicted the spectre of the sewerage works upon the nearby Clooneen Wood (or wood of the little meadow), the outflow pipe from which noisome plant is routed alongside the River Skane and through the heart of Dowdstown. This pipe now disgorges all sorts of vile effluents into the Boyne several hundred yards downstream from Bellinter Bridge. The discharge into the river was placed in midstream, to mask it from public view and hide the evidence, close by the once scenic confluence with the River Skane. Now, while walking the riverbanks of a summer's evening, one is sometimes greeted by the malodorous and less than savoury outpourings of man's detritus, which though unseen creates a foul stink. All this crap is pouring into the river just a short distance upstream from the water intake of Kilcarn waterworks – one wonders if the people of Navan and its environs know the source of the liquid issuing from their fancy modern and sometimes gold plated faucets?

Then along came the N.R.A. and their buddies in Eurolink tollroads to complete the desolation of the landscape by cutting the swathe of the M3 through the valley and throwing an ugly blue-hued bridge across the Boyne. In doing so, this seemingly non-accountable and unelected representative of 'official Ireland' caused to be buried forever the remains of at least two ancient heritage sites alongside the river, namely a motte and bailey behind Oak Lodge and a circular burial plot in Ardsallagh. To slavishly follow the computer-generated line and eliminate the need for the motorway to surmount a slight ground undulation, the road builders gouged a wide deep gash through the landscape from the Skane to the Boyne. This eradicated the site of the previously mentioned settlement and dwarfed the legendary double ditch supposedly dug by John Preston all those years ago. But unlike Preston's boundary, the M3 will keep the people of Dowdstown and Bellinter apart, as will the many miles of motorways sunder other communities throughout Ireland. On the northern riverbank a deep cutting was made through the bluff and the old oak woods felled to make way for the tollroad, supposedly the symbol of the new progressive Ireland and its charging Celtic Tiger. This despoilment of the landscape took place within the short stretch of the Boyne Valley between Bellinter Bridge and the big bend of the river at Ardsallagh, a distance of less than half a mile. Well might one wonder what Sir William Wilde would make of it all should he return to the now desolated scene of inspiration for his eloquent writings of former days?

# 10

# Dowdstown Demesne – Philpotstown Crossroads (Garlow Cross)

Dowdstown in early times – the lost townland of Phillips Towne – Dowdstown's ancient church – lakes and dams – woodlands and Waterloo – modernity and pollution – Dalgan Park – River Skane and origins of its name – Tobar na Mias – Garlow Cross and its origins – Reids (Reads) and The Sibin – Miss Robinson's shop and P.O.

The Civil Survey of 1654/56 shows that the propriators (sic) of the townland of Dowestowne (Dowdstown) were Lawrence Dowdall of Athlumney and Wm Baggott of Dublin – it also states that they were Irish Papists. The survey shows that the townland was one-third part of a plowland and consisted of 184 acres. Other sources say that neither of the previously named gentlemen resided there, the estate being run by a steward who lived in what was described in the Down Survey of 1645/46 as a cottage style residence – possibly the original part of Dowdstown House. Dowdall supported the losing side in the rebellion of 1641 and the consequent Cromwellian wars, so he forfeited his lands during the confiscations that followed. He regained them upon Charles II being restored to the throne, but lost them once again after the Battle of the Boyne and the subsequent Williamite land seizures. Apparently the first member of the Taylor (Taylour) family to hold land in Ireland was a

*Dowdstown House*

military man, an assistant to Sir William Petty who conducted the Down Survey. The primary purpose of this survey being to map the land seized from its owners so that it could be appropriated and reassigned to soldiers and mercenaries as payment for services rendered to the Parliamentarian Army in the recent conflict. Supposedly, Taylor sold his estates in Sussex and came to Ireland where he obtained over twenty thousand acres at this time, including much of the land at Kells and its environs, also the lands around Bective. He may have gained possession of Dowdstown then, but the best information available suggests that property seized from the Dowdalls was assigned to a man named Robert Rochfort. It seems that the Taylors came into possession of Dowdstown in the second half of the 18th century, possibly around the 1770s.

The ancient graveyard and ruins of Dowdstown Church stand on the hillside adjacent to the old turnpike road, nowadays the back-avenue, and commands the once beautiful vista of the River Skane's confluence with the Boyne. Very little remains nowadays except the remnants of the square belfry and a more modern wall surrounding the churchyard; with a couple of ancient gnarled beech trees brooding over the scene. This was once a Cistercian Church, which contributed part of its tithes to Saint Mary's of Dublin: the church being supposedly built during the 1180s by a Norman Knight named Sir Walter Duff. Legends say the area derives its name from his surname and was called Duffstown in olden times – equally it may have been named after Dowdalls of Athlumney, who owned the parish/

144

*Ancient church ruins at Dowdstown*

townland in times past. Several more supposed derivations of the name exist but constraints of space do not permit me to enlarge upon these. The old building was once the church for the parish of Dowdstown, comprising of Dowdstown and Philpotstown townlands; which no longer form a parish but are part of the larger conjoined parishes of Johnstown and Walterstown.

The Down Survey Barony of Skreen map shows a small townland named Phillips Towne within the parish of Dowdstown (spelled Dowestowne). The tiny enclave was roughly 'L' shaped and clearly marked as a separate entity to the remainder of the parish – its boundary ran from the approximate area of the later day Dowdstown Bridge to Bellinter crossroads and from there followed the Barony boundary (the double ditch) to the Boyne, near which it skirted eastwards around the site of Oak Lodge. The eastern boundary was possibly formed by the River Skane, from the area of the bridge to the Boyne. The map shows the townland of Dowestowne as number 58, the townland of Phillpottstowne as number 59 and Phillips Towne as number 58(2). The route of the M3 is now gouged through this former enclave, in the centre of which a pre-construction archaeological dig during 2005/2006 uncovered an ancient circular motte and a square bailey-like enclosure – these being variously described by the archaeologists on site as dating from 700 AD to one thousand years BC.

During the dig at the ancient motte I saw the remains of an old buried stone paved pathway that headed northwestwards towards Bellinter and

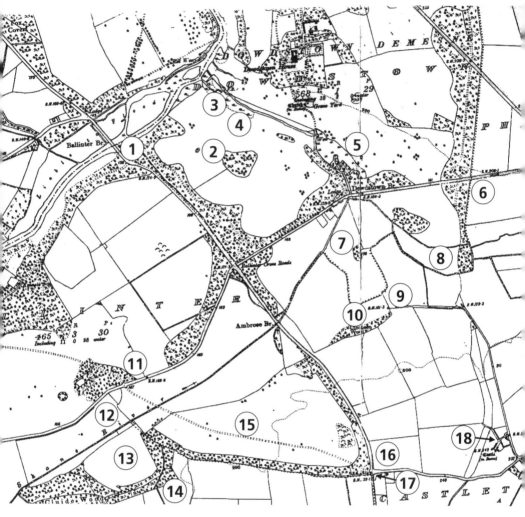

The 1911 OS map of Bellinter and Dowdstown. Note the large areas of woodland which were there until the 1950's.

1. Site of Oak Lodge
2. Site of Ancient Motte and Bailey
3. Dam and spillway
4. Site of Lower Lake
5. Dowdstown Upper Lake
6. The Sally Wood
7. Clumpwood in "River Field"
8. The Gabhra Island
9. Iron gate on Old Turnpike
10. Clooneen Wood
11. Decoy Gate at Bellinter
12. Butler's Bridge
13. The White Field
14. Cluide Wood
15. Old Drive through Deerpark o/s 1882)
16. The Green gate of Bellinter (1800)
17. Castletown Forge
18. Cheevers Castle (1690)

southeastwards towards Walter Duff's old church across the Skane – it was perhaps five feet or so in width and well paved with stones similar to cobblestones. The orientation of the pathway suggests that it once ran from the aforementioned right of way through the old Barony boundary behind Oak Lodge and intersected the line of the defunct Bective/Trim road at the ancient bridge near the ruined church. Perhaps the following presentment in the Barony of Skreen Query Book of 1802 related to this long gone track: *Item 521 Wher £2,, 2,, & £2,, 1,, be raised as before & Acc for by Lord Tarah To's King W Warren & P King to rep' 84 per of footpath from Trim to Drogheda bet'w Balinter & Phillpotstown on the lands of Dowdstown @ 6* (sic).

Several artefacts were uncovered, including the remains of a stone bracelet, part of a 7$^{th}$ cent' iron shears, some bronze studs and a modern scout's knife and whistle. Though I can only guess at the origins of the older items, I know the source of the knife and whistle, as boyscout encampments occupied the site of the old motte several times during my boyhood years. The site has now been gouged from the landscape and its remains lie buried beneath the all-pervasive motorway.

There's a commonly told story that General Robert Taylor, to commemorate his participation in the event, had the woods of Dowdstown Demesne planted to mimic the pre-battle disposition of the British armies at Waterloo in Belgium in 1815. I am not an expert on such military matters, therefore, cannot give an informed opinion on the subject, but some students of that conflict dismiss this suggestion and state that the actual layout of the woods, as shown on the OS maps, is different to the battle formations. Whatever the truth of the matter, the plantations of the Dowdstown Demesne were many and covered in excess of two hundred and fifty acres. Most of the woods were still there during my early years, but many were cut down during the 1950s and the land bulldozed.

For reasons stated earlier, it appears that the development of the Dowdstown Demesne started post 1822. By then all the public roads through the estate were defunct and the old 1730 line of the turnpike transformed into an avenue, with an entrance gateway close by Dowdstown Bridge on the new line of the Trim/Drogheda road. The old stone arched bridge was blocked off and a dam built to replace the embankment, which formerly carried the turnpike from Dublin across the swamp towards the churchyard and Kilcarn. The blocked off River Skane now formed an artificial lake upstream towards Dowdstown Bridge. The avenue ran atop the new dam, or rampart, and the course of the river was altered. A new stone arched bridge, later known as the swimming pool bridge, was constructed as part of the rampart, with a weir being built to maintain the water level in the new lake and forming an ornamental outflow into the re-routed river. At the northern end of the dam was a sluiceway to control the level of the lake and I suspect that this was used as a water conduit to operate an hydraulic ram or hydrostat, because during our childhood the area was known as *the ram*. Some of these features, the lake, the weir and sluice channel, together with the new bridge can be seen on the 1837 OS map. The remains of the sluice winch, the sluice and stone built conduit are still there as I write.

The artificial lake was quite large, extending from the weir by the new bridge southward and almost to the new line of the road – at its southern end was a small promontory on which a stone boathouse was built. This was accessed from the avenue by a wooden bridge spanning the river about one hundred and fifty yards downstream from Dowdstown Bridge. The remnant of a wooden bridge crossed the river there during our youth and was known to us as *the Kesh*. The Kesh had stone abutments on each side of the river – with slots into which wooden beams could be inserted to vary the level of the river and lake. We had many fun times playing at the old Kesh and often gambolled in the rocky ruins of the old boathouse, by then surrounded by a swamp. All this disappeared many years ago with the cleaning of the river and not a trace remains today. The old stone bridge is not shown on the maps because it was blocked off to maintain the water level in the lake.

Another artificial lake existed in the lower valley of the Skane immediately upstream of its confluence with the Boyne. This lake was almost a third of a mile long and formed by a weir, built to hold back the river where it flowed through a gap in the dam. The dam is still there at time of writing, where the river flows under a footbridge and through a narrow rocky defile into the Boyne. It was a beautiful picturesque and idyllic place beside the Skane's confluence with the Boyne, where we sometimes had picnics

Left: *The sluice winch at the site of* The Ram *in Dowdstown*. Right: *The arch of the spillway outflow - lower lake in Dowdstown*.

during our youth. Many people, who walk through this once pastoral scene along the river paths and over the footbridge, fail to realise that the embankment was a dam blocking the valley to form a lake upstream. But the evidence is there for the discerning eye. Downstream of the dam stands a small stone arch, which appears to be an old well, but though often flooded, it's not a well. The little arch is the outlet of a sluice tunnel, or spillway, built in olden times to drain the artificial lake. During our childhood picnics my brother Tom and I spent time exploring this little narrow tunnel. The spillway ran from upstream of the former location of the weir through the tunnel and out into a little stream that ran into the Boyne. The stone slots for the sluice gate can still be found on the ivy-covered riverbank by the dam. In 1956, following the great flood of 1954, the remaining traces of the weir and part of the rocky defile were blasted, the river being widened and deepened and the upstream end of the tunnel blocked off. Neither the 1837 nor the 1882 OS maps show the dam across the valley, but it's shown on the 1911 OS map, though it doesn't show the lake. So it would seem that the dam was built post 1882 and prior to 1911.

But as mentioned, this idyllic spot has now been officially vandalised. The once beautiful pastoral setting fell victim to progress – it is now

*The limekiln in Dowdstown located alongside the old line of the turnpike near Brian Boru's Bridge*

overlooked by the ugly new Boyne crossing of the M3 and is home to the foul sewerage discharges from upstream developments in Dunshaughlin, Killeen and Kilmessan.

The section of the old Dublin to Navan turnpike road through the Dowdstown estate generally merged with the avenues of the demesne. The avenue, from the back lodge on the Trim/Bective road to the farmyard at the rear of Dowdstown house, is built over the ancient route of the turnpike and, if some historians are to be believed, possibly over part of the even more ancient route of *An Slige Asail.* In my previous book *Where Toll Roads Meet*, are included my thoughts on a possible ford on the River Boyne which may have linked Ardsallagh to this ancient route from Tara to Kilcarn.

Prior to the construction of Dowdstown Bridge the river Gabhra mingled with the Skane further to the north and within the area later to become the upper lake. I make this assertion based on local knowledge, which includes early recollections of certain excavations taking place on the riverbed and traces of the old line of the Gabhra still existing long ago. I suggest that the diversion of the river, sometime between 1801 and 1802, was to avoid the building of an extra bridge. With the Gabhra diverted onto the new course, it was necessary to build just one bridge to carry the new line of the road across the commingled streams. At time of writing, if one stands on the little concrete bridge spanning the Gabhra near Dowdstown Bridge, it can be seen that the course of the river is hewn through solid rock. Hence the sudden change in the river's direction of flow was not natural. This, to quote an old saying, was a very practical way of "killing two birds with one stone". Therefore, quite a lot of time, money and effort were saved in building but one bridge across the merged rivers.

Nowadays the opposite modus operandi seems to prevail – this new and different approach to time and money expenditure is demonstrated in the very same field just a few metres away. Here, the collective *wisdom* of Eurolink, Meath County Council and the NRA, completed the destruction of the valley's landscape by building nearly a mile of new roadway and three new bridges. In doing so they caused long-lasting disruption to the local community and environment, squandered vast sums of ever-scarcer money and wiped out the beautiful view of Tara, once to be seen from Dowdstown Bridge. All this unnecessarily invasive work was done to carry a new line of the Trim to Drogheda road across the Gabhra, the M3 motorway and the Skane. Previous to construction of the motorway, the Trim to Drogheda road entered Dowdstown at Bellinter crossroads and passed through the townland – it crossed Dowdstown Bridge and ran on up *the well hill* to Philpotstown crossroads. The local landscape has been altered completely by the M3 motorway bisecting the road a short distance to the east of Bellinter crossroads and the old road of our childhood years has become a cul de sac at both ends. As mentioned, a new section of road was built on a high embankment to the south, which now takes the route over yet another ugly modern and graceless concrete construction across the motorway. The new Bellinter crossroad carries this new line across the Kilmessan road at a staggered junction beside Ambrose Bridge. This new line rejoins the old Trim road near the Decoy Gate in Bellinter. The defunct route will provide an access for a few houses and remain the rear entrance to Dowdstown.

If still resident in my old home near the bridge, in the future should I wish to visit my neighbours up the road, I would be forced to travel over a mile to arrive at their gate. Whereas, previously I could walk a couple of hundred yards up the road to do the same, how is such a retrograde development deemed to be progress? This type of situation prevails in many places throughout Ireland since the advent of motorways and reinforces my belief that these super highways are a divisive influence on rural communities. One might ask if such social implications are considered during the conduct of so-called environmental impact studies and public enquiries? This subject is discussed further in the postscript.

The Columban Fathers bought Dowdstown from the Taylor estate in 1927 for the sum of £15,000. I'm told that at the time the deeds prohibited the sale of the property to papists, therefore, some adroit manoeuvring took place to circumvent the ancient prohibition. Dalgan Park College was built in the 1930s and opened in 1941, with about one hundred and seventy students attending there during its peak years. The name Dalgan Park originated from the Columban's former house near Shrule on the Mayo/Galway border. Dowdstown House remained the international headquarters for the Columban Fathers until 1967, when this organisation moved to Dublin. Nowadays the house is named after Father John Blowick, one of the founder members of the Columban Society. Since 1981 it has been leased to the Meath Diocese and is used as a retreat and conference centre.

Ere we depart the Skane valley, I will add my thoughts on how the river came to be known as such and the probable derivation of the name, which as a child I always spelled *Skein*. I can't recall where I learned that particular spelling, but it was probably from my father who spelled it thus. We came to know that a *Skein* was the name given by the old folks to the portion of wool we held on outstretched arms whilst our mother or sisters rolled it into a ball of wool for knitting. But more significantly, we learned that a flight of geese is called a *Skein of Geese* – especially when flying in a shallow 'V' shaped formation. Many times I saw such bird formations winging their way across the wintry sky, past our house and on up the river valley, to which river I suggest they gave the name. The Skane rises in Gaffney's Well in Dunshaughlin, and completes its journey at a confluence with the Boyne at Dowdstown. First it flows to the northwest towards Kilmessan and onwards to Bellinter. At the Cluide Wood which once graced its banks, the river turns and flows towards the northeast – effectively rounding a corner, thereby changing the shape of it's course into a giant 'V' shape or *Skein,* which is well defined on the old OS maps. In his writings of 1836, John O'Donovan refers to Cluide as meaning 'the corner' or nook. Various dictionaries confirmed my earlier understanding of the meaning of Skein and also indicated its pronunciation is Skayn, the same as Skane. I could find no definition of the word Skane in the English language, except that it's a province in southern Sweden.

I discovered various spellings of the name, including Skane, Skein and Skene, but the spelling on the 1837 OS map is Skane, which seems to have laid a marker for the future. This is not unusual, as many Irish place names were anglicised and their pronunciation altered during various surveys. I note that the latest Discovery map shows the name of the river in both English and Gaelic – in English it's spelled *Skane* and in Gaelic the spelling is *Sceine*. I wonder where the word *Sceine* originates, the closest definition I can find is in Collins Irish/English dictionary, which defines *Scein* as meaning terror, or a glare in one's eyes, but I found no reference to *Sceine*. It's interesting to note that the Grand Jury records, prior to the Ordnance Survey of 1837, spell the river's name as Skeene or Skeine, with no 'a' included. On the 1650s Barony of Lower Deece Down Survey Map, the name is spelled without the letter a, hence there are official records showing that this was the earlier spelling of the name. So it's my personal belief that the river of my childhood derived its name from the many flights of geese soaring over its beautiful valley in times past.

Leaving the Skane valley, the road traverses a hill known to us in our youth as *the well hill*. In his field notes of 1836 John O'Donovan, whilst describing the parish of Dowdstown, noted a well bearing the name *Tobair Na Mias* – he translated this to mean 'the well of the dishes' and wrote that the well was not of religious significance. He further added that this well was located to the south of the old church, which placed it on a direct line between the Hill of Tara and the churchyard in Dowdstown. Several spring wells are located in the immediate vicinity, two of which are in the well field between the church and the River Skane to the west – these have been used for many years as a water supply for Dowdstown and Dalgan Park College. There was a spring located about a hundred yards to the south, which flowed into an old drinking trough in the field. As children we knew this as 'the frogs well', mainly because the trough was sometimes filled with frog's spawn and tadpoles. Nothing at this spring indicated that it might be the well referred to in the field notes.

Further research uncovered nothing in addition to that one rather cryptic reference in O'Donovan's notes. Then another childhood memory came to my aid – I recalled the old well behind the ditch on the well hill and the many times I drank its cool water on hot summer days during my youth. Oftentimes my brother Tom and I, while walking down the road from Garlow Cross on our way home from school in Navan, climbed over the hedge and down into the deep dike (ditch) to slake our thirst. We knelt on the moss covered round stones at the edge of the little spring to sup the cool clear water. Sometimes we couldn't get close to the well, as from time to time it was surrounded by a Tinker's encampment. These 'Knight's of the road' camped frequently in this spot whilst plying their skilled trade and availing of the sweet well water and the largess of the nearby college. When I mused over these memories, as seen through the misty window of time and nostalgia, I realised that the clue might be in the two round stones on which we so blithely knelt all those years ago. If I recall correctly, these stones were perfectly circular and measured about thirty inches in diameter by roughly nine inches thick. As no likelier explanation could be found, I would suggest that the round stones provided the ancient name for the well – they could be likened to platters or plates, otherwise referred to as dishes. Following the construction of the road around 1802, some effort was made to preserve the well as a source of drinking water, but it fell into disuse and its name was lost. This well was sited on the eastern side of the valley close by the previously described ancient route (pre 1730) of the road between the Hill of Tara and Navan.

In another book, *Where Toll Roads Meet,* I mention an old mill located on the river Gabhra beside its confluence with the Cardiffstown stream at a place we called the Gabhra Island, the mill was accessed by a small laneway leading from the old turnpike road near the Clooneen Junction; further information about the location of this mill is included in chapter thirteen. Millstones being concave or dished on one side, therefore, it's possible that the grinding stones from this long gone mill gave rise to the name by being placed at the well when the mill ceased operation. Another possibility is that the stones located at the well during our youth were corn stones, formerly used to stack corn for spring threshing – these had a dish shaped depression on one side. The reader will find further data on these

*Dowdstwon Hurlers of 1943.* Front left to right: *G. Shiels, Finbar Holten, M. Devine, D. O'Brien, R. Farrelly, N. Bowens, Frank Doyle, Paul Farrelly, Jim Cunningham.* Back left to right: *K. Boylan (hidden), Tom Ruddy, Brendan Farrelly, Jack Husband, Leo Boylan, Kevin Holten, Sa' Murray, Mick Lynch, Miler McGrath, J. Swan, Eric Doyle, Jack McGrath, Anthony Holten, K. Farrelly, Frank Swan* (Picture courtesy M. O'Brien)

corn stones included in the chapter on Glanuaigneach. The site of the mill was a few hundred yards to the south of the old well. Unfortunately, the great swathe of the M3 has been gouged across the Gabhra Island and much of the ancient mill site.

I searched for the lost well in 2006 and found only a trickle of water flowing in a shallow channel, the old well was gone, the deep-ditch of yesteryear having been filled by the detritus of the bulldozed woods. Following a few hours hard work with a slashook and spade the lost spring reappeared, still bubbling from the same place as of old. But the two round stones were gone and though I dug as deep as possible not a trace of them could be found. When the water cleared I took a few sips and found it to be sweet and cold as of old. I have no idea what happened to the stones, perhaps they were buried deeper or taken to adorn someone's garden or rockery.

During my early years the road was enclosed by woods, from here to the end of the Dowdstown estate near Philpotstown Cross. Most of these were cut down and bulldozed in the 1950s. To the south, the Sally Wood ran from the Trim to Drogheda road down to the Gabhra and formed the mearing with Read's Farm, (Philpotstown). The Civil Survey shows Philpotstown townland being occupied by a family named Doppine in 1654/56. In 1836 this farm was owned by Doppings, then in later years by Reads – in the 1950s it was bought by Donnelley's from Dublin and at present is owned by a business man. To the north, the college wood, one of the survivors of the original demesne, forms the boundary nowadays. This was once a huge wood running from the Gabhra up to and beyond the N3 to the Yellow Walls Lane. Part of it was known as the fox covert and remains to the north of the main road – it runs from the N3 to the Yellow Walls Lane near where Blake's house stood in years gone by. In former days no houses were sited on the stretch of road between Dowdstown Bridge and the immediate vicinity of the crossroads. A cottage was built on the Philpotstown side of the College Wood in the early 1950s – Dan Norton and his family occupied this cottage for many years. Later in the 1950s a schoolmaster named Cullen built a bungalow in the remains of the Sally Wood and in the early 1960s another schoolmaster named Ferris built a bungalow alongside this.

Next we come to the oft' mentioned and well known Philpotstown Cross, colloquially referred to as Garlow Cross. Many local jokes and legends are told about the 'characters' living around Garlow Cross and the antics they got up to over the years. I can recall the groups of men and boys playing 'pitch and toss' at the crossroads and heard about the

*The gathering of the hunt at Philpotstown cross, Garlow, in the early years of the Twentieth century* (Courtesy M O'Brien)

crossroad dances that took place there in days of yore. What I remember most are the old 'pisoiges' about Saint Patrick and some of the things that reputedly happened to the Saint on his fabled journey from Slane to Tara, supposedly to attempt to Christianise the pagans on the famed hilltop. The following are some of the stories I heard over the years.

When St Patrick was on his first trip to Tara to see the High King, he came to a crossroads where a bunch of men were playing pitch and toss. Being a bit lost and not possessing a Discovery road map or G.P. navigation aid he asked for directions, saying: "My good men can you direct me to Tara". The reply was unprintable, but went something like: "Ah f*** off you hairy auld b******", to which Patrick replied, "Well, at least I know I'm at Garlow Cross" and proceeded on his way with dignity. Another yarn went as follows: When St Patrick was passing the crossroads he decided to have a rest and sat at the bottom of the wall where he fell asleep. Awakening from his slumber, he found that someone had stolen the laces from his sandals. Whereupon the good Saint lost his rag and laid a curse upon the place, saying "That forever more there would be a thief at Garlow Cross"! Yet another yarn was told that when St Patrick travelled to Tara from Slane, he walked through Navan and Kilcarne but he *ran* through Garlow Cross.

*Tobar na Mias - The well of the dishes, Dowdstown, 2006*

*Prospective buyers? Joe Read, third from right, with potential buyers. Holding the horse is Pa Kennedy* (Courtesy M O'Brien)

Obviously these are but colloquial yarns, they couldn't have occurred at the crossroads nowadays known as Garlow Cross, because it didn't exist until almost fourteen hundred years after the venerable Saint passed by. Maybe the supposed events happened at Garlagh Cross (Old Garlow Cross) or perhaps at the ancient crossroads by Dowdstown Churchyard – while the Saint travelled along the legendary *Slighe Asail* on his quest to convert the heathens of County Meath.

Patrick Ward, who hailed from Moynalty, opened a public house at the crossroads in the 1960s; on the site of the old shop run by Cathy Robinson during our youth. Anecdotes tell of a pub at the crossroads in earlier times – this pub being reputedly run by a McKenna family who owned an establishment on Ludlow Street in Navan. I checked with some of the present day members of this family, together with a few older inhabitants of the area and all said that this was not so: no such official pub stood at the crossroads. A man named McKenna supposedly once ran a pub on the hill of Skryne; perhaps this explains the origins of the story.

While no proof exists of an *official* public house being located at Garlow Cross in times past, many anecdotes were told about the famous, or infamous, *Sibin* supposedly operated there by the Reads (Reids) in the good old days. Though I suspect that these legends lost nothing in the telling, yet there seems to remain a hardcore of substance in the many yarns proliferating during my youth. Amongst the stories told at the firesides of yesteryear are those of card games held in the backroom or back kitchen long ago. These tell of high stake games taking place there and how some players came close to losing the very shirts from their backs – supposedly farmers and cattle-jobbers lost many a prized bull, cow, or even parts of their farms when the cards ran unkindly for them. Many tales were told about the exploits of Joe Read (Reid) and his brothers, John, Matt *The Slogger*, and Thomas, *The Yankee*. The brothers, in addition to being involved in horseracing and trading, were renowned members of the local GAA scene – it's said that they played for the Dowdstown teams of the past. John Read reputedly owned a famous racehorse, which won the Galway Plate in 1906, but was awarded the trophy following a stewards inquiry – I heard that this horse was named *The Royal Tara* and the Read's racing colours were scarlet and blue; the old Dowdstown GAA colours.

Miss Robinson (Cathy) opened a shop in the same building that once housed the *Sibin*. This building belonged originally to the Read family, together with the stone farmyard buildings nearby. The 1837 OS map indicates a building at the crossroads and the out offices to the rear, but Larkin's Map indicates no buildings at the new crossroads. Both maps show a building at the site of the former forked junction a few hundred yards to the west. This was on the north side of the Trim road leading towards Dowdstown Bridge and at the original meeting point of the Ratoath/Skryne road and the realigned Dublin to Navan turnpike road. The building doesn't appear on any of the later maps and has disappeared from the landscape – people who ploughed the field in the past fifty years said they never came across any traces of ruins on the site. From the foregoing it can be deduced that the buildings at Philpotstown crossroads were probably constructed sometime between 1817 and 1837. I have no idea what the building to the west was used for, but because of its location on the ancient road from Skryne, it may have been a hostelry of some sort.

Cathy Robinson ran the Post Office in her shop at Philpotstown crossroads from about 1940 until 1966, when she sold the building to Pat Ward for his public house. She remained in charge of the P.O. for several more years and operated it from her nearby bungalow until her retirement a few years later. Nancy McCabe (nee Kennedy) later operated it from her shop up on the Gilltown road near 'the Coille' (Cuillier) until it was eventually closed down. I also heard that for a time the P.O. was run from a house at Garlagh Cross, but I can't establish the veracity of this tale. The original Post Office for the area was opened at Dillon's Bridge in 1880 and was run by the Gartland family, together with the Smithy. The closure of the local Post Office was a sad ending to a long and proud tradition of a locally run public amenity.

I well remember Miss Robinson's shop during my younger days and the kindly lady who sometimes gave us a free 'poke' of sweets during those rare old times – this poke consisted of a twist of newspaper rolled into a cone and filled with a few boiled sweets or bullseyes. At Christmastime she presented the family with a fruitcake in appreciation of our custom. In those days the Trim/Drogheda road ran close by the buildings and there was a little 'island' in front of the shop: on this island grew a hawthorn tree and a lilac bush with a big flat stone beneath, here we sheltered while awaiting the bus to Navan. On warmer summer days we sometimes sat on the stone, but on wintry days we stood under the big bush, shivering in the cold east wind whistling down the road from Jock's Cross.

The crossroads has undergone many changes since those far off days – the island with the bushes and rock has disappeared like the snows of yesteryear. The shop became a pub and the road was re-routed to facilitate staggering of the crossroads. The N3 has become a death trap, almost a feeding frenzy of traffic and chaos. But the greatest change of all is taking place as I write, the M3 motorway is being built across the line of the N3 at Dillon's Bridge and new slip roads are under construction to feed the great maw of the motorway. The area is unrecognisable as the Philpotstown crossroads of old; so far all that progress has achieved is to turn it into a veritable nightmare for travellers, with several people being killed there in recent years. I wonder if these most recent changes will make any improvements: those who live long enough can only wait and see what the next edition of Garlow Cross holds in store for future generations.

# 11

# The Yellow Walls &
# Old Garlagh Cross

The road to Jock's Cross – The Cuille and Conlon's Field – The Yellow
Walls – Rev. Phil Barry's road and Kilcarn Churchyard lane – The Polo
Field – ghosts and Philpotstown Castle – Garlagh Cross – The Green
Road – Lismullin and Saddle Hill – Clonardran and the Deerpark –
Corballis, the Black Church and Templekieran.

From Philpotstown crossroads our road heads eastwards towards
Duleek and away from the Hill of Tara – on this stretch the Hill of
Skryne becomes the dominant feature and can be seen on the horizon
to the south. This section of road, from Philpotstown to Garlagh Cross
Bridge, was cut and widened in 1802 or shortly thereafter. The Grand
Jury Query Book records a presentment made to the summer assizes of
that year which reads: *Item 295, Wher £22,, 16,, & £1,, 2,, 9 wages be
raised off Bar'y Skreen & Acc for by Lord Tarah Cha' Drake Dillon Esq.
J Read Tho's Muldoon to fence & mould 152 per's new road from Trim
to Drogheda betw'n the new turnpike road & Garlow Cross Bridge @ 3s
p* (sic). The distance presented for matches the actual measurement on
the ground (152 Irish perches = 1064 yards or 0.6 mile statute measure),
which proves that the presentment was made for the section between the
1796-1815 new line of the turnpike and Garlagh Cross (Old Garlow). The

T&S maps show the Dublin/Skryne road running on this line in 1778, therefore, it's likely that the existing road was realigned and upgraded.

Approximately a quarter mile to the east of Philpotstown crossroads is a 'T' junction with a sideroad leading northeastwards, this junction is known locally as *Jock's Cross* and the sideroad as the Gilltown road. Local legends tell of how the crossroads came by its name, including yarns of a Scotsman residing there at one time and the place being named after the well-known Jock Wilkinson, but not much substance can be found to most of these tales. A rather ribald story was told about a lover's tryst being the source of the name – of how the parish priest disturbed a couple carrying on in the bushes, whereupon the man ran off but left his underpants, or jocks, behind him. The story goes on to relate that the irate priest hung the said jocks on the bushes as a warning to other prospective flighty couples. This yarn is but a figment of an overheated imagination, as it's a very old name and men didn't wear jocks in those times. The most credible anecdote concerns a family who resided in a house nearby opposite the Yellow Walls Lane: until recent times, the small triangular field in which their house stood was known as *Conlon's Field*. Each generation of the Conlon family produced at least one jockey, which tradition lasted from the second half of the 19th century and into the 1950s. One famous jockey became known as Mutt Conlon and I'm told that this name passed down through the generations. A family member was tragically killed while riding in Kilbeggan races, possibly sometime in the 1950s. The anecdote says that the cross was named after this family of jockeys. However, because of the passage of time I suppose we shall never know for sure how the place acquired its rather odd name.

A junction is shown in this area on the Taylor and Skinner road map of 1778, with the side road marked as the Slane road. Though this map is essential for tracing the main routes of its era, it is unreliable in determining the secondary roads, as the scale and orientation is not great for such purposes. In this instance the map is possibly correct, because the side road leads on through Gilltown to Kentstown and links with the route of the old Dublin to Derry road at Somerville, which continued onwards to Slane. It's possible that the side road shown on this map represents the road leading from Garlagh Cross (Old Garlow) to Gilltown – further mention is made of this road later in the chapter. Jock's Cross 'T' junction is shown on Larkin's Map and the 1837 OS map, with both maps showing several buildings in its vicinity.

Now we'll take a little diversion and travel a short distance up the Gilltown road to a place known locally as the Cuille (Coille or Cuillier). Here, about a quarter of a mile from the Trim to Drogheda road, another little sideroad leads off to the left in a northwesterly direction. This narrow roadway is known as the Yellow Walls Lane (Baille Buidhe – O'Donovan 1836) and the old maps show it crossing the line of the present day N3. On its short route of about two miles it forms the boundary between Philpotstown townland and Corballis and between Corballis and Dowdstown. Larkin's Map names an area to the north, between the lane and Corballis Vale farmhouse, as Yellow Furze. O'Donovan in his field notes of 1836 concludes that the name Corballis derives from the Gaelic Cor Bhaille, meaning the odd town. Another possible meaning is *the place of the weir*, as the Gaelic word Corr means weir and a small river flows through the townland.

As stated, the Yellow Walls Lane at one time ran across the route of the new line of the Dublin to Navan turnpike road (now the N3). It joined up with the old route of the same road through Dowdstown at a place known to us as Brian Boru's Bridge, which is directly across the Boyne from Ardsallagh House and carried the old turnpike across the Follistown River, which forms the mearing between Kilcarn and Dowdstown. Larkin's Map and the 1837 OS map show the link up, but in addition to showing a junction, the Taylor and Skinner map indicates that the by road leading northeastwards was the Drogheda road. This was probably correct during that era as it joined with the Trim to Drogheda road at Garlagh Cross (old Garlow Cross), but more about this presently. The cutting of the new line between Philpotstown and Kilcarn isolated the former connection to the turnpike road at Dowdstown and this section of road to the west of the present day N3 has merged with the landscape and not a trace remains today. I'm told that in more recent times the name Yellow Walls was deemed to be slightly downmarket, hence some of the swanks living thereon renamed it Kilcarn Heights Road.

Both Larkin's Map and the 1837 OS map show a village or hamlet on the lane – the OS map names the site as the Yellow Walls and indicates that it was just west of where the lane crossed the Folistown River. This map also names another location as the Yellow Walls: the second such named spot is where Allen's old farmhouse once stood. O'Donovan's field notes mention the Yellow Walls by name and states that it was a farm with offices and a village of 8 to 10 houses. These field notes also referenced that the name Yellow Walls appears on Larkin's Map. Local legend says the name derives from an ancient dwelling at this location (Allen's farm), which had yellow walls, possibly mudwalls built from yellow, or yallow, clay. While Larkin's Map doesn't show a specific location, it names the area Yellow Walls and shows a small cluster of buildings at the same site depicted on the OS map. Some of these houses were on the opposite side of the lane in a spot we called Blake's Fields. This is close to where the famous 'Shed (Christy) McGrath' lived during our early years, in a cottage beside the little bridge. Supposedly, in olden times a mass path ran from the lane near the hamlet and across the fields to Kilcarn Church lane, in more recent years the inhabitants of the Yellow Walls used the path to attend mass in Johnstown chapel.

But in my opinion, the Yellow Walls Lane has a greater story to tell in terms of the area's road networks during times past. One of the inaccuracies in Larkin's Map shows up here: both the line of the Yellow Walls Lane and the Follistown River are shown incorrectly and do not match the topography. While it may be argued that the line of the road has changed over the intervening years, it's unlikely that the route of the river has altered, as it runs in a deep natural glen which probably eroded into the limestone over many centuries. There's a simple explanation for these inconsistencies, however, as the map was surveyed and drafted prior to the cutting of the new turnpike road from Philpotstown to Kilcarn, the route shown was more conceptual than actual. This map indicates an avenue or roadway connecting Upper and Lower Kilcarn estate houses and the avenue from Lower Kilcarn running to both the old and new lines of the turnpike road, but it does not show the old church and graveyard or the churchyard laneway at Kilcarn.

The 1837 OS map indicates the aforementioned connecting roads between the two estates at Kilcarn, including the old church and graveyard and the churchyard laneway – both routes are shown truncated i.e. roads to nowhere. But the field boundaries in the vicinity of the Yellow Walls Lane are interesting on this map, as they indicate the possible continuation of this road in a different direction. At time of writing, there's a sharp ninety degree bend taking the little road towards the southwest and its intersection with the N3 close by Ms Haley's farm: in earlier days it connected to the old line of the turnpike road, as described. The field boundary lines show that the road may have run on a curving route northwestward and joined with the old turnpike at Upper Kilcarn, rather than at Brian Boru's Bridge. This map also shows a road linking the two lines of the turnpike and passing very close to the house at Upper Kilcarn. It's possible that the sudden ninety-degree bend in the Yellow Walls Lane of the present day was at one time part of a 'T' junction, with the main line running on towards the front of the house at Upper Kilcarn. The other leg of the 'T', the road of the present day, would have run south to link up with the old turnpike at the bridge. It's possible that in later years the layout was altered to remove the road from the precincts of the demesne at Upper Kilcarn, perhaps in the period prior to the survey of the T&S map in the 1770s.

The Longfield estate (1822) map of Kilcarn Demesne, when studied in conjunction with the other maps, provides the final clue to the maze of old and long lost roads in the Kilcarn area. Although now barely legible, it yields some information which I could not find elsewhere, including: details of the old mill (the Big Mill) and millrace at Kilcarn, the old bridge at Kilcarn, many field names of the estate and the old road network around Johnstown. In addition to the aforementioned roads and avenues of the estate, it indicates a road running from the old line of the turnpike in front of the house at Upper Kilcarn, crossing the new turnpike and running through the estate to link with the road from Johnstown to Kentstown near the Rath at Oldtown. A note on the map says of this road: *taken by Rev. Phil Barry in 1819*. In my view, this long gone road was once part of the main road from Navan to Duleek previous to the construction of *The New Bridge* across the River Boyne sometime between the 1730s and 1756. This road makes sense of the disconnected old roads shown on the other maps, as it provided a link to the turnpike for the avenues of the

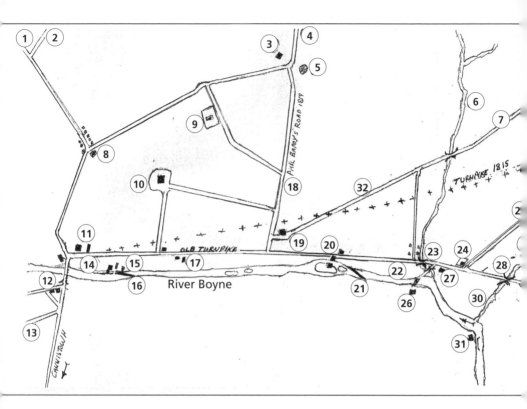

*Author's reconstruction of road layout Kilcarn/Dowdstown circa 1800   Not to scale*

1.  Road to Killagrin (Babe's Bridge?)
2.  Old Road to Kentstown via Realtogue
3.  Pastor Hill
4.  Duleek/Navan Road via Oldtown
5.  Rath
6.  Follistown River
7.  Yellow Walls Lane
8.  Johnstown Village
9.  Kilcarn Churchyard
10. Kilcarn Lower (park)
11. Kilcarn Lodge (kennels)
12. Kilcarn Turnpike House
13. Bothar Ailling
14. Kilcarn Bridge
15. The Big Mill, Kilcarn
16. Kilcarn Weir
17. Ruins of Inn
18. Rev. Phil Barry's Road (1819)
19. Upper Kilcarn
20. Upper Kilcarn Mill
21. Upper Kilcarn Weir
22. Ford on Boyne
23. Brian Boru's Bridge
24. Ruins of Dowdstown Church
25. Old Skreen Road
26. Ardsallagh House
27. Dowdstown House
28. Old Stone Bridge
29. Old Tara Road
30. River Skein
31. Ardsallagh Mill
32. Old Line of Yellow Walls Lane

two estates, the Kilcarn churchyard lane and the Yellow Walls Lane (see further references in chapter 15).

During our younger days the Gilltown road was still untarred and remained as a gravel road until surfaced with tar and chippings in the late 1950s. We sometimes drove along it by pony trap in those far off days on our way to Granny's house over in Oldtown – many potholes adorned its gravelled surface then and Dad often joked about it being the birthplace of all the potholes in Ireland.

The Cuille (Coille or Cuillier) is a large field opposite the junction of the Yellow Walls Lane and the Gilltown road, many local legends are told about ghosts in its vicinity. Some said that a monastery or convent once existed on the location, perhaps these legends emanate from tales told about the ancient abbey (priory) of nearby Lismullin? People wonder at the source of the name, but a clue can be found in the OS map of 1837: this show an extensive area of woodland to the east of the Gilltown road and along the small stream running from Clonardran to Garlagh Cross. As the Gaelic name for forestry or woodland is Coillte, it's reasonable to propose that the name Cuille, Coille or Cuillier derives from the woodlands occupying the area in olden times and the variations in spelling can be attributed to colloquial usage.

The old maps indicate a road leading southeastward from the Gilltown road at its junction with the Yellow Walls Lane and down to Garlagh Cross (Old Garlow) - in my view this junction was the origional location of Jock's Cross. The section of road provided the link between the old turnpike road and the road to Drogheda, via the Yellow Walls Lane, which possibly explains the reason why it was named 'the Drogheda road' on the T&S map. In earlier years some traces of this linking road were still evident at both ends, as were the ruins of several old houses along the short route. Nowadays there's merely an entry from the Gilltown road to a few outbuildings located at the site of the previously mentioned Conlon's field. It's likely that the section of the Gilltown road from here to the present day Jock's Cross on the Trim/Drogheda road was cut in 1802 during the same period as the widening of the road from Philpotstown crossroads. It's much wider than the remainder of the road running through Gilltown and in older times was known as *the new road*.

The OS map of 1837 shows several buildings along the section of now defunct road to old Garlow Cross and it was obviously a very populous place then. Larkin's Map shows a similar number of dwellings in the area, and also depicts a lane leading up into the woodland in the Cuille to a couple of large buildings close by the old woods. This map also indicates that the section of road running up from Garlagh Cross continued on across the Gilltown road. It ran alongside the Yellow Walls Lane to the back of Clarke's old stone house and close to the well, where it came to a dead end near *The Polo Field*. A number of houses are shown on this cul de sac, about eight in total forming a small hamlet, which tends to explain the presence of a spring well complete with stone surround and capping. All this suggests that Garlagh Cross was once a well-populated area in times past, long before the later day Philpotstown/Garlow Cross, usurped its position of being the principal landmark in the area.

The previously mentioned polo field was a well-known gathering place for GAA football teams over many generations. Though there are differing views as to its exact location, most people are of the opinion that it was to the south of the Yellow Walls Lane near where May Clarke lived during my lifetime. I'm not sure of the origins of the name, but would assume that the gentry played polo there in bygone days. I heard many tales from Dad and my uncles about the times when the Dowdstown teams of old played hurling and football on its flat green sward, but like everything else all these are but ancient memories now. In later years local lads used the Cuillier as a training area thus carrying on the tradition.

It's opportune to mention here the legends about a castle in the area, which has been speculated upon by historians over the years. There's a belief held by some that a castle once existed in the present day townland of Dowdstown. Many noted castles were to be found in the area, such as Riverstown castle, the ruins of the castle in Castletown Tara and the old ruined castles at Walterstown (Monkstown) and Asigh (Assey), Balsoon, Trubley, Craystown and Scurlockstown. Though some of these have entirely disappeared yet they are well recorded. There was also a castle across the Boyne in Ardsallagh at one time, as well as the castles in Athlumney and Skryne – so the area was well endowed by castles and towerhouses. But where was the supposed castle in Dowdstown? The Down Survey of the

1640s refers to a *cottage style residence* on the estate; there is no mention of a castle. So, at least from around the middle of the 17<sup>th</sup> century, there appears to be no evidence of the presence of a castle on the estate or in the townland, as we know it today. A clue to the missing castle can be found in the oft' mentioned Taylor and Skinner maps. One prominent historian supposes that a castle once existed in Dowdstown because one such ruined castle is shown on this map of the area, which was surveyed in the 1770s. In my opinion, these are the ruins of the old church, as so depicted on all the other maps; perhaps the surveyors mistook these ruins for a castle. There is another possibility, which I think is highly unlikely, that either Dowdstown House or the ancient church was built upon the site of an existing castle – but we shall never know for sure.

Further research provided another possible solution to this riddle from the past and indicates how some items of local knowledge can persist through the generations. Close perusal of the 1654/56 Civil Survey of Dowdstown Parish failed to yield any mention of a castle under this heading, but in the section on Philpotstown I found a clear reference to a Castle and a thatched house in that townland. This appears to indicate the presence of a castle in the ancient parish of Dowdstown, but it was located in the townland of Philpotstown … where was it sited?

Over the years, stories have been told of stone ruins standing in the fields near the Cuille (Coille) and close by Conlon's Field. The reputed site of the ruins coincided closely to the buildings shown on Larkin's Map at the end of a lane leading off the defunct road from Garlagh Cross to the Gilltown road. Although these were sited in the townland of Gilltown, they were on the edge of Philpotstown – but as shown elsewhere, the boundaries of townlands varied considerably over the years, hence the old ruins may have been in Philpotstown at one time. These ruins were variously described as 'the dovecote', or pigeon house and 'the castle'. Many tales were told about the ghostly figures of nuns seen roaming around in the moonlight near the old ruins, and inevitably, late night travellers saw the black hound with fiery red eyes. Perhaps these stories gave rise to the tale of a monastery supposedly located on the site long ago. Some of the more elderly residents of the area have described the ruin as being about twenty or thirty-feet-square and the same in height, others said that it was circular shaped and called the pigeon house. During the passing years many of the stones were removed and used for buildings elsewhere. I'm told that the remains of the structure were demolished and the site bulldozed sometime in the late 1950s or early 1960s. From the descriptions given, it seems possible that these ruins were once part of the castle mentioned in the Civil Survey of 1654/56 as being located in Philpotstown. Perhaps they were the remains of a *watchtower of the Pale* or another towerhouse and may have been the old home of the Doppings (Doppines), named in the Civil Survey as occupiers of the townland. The Down Survey Barony Map of the 1650s indicates a large building, possibly a castle, located near the junction of the three parish boundaries, which place later became known as Garlagh Cross. Griffith's valuation of 1854 indicates the presence of ruins in Philpotstown townland. It shows that Catherine Smith had a house and ruins, with no significant amount of land attached, leased to Patrick Fagan at an annual rateable valuation of 4s. 0d.. The ruins are specifically listed and don't appear to be farm buildings, which were normally shown as 'offices'. Could these have been the ruins of the lost castle, the source of so many stories during my boyhood years?

Following the Trim/Drogheda road eastward from Jock's Cross we top a little knoll from which there is a great view of the surrounding countryside, to the right is Lismullin (the fort of the mill) and the hill of Skryne. Looking back, the Hill of Tara and wooded valley of the Skane can be seen, whilst straight ahead lies the hill of Clonardran, known in Gaelic as Cluain Ard Rathin: which name is interpreted by John O'Donovan as 'high lawn or the meadow of the ferns'. Unfortunately, this pastoral scene is blighted by the wide swathe of the M3 and the spaghetti junction of Blundelstown interchange, sprawled over the lower slopes of the ancient hill. In the hollow beyond the knoll is the oft' mentioned Garlagh Cross or 'the Cross of the Babies'. O'Donovan's field notes interpret Garlagh (Garlach) as meaning *the place of the babies*. He concluded that it might be a place where stillborn or other unbaptised infants were interred in previous years. Nowadays, the former 'crossroads' is but a forked junction, with the Trim to Drogheda road leading straight on up the hill of Clonardran towards Walterstown and the road to Skryne branching off to the right.

Between the two roads lies a small triangular grassy patch where stood a stone cross in days of yore, supposedly to commemorate the interred infants of yesteryear. It was a common enough practice in olden times to have such burial places for infants located where several parishes shared a common boundary. At Garlagh Cross, the boundaries of the ancient parishes of Dowdstown, Lismullin and Templekeeran (Templekieran) met. The old maps show a building located at the southeastern edge of the green. Larkin's Map names this crossroads as Garticross – the meaning of this name eludes me, but it may have been a misspelling or a colloquialism of another name, as O'Donovan's interpretation seems to stand up to scrutiny.

A modern Collins Irish dictionary defines the word Garlach as meaning a child, urchin or brat. The word Gar is described inter alia as meaning a favour, proximity, near, while Laige means small, frail or early childhood. So, whether the spelling Garlagh or Garlach is used, the name of the ancient crossroads may be associated with childhood. As a point of interest, a similar sounding word, namely Garbhlach, is described as meaning rough ground and the word Gabhlaigh is defined as a fork, or something that branches out.

In recent times, the local community has done a great job in upgrading the little green at the crossroads – they have mounted a sundial, together with a marble plaque depicting some of the history of the place and keep everything in pristine condition. The little stream from Clonardran has been named *The Garlach* and plaques bearing that name placed on the breast walls of the bridge. The restoration of the green is a nice gesture to the memories of past generations, a rare enough occurrence in the progressive Ireland of the present day.

Across the road from the green there's an old house, which at time of writing is owned and occupied by Liam McCarthy, a well-known local historian. As the building is sited on what was a strategic junction of two main routes, I suspect that it was once an Inn, but I have no proof of this: the old maps tend to lend substance to the antiquity of the house, as they show a building on the site in olden times. Liam has a record of tenants who leased the premises since the 1850s. These include Matthew Montague, a Maguire family, John Robinson (Jack), Neddy Quinn, Freddie Welsh, who once owned a pub in Navan and Mickey Cook – the Cooks later moved into the house next door to us in Dowdstown in 1949 and were our neighbours until 1955. If I recall correctly, the old corner house had a thatched roof during my youth and it always looked quaint standing there on the roadside by the bridge. This bridge carried the road across the little stream flowing down from Clonardran, through the garden of Liam's house and into the Gabhra close by the site of the King's Mill. A local anecdote says that some ancient stones, perhaps altar stones or some such from the nearby Templekeeran church or the long gone nun's priory of Lismullin, were built into and concealed within the structure of this small bridge during olden times when a purge was in progress. In my early years a shop was located in the house and operated by various people over the years, including Welshs and Robinsons – Jack Robinson sold paraffin and lamp oil there in the days before rural electrification.

The present day road traversing Clonardran hill and leading from the crossroads to the Decoy was known as *The Green Road*, because grass reputedly grew upon its centre at one time. Another possible source for the strange name is that it led to and from the little green at the crossroads. In my view the name stems from much earlier times, and I suspect that until 1800-1801 this section of road was but a grassy/muddy track providing access to the Deerpark at Clonardran and leading onwards to the Decoy. I suggest that until the early 1800s, the Trim/Drogheda road was routed via Lismullin crossroads, where it joined the road from Tara and Castletown (once the Summerhill to Drogheda road), which passed through the Lismullin Demesne and on to the Decoy. When the green road was upgraded it became part of the new main route from Trim to Drogheda. Both Larkin's Map and the 1837 OS map show the line of the road from Garlagh Cross. Though the maps do not provide a precise date for the upgrading of the section between the crossroads and the Decoy, the Grand Jury Books contain records that provide a fairly accurate date for the green road being upgraded to its modern day aspect.

The first relevant presentment is in the Query Book of 1800 under the Barony of Skreen and reads: *Item 200 Wher £32,, 17,, & £1,, 12,, 9 wages be levied off Bo'y of Skreen & Acc for by Char's Drake Dillon Esq. J Wilkinson & Jo'n Carthy to widen 146 perches 32ft wide road from Trim to Drogheda betw'n Garlow Cross and Walterstown @ 4s 6d* (sic). The second presentment is in the Lent assizes Query Book of 1801 under the Barony of Skreen and reads: *Item 562 Wher £38,, 17,, 3½ & £1,, 10,, 10½ wages be raised as before & Acc for by Cha' Drake Dillon Esq. Jo'n Carthy & Jos' Holmes to widen & fence 205 Per's 32 feet wide from Trim to Drogheda betw'n Garlow Cross & Decoy of Lismullen @ 3s 9½ d perch* (sic). Because the present day Philpotstown (Garlow) crossroads didn't exist until about 1814/1815, these two presentments seem to provide irrefutable proof that *the green road* was upgraded during the years 1800 to 1802!

Now let's journey along the green road and make a brief visit to the Deerpark at Clonardran, once part of the Dillon estates. The road that climbs the hill at Clonardran is obviously a new line, as it runs straight and true from Garlagh Cross to the hilltop: this stretch formed the boundary between the parishes of Templekeeran and Lismullin in olden times. Here, in Kierans (Kerin's) field to the right of the road there's an old Fairy Rath known locally as Saddle Hill – some say it's called such because it was shaped like a saddle. In our youth my father leased these fields from old Dicky Kierans (Kerin's) and grazed cattle there. During those times I often played at the little hill, but was ever careful not to break any of the shrubbery growing thereon, being very fearful of invoking the wrath of 'the little people' whose home it was supposed to be.

The ancient parish name of Lismullin derives from the Gaelic Lios Muillinn, meaning 'the fort of the mill': in Gaelic, Lios means a ring fort, fairy mound or an enclosure and Muileann is the name for a mill. Many people believe that the source of this name is the ancient fort of Rath Luga, located about a mile further up the road from the mill and towards the hill of Skryne: the mill was on the nearby River Gabhra. Whilst little doubt exists that the mill part of the name derived from this mill, the location of the fort included in the parish name is a moot point. O'Donovan's 1836 field notes on the parish of Lismullin contain a reference that may connect the source of the name to the little fort, locally known as Saddle Hill and located a few hundred yards from the site of the old mill. The reference goes as follows: 'There is a fort near Templekeeran Mill called Lios a' Mhuilinn" (sic}. This may be a reference to the small Fairy Rath and could indicate that in earlier times it was known by the Gaelic name for the parish. The reference to Templekeeran Mill, instead of Lismullin Mill, might mean that the mill was also known by that name. I note that elsewhere in the field notes the River Gabhra is referred to as the Templekeeran River, and was possibly named such because it formed the northern boundary of Blundelstown, a detached part of Templekeeran parish.

The new Lismullin School was built in 1957, in the same field and adjacent to the Rath – this replaced the old schools in Walterstown and at Dillon's Bridge on the Dublin Road.

Mention of the school and Dicky Kierans reminds me of how folk memories are so important to the preservation of local history. In 2007 a booklet was published to commemorate the fiftieth anniversary of the opening of Lismullin School. Whilst browsing through this I came across an item in which Dicky tells his daughter Mary about the local roads – this excerpt was extracted from the folklore surveys of 1938. These surveys were conducted in the schools throughout the country and consisted of local stories being told to the schoolchildren by the older generation, which stories were written down by the pupils as a school exercise. The objective being to preserve some of the local folklore and heritage, which was perceived to be dying out at the time. The records were gathered and archived in University College Dublin: there is a marvellous microfilm collection in the library in Navan. In the extract referred to, Dicky recounts tales of the local roads to his daughter Mary: which references I found to be amazingly accurate, containing details which took many hours of research to discover. Perhaps now would be an opportune time to carry out another folklore survey in the rapidly changing Ireland of today.

Further to the east of Lismullin School the Deerpark lane leads off to the left and runs for about a half mile northeastwards into the fields – it terminated at John Farrelly's farm, known as the Deerpark farm when the area was owned by the Dillon's of Lismullin. Nowadays the old lane is a well-maintained entry to several modern houses but it wasn't always so. In my youth, this lane would have been a prime candidate for the title of the green road, as it was then a twisty muddy laneway with practically a

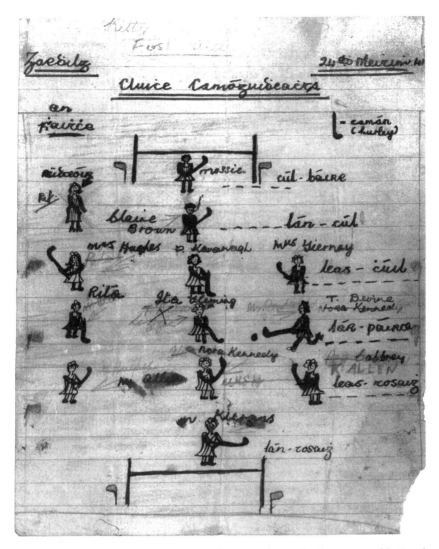

*This team sheet was compiled by Mary Kierans (later Quinn) in 1941, then captain of the Dowdstown camogie team.* (Courtesy Cynthia Nolan)

meadow growing upon its surface. Dad had some land leased here from Shed (Christy) McGrath) for grazing cattle. At one time, 'The Shed' owned a racehorse named Boyne Rover, which he sometimes kept in a real shed up on his land in the Deerpark. There are many yarns and stories about this horse and its renowned owner, which could take a whole book to recount, but as my space is limited I will refrain for the moment. Suffice to say The Shed was famous for these and many other exploits, especially on

175

the GAA scene and he will live on for many years in local memory. I recall the dry hot summer of 1959 when the grass in the Deerpark withered and died and the streams dried up. We had to haul drinking water for the cattle up from the Skane at Dowdstown in the van, but eventually it became so bad that Dad moved the cattle from the Deerpark to another little farm down on the shores of Lough Sheelin in County Cavan.

Some people speculate that the Deerpark lane once ran onwards and joined with the road over at Gilltown. A study of the maps, including the latest Discovery series, would tend to support this proposition. There are at least two possibilities: the first being that it may have turned to the west and ran across the bottomlands, then crossed the Gilltown road at Grey's old farmyard and run on across Corballis through Dodo Flanagan's farm. I have heard anecdotes that a road once ran through here and passed by 'the Black Church' and on towards Oldtown, where it joined the road to Johnstown beside the old stone house where Commandant (Captain) Kelly lived during my early boyhood. Alternatively it could have turned slightly eastward and linked with the lane leading off the road near Gerrardstown Cross (Gilltown) – this is an old lane, as it shows up on some old maps and could once have been an entry to Gerrardstown Castle. However, that's a story for another day, but so far I haven't found anything that would prove or disprove either scenario.

Larkin's Map shows a place named *Garringlais* located between Dodo Flanagan's farm in Corballis and Lynch's farm in Oldtown – Dodo told me that the farm at Corballis has been in the possession of her family for seven generations. Collins Irish dictionary defines the word garran as a grove and glas as meaning green. With a slight change of spelling and a little imagination this name could be interpreted to mean the Green Grove, perhaps the name as spelled on the map reflects an older form of spelling. I can find no person, including local historians, with knowledge of the placename. This seems to be the approximate area where the site of the Black Church was supposedly located in the distant past. The old OS maps and field notes show that the ancient parish of Templekeeran encompassed the area comprising Corballis, Gilltown (Gillstown) and Clonardran, with the townland of Blundelstown being a disconnected part thereof. This old parish extended from the Yellow Walls Lane and included Flanagan's and Grey's farms and the Clonardran stream, nowadays named the Garlach. As stated, in olden times it adjoined the parishes of Dowdstown and Lismullin at Garlagh Cross. O'Donovan's 1836 field notes define Templekeeran as meaning *St. Kieran's Church* and also mention that no ruins existed in the parish.

The OS maps and several other old maps show that the remains of the church and graveyard, presently known as Templekeeran, is actually located in the old parish of Lismullin. It seems likely, therefore, that this ancient site was at one time the church and burial ground for Lismullin parish and may have been destroyed during the times of the reformation or the rebellion of 1641. Possibly it became known as Templekeeran through local usage. Or perhaps this name originates from the name 'Templecairn' (Cairn or Carn, a pile of stones, as distinct from St. Kieran/Keeran), which is shown in this area (Lismullin) on Larkin's Map: the old OS maps do not show this name in Lismullin parish. Because of its location on the edge of the mearing with Corballis, one wonders if the fabled Black Church was once the church for Templekeeran parish, as it was unlikely that the parish existed without a church? The Down Survey County Map (1645) indicates a church sited within the boundary of Corballis and close to the mearing with Kilcarn/Oldtown. It also shows half the townland of Loghtowne located between Lismullin and Balgeeth with the other half shown as part of Blundistowne (Blundelstown), this townland has disappeared long since. The Civil Survey of 1654/56 refers to Templekeeran parish as follows: "On ye premisses a chappell & a quarry (sic), and notes that Balgeith (83 acres) and Loghtowne (63 acres) are townlands of the parish. Referring to Loghtowne (possibly meaning Loughtown or the town of the lake), the late Kitty Farrelly from Walterstown referred to an area between the Decoy and the Gleann Lane as Streamstown. Which name may once have been associated with the Decoy Lake, a possible location of Loghtowne.

There's nothing of great significance between the Deerpark lane and the Decoy. The Glebelands of Lismullin, as distinct from the Glebe of Skryne, were possibly located in this area, perhaps near the Decoy. I have seen records dating back to the times of King Edward VI in the 16th century, which mention the Glebelands of Lismullin, but so far have been unable to ascertain their exact location. Some historical writings associate these Glebelands with the aforementioned Templekeeran churchyard: which tends to support the proposition that this church was part of Lismullin parish. Local anecdotes say that a field, which ran towards the five roads of Skryne at the back of McDermott's farm, was known as the Glebe field. Because of its location, as described on the Civil Survey of 1654/56, the area near McDermott's farm is possibly part of the previously mentioned long lost townland of Loghtown. In my opinion, this disappeared townland is the key to the mystery of how the old churchyard became known by its present name.

As a boy I loved travelling the stretch of the Skryne road where it runs in the Gabhra valley from Garlagh Cross up to Lismullin old church (St. Columba's church of 1809). Its twists and turns, leafy shade and moss covered stone walls are steeped in history. Just to the south of Garlagh Cross, the road passes through a twisty glen and into the wooded section along the Gabhra Gorge. At the first bend, to the right of the road a little laneway leads off into the fields to a farmyard close by the River Gabhra. This farmyard is built on the site of Lismullin Mill, which supposedly gave

The Mill Lane *former entrance to Lismullen Mill - supposed site of the legendary King's Mill.*

the ancient parish its name, the fort of the mill. The mill here was referred to as 'the King's Mill'; its known history is covered in the chapter titled *The Mills of Gabhra*.

In bygone days, at the entrance to Farrelly's old gravel pit across the road from the mill lane, stood a Smithy (forge). Though no trace of it exists now, the 1837 map shows two buildings on the site. Jack Farrelly, Brendan's father, was the last of this family name to operate the Smithy on the site. Brendan told me that in his grandfather's time the roof was blown off the forge during the night of The Big Wind (oiche an gaoithe mor) which event I believe occurred in the 1880s and not during the more infamous storm of 1839. According to anecdote, some of the roof slates were found above at Saddle Hill.

From here we'll journey along the road winding through the Gabhra valley between the meadow of the ferns (Clonardran) and the hill of the fox – then to the east of the heavily wooded Gabhra Gorge until we come to Lismullin crossroads. Here in olden times I believe the Trim to Drogheda road joined the Summerhill road and turned east towards the Decoy.

*The plaque at Garlagh Cross*

# 12

# Through Lismullin and the Gabhra Valley to the Decoy

Lismullin crossroads and Billy's Road – Sunday Well and The Nun's Priory – the River Gabhra and the wells of Tara – preserving by record and modern vandalism – Rath Luga and Gabhar Aichle – St Columba's Church – lakes and icehouse.

In olden times the road from the present day Royal Tara Golf Club passed through Castletown Tara crossroads and Lismullin to the Decoy. This road was at one time part of the old line from Summerhill to Drogheda and ran from west to east through the area where the 'new line' of the Dublin to Navan turnpike road (now the N3) was cut during the major realignment in the 1790s. The road ran on through Lismullin Demesne, where, behind the R.I.C. barracks, which stood near the top of soldier's hill on the turnpike, it joined the road running northeastwards from Tara. The realignment of the turnpike caused crossroads to be formed at the present day Tara Cross and the 'T' junction near the top of soldier's hill. These crossroads remained until the line of road through Lismullin was closed in 1808 – this road was replaced by a new line of the Summerhill to Drogheda road, cut from Batterjohn (big) through Dunsany, Ballyna, Ross Cross and Oberstown to Edoxtown in the years between 1801 and 1804. The closing of the road through

*The Lismullen Bridge across river Gabhra on the old line of the Summerhill/Drogheda road*

Lismullin is recorded in the Grand Jury Query Book of 1808. In the Lent assizes of that year, under the Barony of Skreen, item 416 reads: *Sir C.D. Dillon and Tho's Carberry presented for 5s 0d to stop the old road in lands of Jordanstown and Lismullen from Summerhill to Drogheda.* (not quoted verbatim).

From the former junction behind the barracks the merged roads passed eastwards through the demesne and crossed the road to Skryne, thus forming the crossroads referred to in these writings as Lismullin crossroads. The route carried on northeastwards and joined the line of the green road at the Decoy farm. Some say it ran on towards Staffordstown in olden times and that traces of it have been found in the fields between the Decoy and Gerrardstown – while this may be true, there are no indications on any of the old maps.

The previously described old road layout can be seen on Larkin's Map, but it's not shown on the 1837 OS map: although the route can be traced by the field boundary lines and avenue network within the old Lismullin Demesne. To the south of this road a holy well was located in the middle of the estate, just east of the Gabhra and reputedly on the site of the ancient *Priory of the Holy Trinity,* an Augustinian institution. This well was named Sunday Well (Tobar Domnaig fons Sabbathi – J O'Donovan

181

1836) and described in the OS field notes as being located 'forty perches' (220 or 280 yds) to the east of the priory.

As mentioned, the rear entrance to the Lismullin Demesne was once the continuation of the joined roads from the Hill of Tara and Castletown Tara. Part of the road from the Hill of Tara being reputedly built on the route of one of the ancient *Slighte, an Slighe Mhidhluchra* or the road to Ulster. The section from the Skryne road to the Decoy is known locally as Billy's Road. At least two possible sources exist for this name – according to one local legend King Billy (William of Orange), following his victory at the battle of the Boyne in 1690 travelled along this road on his way to stay at Dillon's Manor in Lismullin. Another local legend says that a man named Billy Weldon once lived somewhere along the road and that it was named after him. According to Griffith's valuation of 1854, a William Weldon lived in Lismullin at that time.

It's impossible to cover adequately the story of Lismullin without relating the history of the oft' mentioned River Gabhra, which flows through this once beautiful landscape. To many it was an unnamed stream, but from my boyhood days I've heard this little river referred to as the Gowra, or the Gabhra, and in those times I thought it was named after a goat, or Gabhar. In the 1950s and 1960s, the name of the river seemed to exist in folklore only and I never saw it in writing until relatively recent times. But I was familiar with the name in the context of the Fianna and the battle reputedly fought on *the fields of Gabhra*. Therefore, it's worth devoting some space to show what research has uncovered and allow the reader to form his or her own opinion on the subject.

First I'll describe the route of the ancient stream and then some of the anecdotes and folklore pertaining to its rather short passage through the area. It rises in the vicinity of Branstown, close to the old road to Trevet (supposedly one of the oldest Norman burial grounds in Ireland) and the former Collierstown Bog. From here it flows to the east of Clowanstown (Clownstown) in a meandering course to the northeast. Passing under the Ross Cross to Oberstown road it enters the townland of Baronstown, where it's joined by a small tributary flowing from the west and under the main Dublin road near the old Post Office at Ross crossroads. To the northeast of the crossroads and close to the junction of the two streams, the 1837 OS map shows a large country house named Maryville: Larkins Map indicates a cluster of houses forming a hamlet in approximately the same area, which on this map is named Thorntown. Local folklore yielded no anecdotes about either the manor house or hamlet, but Mary Wilkinson (nee Lynch of Oldtown) provided me with a snippet of information. She told me that in her home in Baronstown, the residence of the well-known Jock Wilkinson, is an old door reputed to have come from the former house named Maryville. As neither time nor space permits, perhaps this is yet one more story for another day.

Passing under the little bridge in Baronstown on the old road from Meagher's Cross to Skryne, the stream forms the boundary of Cabragh townland before entering Lismullin, where it's paid tribute by a brook flowing under the N3 from the slopes of Tara. This small river once formed a flax retting pond near the confluence with the Gabhra in Lismullin Park – until recent years the remains of this pond could be seen beside a little wood, known as the pond wood. This stream rises near Castleboy to the southwest of Tara – springs from three of the legendary five (or seven) wells of Tara mingle with its waters on the river's course across the ancient hillside. The first of these wells, *Neamnach* or the *Chrystalline Spring*, rises close to the small five Irish acre townland of Faudeen (or Fodeen, the small sod), which is located near the Odder road, once supposedly part of the ancient *Slighe Dhala*. Next, the fledgling river is joined by a rill formed by the outflow from the largest of Tara's wells – known variously as *Saint Patrick's Well, Dark Eye, the Well of the White Cow or Cormac's well*.

The third well is unnamed and joined the stream near Tara Hall, or Newhall. During the heyday of Tara Hall the stream was blocked by a dam, which formed ornamental lakes that have long since disappeared. The hall was demolished in the 1940s, reputedly by a man named Frame, for the stones in its walls and the lead content of the roof and its many windows. I have heard this stream called by several names, but principally the Odder River and the Nith stream.

The Gabhra continued on past Lismullin Manor and towards the Skryne road, near which it turned northwards towards the gorge. A dam was located here, both in olden times and during my youth, which formed ornamental lakes upstream towards the Manor, but these have disappeared in recent years. Emerging from the wooded glen (Gabhra Gorge) the river flows past 'the hill of the fox', in previous years its waters were diverted into the headrace of Lismullin Mill (the 'King's mill'), where it once powered the millstones. At the mill site, the Gabhra exited through the tailrace flowing to the northwest towards Dowdstown. Along this stretch it commingles with the small stream running down from Clonardran and under the bridge at Garlagh Cross. Then passed under Dillon's Bridge on the main Dublin to Navan Road and merged with a small stream flowing down from Jordanstown through Daly's old farm.

From the site of Lismullin Mill to its confluence with the Skane, the Gabhra formed a mearing between Philpotstown and Blundelstown, then Philpotstown and Jordanstown and finally Dowdstown and Castletown Tara. At the site of the long gone Sally Wood in Dowdstown, the Gabhra split and formed two branches, thus creating the previously mentioned Gabhra Island upon which stood the water mill shown on Larkin's Map. The branches rejoined north of the little island and the river flowed onwards to mingle with the Skane at Dowdstown Bridge.

The entire length of the river is scarcely four miles: much of which is now criss-crossed by the M3 motorway and is no longer a natural stream. But unlike its rather modest length, in terms of Irish mythology and folklore the little river is a giant and punches well above its weight, as it could be so described in boxing parlance. Anecdotes are told of the *Battle of Gabhra,* supposedly fought in the valley alongside its banks and in which Finn and the Fianna were vanquished. This event signifying the end of this army of Irish mythology, whose slain were buried in the Rath of Gabhra, which burial place may be sited either in *Rath Luga* or *Rathmiles.* Since time immemorial these ancient forts graced the Gabhra's banks in the relatively silent pastoral landscape, but soon they will suffer the thunderous discord of the new motorway.

The desecration caused to the ancient sites in the valley in bygone days could perhaps be attributed to unenlightened people living in unenlightened times – but to what or to whom can we ascribe blame for the present day ravaging of the valley and the once historic river? While the destruction of the King's mill and Priory of the Holy Trinity were events that should not have occurred, they scarcely left a mark upon the landscape of the beautiful valley. These former acts of unenlightened vandalism are now being compounded by acts of officially sanctioned modern day vandalism i.e. 'the preserve by record brigade', whose motto is to take pictures and then bury history beneath developments. The gouging of the motorway through this beautiful area will scar the landscape forever and perhaps future generations will ask how we, the so-called enlightened people of the era, allowed it to happen?

Regarding the River Gabhra, I have never seen it marked such on any map, though, as mentioned, I thought the river was named after a goat because of the similarity of the names in Gaelic. In this context I will first refer to O'Donovan's 1836 field notes on the parish of Templekeeran: *Gowra River – local ……. Gabhra, the genitive case of Gabhar largely used as nominative. c.f. Gabhar Aichle, Gowra of Aichle, now the Hill of Skreen, near Tara. This little river rises in a bog near Stranstown (sic) in Skreen Parish. It flows along the northern border of the detached portion of Templekeeran ph. And continues westwards to join the Boyne at Ardsallagh* (sic).

*End of Parish of Templekeeran.*

*Note*
*Of the name Gabhair or Gowra, Eoin Mac Neill could find no definition in any dictionary or glossary; but from a study of its usage he concluded that it meant "a low broad ridge between two river valleys." (see phases of Irish History, p. 107). The Templekeeran River probably takes its name from the neighbouring Gabhar Aichle, the ancient name of the Hill of Skreen* (sic).

From the foregoing it would seem that little certainty existed amongst O'Donovan and his team of scholars as to the origins of the name Gabhra in the context of its application to the small river flowing through the valley. I note with interest that O'Donovan called the river 'the Templekeeran River'. Also, at time of writing, there has been much discussion on this subject and quite a divergence of opinions amongst renowned historians, but in my view there's still little more clarity on the matter. If the upper echelons of historians cannot agree on the origins of the name, what hope have I, a mere rookie, of discovering a definitive solution to the riddle? It's fairly certain that the name Gabhar Aichle was the ancient name for the Hill of Skryne. But the definition of this name, stating that it means *a low broad ridge between two river valleys*, could apply equally to both Tara and Skryne. Tara is located between the River Skane and the Gabhra, while Skryne is sited between the River Gabhra and the Hurley (Herley/Caman) River. Hence this name could be applied to many places where ridges are formed between river valleys and the name may once have been used in a generic sense.

Whilst researching the history of the Taylor family in Dowdstown, I discovered a reference to a river in India, which might have some relevance to the river in Meath named the Gabhra. Sister Rose D. King, of Dalgan Park, compiled a resume of the Taylor family and the various members thereof who owned Dowdstown estate over the years. Browsing through this document I noted a reference to the name *Gogra*, which was included in a letter written in India by Richard Taylor to his brother Thomas Edward. At the time, Richard was serving as an officer in the British Army in India, helping to suppress the Sepoy Mutiny of 1858. The address on the letter was Camp Bulrampore and the date December 1858. The part of interest to me goes as follow: *There is good tiger hunting not far off. If my brigade is left on this side of the Gogra, I hope to have some sport bye and bye. There is a friendly Rajah here, a mighty hunter with good elephants* (sic).

The reference to the *Gogra* intrigued me and I wondered if it was a river, as it appeared such from the context and sounded similar to the name of our local river Gabhra. Research revealed that it was indeed a river in upper Nepal and northern India – which rises at an altitude of about 13000ft in the Himalayas and flows through Nepal as the *Karnali River*. The river is an important inland waterway, which commingles with the Holy River Ganges near the town of Chapra. On its six hundred-mile passage through India, it's known as the *River Ghaghara* (or Gogra) which name has a similar spelling to that of the little river *Gabhra*, thousands of miles away in County Meath. In 1859, Thomas Edward Taylor inherited Dowdstown upon the death of his mother and Richard inherited Ardgillan Demesne near Skerries in County Dublin: the brothers exchanged properties and Richard became the owner of Dowdstown – through which flowed the river Gabhra. One wonders what Richard Taylor thought of the little obscure river on his estate bearing almost the

*The icehouse at lismullen*

same title as the famous river in India, where he campaigned in some bloody battles against the Sepoys.

Another feature on the Lismullin estate is the old icehouse located near the long gone route of the Summerhill to Drogheda road. This is an ovoid (egg) shaped stone building buried in an earthen mound for insulation purposes: in olden times prior to the advent of refrigerators, some of the country houses had such places built. Supposedly, in the wintertime ice was harvested from frozen rivers, lakes and ponds – this being another reasons for the development of artificial lakes in the big estates.

The remnants of the Church of Ireland parish church of Lismullin (St Columba's Church), stands beside the road leading from Lismullin to Skryne: it was built in 1809 and mostly demolished in the 1970s. A famous stained glass window, which originated in Trim, once adorned this church. In recent years this window fetched a large sum of money in one of the great auction rooms in London. On the crest of a hill across the road towards the east stand the remains of the previously mentioned ancient ruined church and graveyard of Templekeeran, which commands a beautiful vista across the Gabhra valley towards Tara. The burial ground is still in use at time of writing and some of the church remains in situ. The local community has done a wonderful job in cleaning up and restoring the once run down site.

In the Gabhra gorge close by the old Lismullin crossroads, the remains of an old souterrain can be found in the eastside bluff. The entrance is approximately two feet square and local people say that it extends for about twenty feet underground towards the Skryne road. Nobody is sure of its history and it attracted little attention during the recent furore over the eradication of other historical sites nearby. Perhaps some day it may be explored and its origins discovered?

The most interesting sites in the valley, from an historical perspective, are *Rath Luga* (*Rath Lugh*), an ancient ring fort atop the remains of an Esker Ridge and a nearby Henge. Unfortunately, as I write, this memento of our former history is the subject of great controversy. Despite constant reassurances from the NRA that it would not in any way impinge upon or affect the site, the apron of the new motorway is to pass within a few yards of its edge. Further to the west is a prime example of the modern day vandalism referenced earlier: here was found the remains of an ancient burial site and a *Henge,* both dating back several thousand years. To avoid spoiling the grand computer-generated sweeping curve of the new motorway, these ancient monuments were *preserved by record* and then buried beneath the M3. Recently, whilst walking near the security fence surrounding the motorway sites in Lismullin, I was both saddened and amused to see signs informing all and sundry that the fence enclosed a national monument, then threatening massive penalties and dire consequences for anyone found guilty of *despoiling* the said monument. I wonder what sanctions will be imposed upon those responsible for the ultimate despoliation of the site – the total destruction of the monument by building a motorway over it?

The Decoy, which is not a townland, a parish or an official postal address, has been known by this unusual name for many years: the Taylor and Skinner map shows that the area was named the Decoy in 1778. Previously, the purpose of and methods used in the decoy lakes of the period were described in the context of the decoy at Bellinter, a repeat description, therefore is unnecessary. Larkin's Map indicates the presence of a small artificial lake at some distance to the rear of the residence and the name Decoy can be discerned within the confines of the lake and surrounding woodland, but not in close proximity to the house. It's

*The present day residence of the former decoy of Lismullin* (Courtesy Mary Wilkinson)

obvious, therefore, that the name applied to the wooded lake rather than to the house. A partly rhomboid shaped section of woodland is shown on the 1837 OS map, within which a small lake or pond is marked *Decoy*. Two streams flowing from the south supplied the lake and a single stream flowed from the lake towards *Glean Uaigneach* to the northeast. The OS map of 1882 indicates the name Decoy near the residence and not at the lake in the wood – perhaps this indicates how things change in the landscape with the passing of but a short few years! Larkin's Map depicts a group of about ten buildings between the woodland lake and the road. These buildings could indicate the presence of a small village here in the early years of the 19th century. The Decoy farm was originally part of the Dillon estate of Lismullin. Ancestors of the Wilkinson family, who live in Baronstown at time of writing, owned the Decoy farm in times past. I'm told that in former days one of the Wilkinsons was known as *the Duck Wilkinson*, because he brought ducks captured at the Decoy-lake to the Dublin markets in a horsedrawn wagon. Later, a man named Knox Gore, who hailed from North Mayo owned the Decoy. During my younger days McIvors owned the property, they sold it to a man named Smith around 1957. In the late 1960s or early 1970s, the farm was acquired by the Land Commission and divided into smallholdings.

# 13

# The Mills of Gabhra

The King's Mill and Lismullin corn mill – Dillon's Bridge and the fulling mill at Blundelstown – the lost mill on the Gabhra Island in Castletown Tara.

Three separate water mills existed on the River Gabhra in times past. Lismullin Mill, supposedly the King's Mill of legend is well known, but not much data is available on the other mills, which seem to have faded from historical record. The three mills were located on a one mile long stretch of the little river and all were within the same distance of my old home in Dowdstown. The mill furthest upstream being in Lismullin, the central mill at Dillon's Bridge in Blundelstown and the mill furthest downstream sited in a place we knew as the Gabhra Island. The latter mill was unknown to me until I noted it on Larkin's Map during research.

Previous historical references contain obvious confusion between the siting of Lismullin Mill and the nearby mill at Blundelstown. I came across several references to the King's Mill being located in Blundelstown and some mentions of the mill in Blundelstown that were relevant to the mill in Lismullin. The Civil Survey of 1654/56 makes separate and clear references to all three mills, but a sound knowledge of local topography and the old parish/townland boundaries is required to make sense of these.

Legends say that the first water driven corn mill in Ireland once stood on the banks of the River Gabhra in Lismullin. They tell of how Cormac Mac Airt, High King at Tara, had the mill built to save his favourite handmaiden, Ciarnaid (Ciarnait/Cernat), the onerous task of grinding corn for the king's household with her handmill or quern. Ciarnat being with child by the king, he employed a Pictish millwright provided by the king of Scotland to build and work the mill; this miller's name was Mac Lamha, which translates to Hand. In the 1830s, Christopher Byrne was the miller at Lismullin Mill. His mother supposedly claimed descent from the original Hand family, who according to legend operated the mill since its construction around AD 250 to the coming of the Normans in the 12th century. A man nicknamed Long John Byrne reputedly was the last miller at Lismullin.

It is interesting to note that mention of Lismullin ( Lismullen) Mill is made is George Petrie's presentation of 1837 *On the History and Antiquities of Tara Hill*: From this paper it can be deduced that ancient tradition locates the *King's Mill* on the *Nith Stream*, which issued from the well named Neamhnach on Tara, and that more recent folklore places the same mill on the northern bank of the *River Guara* (Gabhra). As previously mentioned in Chapter 12, *The Nith Stream* rises near Castleboy and collects the outflowing water from at least three of Tara's ancient wells: it then flows eastwards to commingle with the *River Gabhra* within Lismullin Park, upstream of the former ornamental lakes. In my view, Petrie's account of the older and more recent legends can be reconciled with the topography if these rivers are considered as two separate entities.

The following quotation, which may have added to the confusion of locations, is taken from John O'Donovan's 1836 field notes on the townland of Blundelstown: *On ye Premises a ffulling Mill. Civil Survey. The little river Gabhra flows westwards along its northern border. On this river the first water mill in Ireland is said to have been erected on the orders of the High King Cormac Mac Airt to relieve his concubine from the labour of grinding corn with tha quern. On the supposed site of this ancient mill now stands Lismullin Mill , of which a man named Christopher Byrne is the miller. His mother's name was Hand , and she claims descent from the founder of the first mill , who came to Ireland from Scotland* (sic). This reference is somewhat confusing, but when the old maps are studied, it's clear that he was referring to two different mills: the first being a ffulling mill listed by the Civil Survey in Blundelstown. Reference to the second mill, the King's Mill, is made in the context of its location on the River Gabhra, not in Blundelstown townland. I will enlarge upon this topic presently.

Though it's impossible at this remove to establish the veracity of the claims about the Hand family's involvement and the origins of and earlier history of the ancient mill, there are various references to a mill in the area from the early part of the second millennium. Here are some snippets about Lismullin gleaned during research: Following Hugh de Lacy's invasion of Meath in the 12th century the Nangle family came into possession of Lismullin and the mill. In 1223, Richard de la Corner, a Nangle, became bishop of Meath and gained possession of Lismullin Manor and the corn mill. His sister, Alicia de la Corner (or Avice) founded an Augustinian monastery, known as *the Priory of the Holy Trinity*, in the valley alongside the River Gabhra – she received a charter for the manor and the mill. The nuns of Lismullin Priory owned both mill and Manor until the suppression of the Monasteries in 1539. The mill passed to Sir Thomas Cusack, Sheriff of Meath, and his heirs: an inquisition in 1541 listed the mill as one of Cusack's possessions. In 1547 the corn mill is included in a crown grant to Cusack on a twenty-year lease.

The origin of and linkage between the names Nangle and De la Corner is interesting – both names derive from commonly used words describing the same item, namely an angle and a corner. Some dictionaries define these words as deriving from the Latin *Angulus* and state that Angle originates from an area named Angul in northern Germany; inhabitants of which place invaded England in the 5th century. Anectdotes say that the name Nangle originated in Wales, possibly on a peninsula, the residents of this region became known as *the people living in the corner*, or Nangles!

In an old issue of *Riocht na Midhe* I found the following item, which purports to refer to the King's Mill in Lismullin: *It was recorded at Navan, in 1636, "that the mill at Blundelstown had been owned by William Rowles of Dublin, who on the 22nd March 1624, made it over by treaty to George Devenish of Dublin, Robert Plunkett and William Pallice of Dublin, and Will' Archbold of Crookestown Co' Kildare, and his heirs. The Civil Survey*

*of 1654/56 lists the mill as part of the goods of William Malone of Lismullin,*
*an Irish Papist"*(sic).

Although the above extract mentions the mill at Blundelstown, the context in which it was written indicates it referred to Lismullin Mill. If, in fact, the reference was to the mill at Blundelstown, it provides names of several people involved with Blundelstown mill in far off times. This is an example of the previously mentioned confusion of the sites.

In 1658 Lismullin Mill passed to Arthur Dillon, founder of the later day Dillon dynasty at Lismullin. It would seem that the Dillons acquired Lismullin as part of lands seized during the land confiscations in Cromwellian times. From then until it ceased operation in 1883 the mill was owned by the Dillons and leased to various operators.

Little doubt exists as to the mill's antiquity because some records show its presence in the area since at least the mid 13th century, but whether it was the King's Mill or not remains a moot point. Some historians say that this mill was sited in Blundelstown, but my view is that its site was in Lismullin, because all the evidence shows that the mill located there was a corn mill: whereas other records indicate that Blundelstown mill was a fulling or textile mill. As mentioned, the name Lismullin derives from the mill and a nearby fort. The former site of the mill is well known locally, being located in an area called the mill farm, which is on the Skryne road approximately a quarter mile from Garlagh Cross (old Garlow). The lane leading down from the road is shown on Larkin's Map and the mill as a cogwheel symbol. This laneway is still there at time of writing in 2007/9. The 1837 OS map marks it as a corn mill and also indicates the buildings on the site and their layout on the riverbank. Both maps show the mill in Lismullin to the north of the Gabhra. It was not sited in Blundelstown, a separate entity comprised of a detached part of Templekeeran parish. The Civil Survey of 1654/56 lists the following in Lismullin, "On the Premises one castle one Abbey, one Mill, one stone house & a few ashe timber trees" (sic). Griffith's valuation indicates that in 1854 the lessee of the premises was Patrick Byrne and that the rateable valuation for the mill, the house and the 26 acre farm was £36 15s 0d. As mentioned previously, the last miller was John Byrne, known as long John Byrne, reputedly he was evicted in 1883 and the mill demolished by its then

*The remains of a millstone found on the site of Lismullen Mill.*

owners, the Dillon family, because of non-payment of rent.

Early in 2008 I photographed part of a millstone, found buried on the site of Lismullin Mill near the ancient well. There's no doubt that it is part of a 'runner' millstone, as two of the rectangular-cut drive and pivot points are visible and concentric marks can be seen on its concave surface. I estimate that the original full stone was approximately four feet in diameter. Like many such places in Ireland one wonders what might have been found had a proper archaeological inspection of the site been conducted in the past. Now it's too late, because a farmyard covers the former location of the mill and much reclamation work took place in the area over many years.

Typically, the mill that gave the name to this ancient parish has disappeared entirely. It was mostly demolished in 1883 and the stones used for buildings elsewhere – in more recent years the last remaining structure on the site was converted for use as a farm building. The mill was situated across the Gabhra from the hill known locally as *Cnoic an Sioneach*, or *The Hill of The Fox*, which is pronounced 'Croc a Tannig' (Crockatanney). There is another possible source for the name, which may relate to the mill: the similar sounding Gaelic word *Sniomhachain* means a spinning-mill. Perhaps this name was once used to describe the knoll as *The Hill of the Spinning Mill*, and may have become associated with the word Sioneach through colloquial usage. On the same site and near the mill was an ancient well, which was used until relatively recent times. A few years ago this well was piped into the Gabhra and the site filled in. The locations of the mill and well are variously described locally as *The Well Field*, *The Mill Field*, or *The Mill Farm*.

A book entitled *The Parish of Duleek and over the ditches* contains intriguing references to the Priory of Lismullin, in the context of that institution acquiring a mill in Clatterstown near Bellewstown. The following are some excerpts:

A report in "*Irish Monastic Possessions and the Dissolution of Religious Houses" by Newport White of The inquisition made at Skryne 1 Oct 1540, one of the King's Commissioners, J Mynne assisted by Robert Cowley and Patrick Barnewell – "Priory of the House of Nuns of Lismullen, amongst other property situate in the town of Clatterstown, 1 Messauge 60 acres arable, 4 ac. Meadow and 6 ac. pasture James Andrew tenant' rent 53s 4d and for customs 5s and 4 hens (8d,) 59s. A water Mill held by Richard Markey on condition of sustaining all repairs to the Mill except as regards timber, iron, and metal (aes) and giving 26 pecks (modia) of corn and 26 measures of Mansetum (fine flour) value 52s."*

Cal. of Inquisitions 111 (1348-1377) &. Cal. Patent Rolls (1367-1370) PP 123/4: *Inquisition before Rich. De Stury Knight at Scryn 28 Oct 1367. Avice de la Corner founded the Priory of Lismolyn in honour of the Holy Trinity & Saint Mary, & established there a Prioress and certain nuns to whom she gave in pure alms" and a "Messauge, a Mill, and a Caracute of land in Norman Clatere ('stown). All this was in the time of King Henry 111 before the statute of Mortmain."*

An entry in Dean Cogan's "Diocese of Meath" states on the authority of Jas. Ware (Ware's Bishops) that, *Avice (or Alice) de La Corner who founded the House of Lismullen was sister of Richard de La Corner who was Bishop of Meath and was Consecrated at St. Peter's Drogheda in 1230 and died 1250 and an entry in the inquisition above quoted specifically states "Richd. De la Corner gave to the Prioress Avice de La Corner the said Property (in Clatterstown) (sic).*

The book goes on to give details of the origins of Norman Clatere but space does not permit its inclusion. Note the two different spellings, Lismullen and Lismolyn and the use of the word Messauge. The term

Messauge or Messuage was seemingly used extensively during Anglo-Norman times and I have found varying explanations of its origins and usage. The most logical of these says that it was a term used to describe a property consisting of a house, out buildings and a courtyard with a parcel of land within its curtilage. Though its origins is uncertain, it possibly derives from the French word *mansio*, meaning a holding, or another French word *menage* and is said to be the origin of the English word *mansion*.

Another mill was sited a short distance downstream at a location colloquially known as Dillon's Bridge. In my view, this was the mill referred to in ancient records as Blundelstown Mill. The bridge presently spanning the river (2007) is of stone arched construction and the span is about sixteen feet. The name and date engraved upon the parapet walls suggest that the incumbent Lord Dillon, possibly Sir John Dillon Bart or Sir William Dillon Bart built the bridge in 1860. These names feature prominently in Griffith's valuation of the 1850s, *Bart* is an abbreviation for Baronet; a minor title. As the first bridge here was constructed in the 1790s to carry the new line of the Dublin to Navan turnpike road across the Gabhra, over sixty years earlier, one wonders about the first river crossing and what happened to the original bridge? Larkin's Map shows a bridge and buildings in the same spot as the later day site of the post office and Smithy to the south of the river, but there is no name on the bridge and the mill is not shown. The 1837 OS map indicates the mill and a bridge, which it names Dillon's Bridge.

In 1796/1798, a stone arched bridge, about five feet wide, was built to carry the new line of the turnpike across the tailrace of the mill, approximately two hundred metres north of Dillon's Bridge at the place where the old mill is shown on the OS Map. From times past I recall a swampy stream running from the downstream side of this little bridge, down the bottoms parallel to the river and joining the Gabhra at the Dowdstown Mearing, upstream from the previously described Gabhra Island. In my view this was once the tailrace of Blundelstown Mill. The Gabhra flows through flat terrain in this area, hence a lengthy tailrace was required to obtain the differential water head to power the mill. Long tailraces were a feature at several other local mills such as Arnold's Mill at

196

*Small millrace bridge at Dillon's Bridge (now buried beneath the N3 (R147)*

Kilmessan, the mills at Bective and Lower Kilcarn and the smaller mills at Rathfeigh and Macetown. The operational efficiency of water mills was drastically reduced during times of flooding; therefore, the longer tailraces led the water exiting the millwheel to a lower river level downstream. The previously mentioned Brendan Farrelly confirms the existence of the old stream, because he recalls helping to clean it out during the times he worked on Donnelley's farm in the 1950s. In earlier days, when a pupil in the nearby Dillon's Bridge School, Brendan remembers trogging (trudging) under the little bridge. The stream has now been buried by local development work.

An archaeological excavation of the mill site at Dillon's Bridge was conducted early in 2007, during which I observed some stonewalls unearthed, but I have not yet seen a report on the findings. I'm told that a clay pipe, some cloth and a quantity of buttons were found during the dig. The cloth and buttons are significant in the context of what I found recorded in the Civil Survey of 1654/56.

Apart from the River Gabhra, there's another possible source for the water that powered the mill at Blundelstown. This could have originated from the small stream, now named the Garlach, flowing from Clonardran and passing under the ancient bridge at Garlagh Cross (Old Garlow Cross). Brendan Farrelly said that in his youth a dry channel ran across the fields from this stream and petered out about fifty yards upstream from the site of the old mill. Perhaps this stream once supplied the lost mill with water to drive its wheel and in later years was diverted into the Gabhra near the site of Lismullin Mill.

Blundelstown was a detached portion of Templekeeran parish and, though bordering Lismullin it was a separate entity with the River Gabhra forming its northern boundary. According to the 1837 OS map the townland consisted of 162 acres 3 roods and 33 perches (statute measure) and part of it was located to the west of the turnpike road, extending to the later day Daly's farm located in Castletown Tara (Rathmiles farm). Jordanstown, supposedly named after a miller named Jordan, was located further south and Lismullin to the east. The 1882 OS map indicates that Blundelstown was more or less unchanged from its 1837 footprint, however, the 1911 OS map shows the western boundary of Blundelstown running up soldier's hill along the Navan to Dublin road and the townland area reduced to 120 acres 3 roods and 3 perches. Concurrently, the area of the adjoining townland of Castletown Tara increased from 799 acres 0 roods and 21 perches to 862 acres 0 roods and 6 perches. These alterations to the townland boundaries and areas indicate that many things change with the passage of time, hence allowances must be made for the changing landscape of the differing periods.

Larkin's Map names the area of Blundelstown as Lunderstown, perhaps it's a misspelling – but an area bearing that name is located to the southeast of Duleek, as indicated on the same map and the modern day Discovery map. Blundelstown Mill is shown on the 1837 OS map sited north of the Gabhra close by the turnpike road, which would suggest that the mill was then located in Philpotstown townland. This is the only map upon which I can find a graphical reference to this mill, marked as an old mill its former usage is unspecified. In my experience, the place being described in such terms tends to indicate it was disused or in ruins at the time of the survey in 1836. It is significant, therefore, that the small bridge was built to carry the turnpike road across the tailrace, which might suggest that the mill was still in use in the 1790s. Had it been defunct at that time, the millrace could have been run into the Gabhra alongside the new road thus avoiding the need for a second bridge. The river was diverted from time to time hence the boundaries could have become somewhat elastic. In those days the site of this mill was possibly located in Blundelstown townland and not in Philpotstown, as it would appear to be at time of writing. Such boundary anomalies can be observed in several places on the maps, especially on the River Skane to the west and south, where the parish and union mearings altered from time to time due to river diversions.

The 1654/56 Civil Survey states the following: *Blundistown 1/3 pte of a plowland, 104 Irish acres* (sic). Under the heading of "Propriators in 1640 and their qualifications" it states *Anthony Dopping a Protestant the one Moyety & William Malone of Lismullin the other Moyety* (sic). Elsewhere it records that William Malone was an Irish Papist. But significantly in the context of mills, it states in the section marked observations *On ye Premisses a ffulling Mill* (sic). Previously, I never heard of a ffulling mill and I thought it was a misspelling. However, initial research indicated it to be a word used to describe a process whereby cloth was made bulkier, or fuller, by this method. The fulling process involved dampening and beating the cloth, with a material known as Fuller's earth being used: this was special absorbent clay also used for filtering liquids and removing dirt and lanolin from wool. I'm told by the older folk that the said Fuller's earth was a well-known poultice in olden times, being employed for drawing wounds and sores and soothing inflamed skin. Fishermen use this substance for treating fishing lines and I have heard of its usage in dyeing cloth. It seems that the common surname Fuller probably derived from this occupation.

Further research yielded more information on fulling mills in County Meath. The following is an extract from Cyril Ellison's famous book *The Waters of the Boyne and Blackwater: Another type of mill once to be found in Meath was the tuck mill or fulling mill, designed to pound the woollens produced by local handweavers in order to compact and thicken them. Such mills were to be found at Kells, Athlumney, Ardmulchan, Dollardstown and Dowth and helped to give the folk along the river that hard-wearing frieze cloak known as a Trusty* (sic). Interestingly, although the book mentions many mills on the smaller rivers in Meath and indeed refers to the King's Mill in Lismullin, no mention is made of any other mills on the Gabhra. Fulling mills date from medieval times and were variously described as Fulling, Tucking or Walking (Waulking) mills. In Wales they were known

*Are these pupils of Dillon's Bridge School? About 1950.*

as a Pandy. Depending on the location, their operators were called, Fullers, Tuckers or Walkers, I have no idea how the Welsh described the operator of a Pandy! As mentioned, the name Fuller probably derives from this occupation, perhaps the names Tucker and Walker had similar origins? In addition to being the source of several surnames, fulling mills apparently gave rise to other terms used in the English language and may have provided the inspiration for an ancient Spanish romance by the author Cervantes, titled *Don Quixote de la Manche*. The ancient legend of Don Quixote supposedly originated from a Spanish grandee driven demented by the pounding hammers of several wind-powered fulling mills located near his castle. The good Don took out his frustration by tilting at the windmills with his lance thus was born the word quixotic, often used to describe someone doing odd things or fighting hopeless battles. The expression *on tenterhooks* derives from part of the fulling process, whereby cloth was stretched across frames and secured by hooks known as tenterhooks.

According to the Civil Survey, a textile mill (as distinct from a corn mill) once stood on the banks of the Gabhra at Dillon's Bridge. This should not be confused with flax scutching mills, such mills being used in the early part of the linen making process to beat the fibres from the flax plants. The fulling process was used much later and only on woollen cloth. An interesting aspect of the textile mill at Blundelstown is that the townland name probably derived from the family name Blundell: a family of this

*Left: ruins of the Post Office and Smithy at Dillon's Bridge, 2007. Right: The Smithy's 'Bending Stone' at Dillon's Bridge, used to form wheel shoeings.*

name became prominent in the flax milling industry around Navan in later years. Perhaps the little mill on the Gabhra was one of their first enterprises in cloth manufacture. I doubt if we will ever know for sure, as one of the slip roads of the Blundelstown interchange is now built over the site of the ancient mill.

In an ecclesiastical history book there's a possible reference to a mill at Blundelstown in earlier times. This states that on September the 23rd 1547, King Edward VI (1537-1553) granted to Sir Thomas Cusack, Knight, the site and circuit of the old Priory and Glebelands of Lismullin and the Manor – together with a water mill and water course in Bludestone (sic) (Blundelstown?), for a fine of £413. 11s. 1d. and an annual rent of £1. 2s.. I wonder could this be a reference to the mill at the later day Dillon's Bridge? This reference also mentions Lismullin Priory as *The Nonnys Priory'*.

In summary, I would speculate that at the time of the construction of the new line of the Dublin to Navan turnpike road in the 1790s a mill existed in the spot as shown in later years on the1837 OS map. Access to the mill could have been gained from the nearby Skryne-Navan road. The smaller bridge was built to carry the new road across the tailrace of this mill. The water supply might have derived from at least two sources: the most likely being the little stream from Garlagh Cross – the other source could have originated from a sidestream taken off the Gabhra somewhere upstream of the bridge.

Dillon's Bridge National School was built in 1860 on the western

*An impression of Dillon's Bridge School as painted by Greta Halpin (Nee Brady)*

side of the Dublin to Navan road. It was the local school for almost one hundred years, being closed in 1957 when a new school was built nearby in Lismullin on the Walterstown road – the new school replaced both it and the National School in Walterstown. Griffith's valuation of 1854 indicates the presence of a schoolhouse in Philpotstown in that year but does not name its exact location. Local legends told of an old hedge school in the area in times past, perhaps these may have derived from the school indicated in the valuation report, although it clearly shows that this school was run by the commissioners for education. The old schoolhouse was located on the downstream side of the bridge and up close to the river. Being in a poor state of repair it was demolished in the early 1960s. Lately, the ruins were excavated and recorded. Though the schoolhouse and the old Smithy are gone and the bridge may soon meet the same fate, the district name is likely to remain for a long time.

At Dillon's Bridge, the modern day 'enlightened' vandals have struck again by demolishing the beautiful old stone arched bridge and replacing it with an ugly concrete box-like structure with no redeeming features. The small bridge across the old millrace has also been buried beneath the realigned embankment. But why should I be surprised, the same unimaginative official mindset has wreaked havoc throughout the

*The western arch of Dillon's Bridge shortly before it's destruction in 2008*

countryside. This trail of destruction includes inter alia the removal of William Augustus Beaufort's house in Navan to make room for a traffic roundabout. Additionally, the old skewed railway bridge beside the ancient cemetery at Cannistown has been demolished: one wonders where the valuable old stones from these bridges has disappeared to, perhaps, like the shoeing stone at Bective crossroads, these too were spirited away to an alien planet. The wanton destruction of Dillon's Bridge was unnecessary and is but part of the previously mentioned annihilation of the Gabhra valley in Lismullin and the destruction of the landscape at Dowdstown and Bellinter. Surely a more enlightened and imaginative approach to the crossing of the M3 at this point could have allowed the ancient bridge to remain in situ. Leaving the bridge as a feature on the landscape would have made sense in our fast maddening world: thereby providing an example to future generations of the work of skilled craftsmen from times past. Perhaps such a sensible gesture might have given pause for thought in the mad rush to destroy our past and demonstrated that there are other things in life besides making money and progress.

I have already mentioned the third mill on the Gabhra, namely the mill at Castletown Tara, references to which I discovered in the Civil Survey of 1654/56 and the cogwheel symbol on Larkin's Map of 1812. Folklore

*The plaque on the eastern parapet of Dillon's Bridge, 2007*

in the area says that a mill once existed at Newhall (Tara Hall) and that this may have been the King's Mill of legend. Local people told me that in older times they saw the remains of a mill on the little River Nith, a tributary of the Gabhra, but I can find no record on the maps or in any of the surveys.

The third mill on the little river was located just across the fields from my old home in Dowdstown in a place known to us then as the Gabhra Island. This Island was formed by the river's course splitting and then rejoining further downstream within Dowdstown.

Larkin's Map provided yet another surprise at the bottom of the old laneway known as the Tara lane. It showed that a water mill once stood on the banks of the River Gabhra close by the old turnpike road. The symbol for the mill was shown on the island, together with several large structures to the south of the river. The mill and buildings were accessed by a laneway leading off the turnpike road near a small stream. This little stream rises over in Cardiffstown at the bottom of the western slopes of Tara and flows through Castletown and close by the ruins of the castle, then under the turnpike before joining the Gabhra at the mill site. Approximately half a kilometre above its confluence with the Gabhra, the smaller stream passed through a deep glen, where it was dammed. In times long gone, the outflow from the dam was used to power a hydraulic ram for pumping water up to the house at the ruined castle – in my younger days the place was used for dipping sheep. Perhaps this dam was employed in even earlier times to form a millpond, thus providing a strategic location for the mill.

It was ever a mystery to me why the Gabhra was routed in such a way. The river flowed from the east through Lismullin and under Dillon's Bridge, then split into two separate branches at the mearing where the tall oaks of the Sally Wood once dominated this corner of Dowdstown. Further on, within the Dowdstown estate, both parts of the river rejoined. The field formed between the two branches of the stream was called the Gabhra Island and shaped rather like Daniel Boon's powder horn. The reason for the split in the river's course had eluded me, but the mill shown on Larkin's Map solved the riddle. Similar to the mill at Dillon's Bridge and other previously mentioned mills, the long diversion provided a head and tailrace for the watermill. In addition to Larkin's Map, the split course of the river shows up on the OS maps, so it's obviously an ancient feature on the landscape.

About sixty mills are depicted on Larkin's Map of County Meath, including the mills on the Skane catchment at Knockmark (Drumree), Arnold's Mill in Kilmessan, and Lismullin Mill on the Gabhra. Three mills are shown on the River Nanny, including McNamara's corn mill near Fairlands crossroads, the mill near Kentstown, which in our youth was known as Daly's sawmill, and the water mill near Balrath. He also included the old windmill at Balrath, the two mills at Clavinstown, Rathfeigh Mill on the Hurley River (Delaney's Mill) and Macetown Mill on a tributary of the Hurley. Clatterstown Mill near the Bolies is marked on the map, but only a few mills are shown on the Boyne above Navan. All the water mills are depicted by a small symbol of a waterwheel; a tiny circle with seven/eight spokes radiating from its centre like a cogwheel. With all these verified mills being marked on his map, it's unlikely that Larkin imagined the mill on the Gabhra Island at Dowdstown.

Upon discovering the 'other townland' of Dowdstown, in Tara parish, as mentioned previously, I rechecked the Civil Survey of 1654/56. Under the heading of "Castletownetaragh", I noted the following entry: *on the premises on stone house one watermill & Divers cottages* (sic). I had found the mill shown on Larkin's Map, or at least a reference to it on paper, which indicates that the mill dated from olden times.

The symbol on Larkin's Map and the entry in the Civil Survey were the first indications I had of the former presence of a mill in this area, but it comes as no surprise because three rivers flow through the valley. At one time a mill stood on the banks of the Boyne in Ardsallagh directly opposite the Skane confluence. The mill being in such close proximity to the Hill of Tara makes one wonder if this was perhaps the location of the legendary King's Mill. The mill site lay alongside part of *An Slighe Asail,* one of the reputed five roads of Tara, upon which the old turnpike road supposedly ran in a later period. Although substantial evidence supports the notion of Lismullin being the site of the King's Mill, such legends can become distorted over many centuries, as evidenced by the confusion of the mill sites at Blundelstown and Lismullin.

In 2007 I took these findings to the NRA archaeologists at their offices in Navan. Whilst the personnel on active duty at field sites were receptive to input from local people, some members of the office staff didn't seem even slightly interested. Perhaps they considered I was merely a crank trying to impede progress or were working to an agenda not based on inclusiveness. I formed the distinct impression that some of these supposed *custodians of our heritage* did not welcome and were obviously unenthusiastic about receiving input from mere amateur historians. They eventually produced evidence from the aerial survey of some ground anomalies and of the site being excavated previously, but nothing was found. Being unaware of the existence of Larkin's Map, which provided the only graphical clue of the former presence of the mill, the archaeologists, therefore, did not know what was built there in olden times. But I still wonder, as I recall seeing some old stone and mudwall ruins on the Gabhra Island when crossing the fields on my many trips to Tara in times past. The M3 route is gouged across the Gabhra Island and much of the old mill site is buried forever. Now we shall never discover more about the ancient mill that stood on the little island in the fields near Tara.

# 14

# The Old Road from the Decoy to the Black Lion Inn

The Decoy – Balgeeth – Darby's lane – Cusackstown/Walterstown – Walter Tuite and Walterstown Castle – The River Nanny – McNamara's and Daly's Mills, The valley of diamond rocks – The five roads of Skryne – The White House and Candle Hill – Banshees and bellringers – The rock road and St. Patrick's well – Proudstown Church and the black dog of the Borrowaddy Road – Kilshinny Lane, Danestown and Blacklion mudwalled chapel.

Heading eastwards from the Decoy the road negotiates a number of twists and turns, which are shown on the old maps. It then passes a laneway leading to the former location of McDermott's farm: Larkin's Map shows a laneway hereabouts with a small cluster of buildings or hamlet at its head. A local legend said that a mass path led from here to Templekeeran (Templecairn) churchyard in times past, but I cannot find evidence of this on any old maps. Further on and to the right of the road, we come to a farmhouse built during my boyhood and occupied by big Larry McCormack. The house was built upon the ruins of an old dwelling known locally as Murray's Walls – some buildings are shown on this site on the old OS maps. I recall the farm particularly as I often helped Dad at sheep shearing there during my youth and I remember Larry and his old Allis Chalmers tractor with the twin narrow-set front wheels.

Larkin's No. 7
1. The Giltown Road
2. Walterstown Crossroads
3. Garlagh Cross (Old Garlow)
4. Lismullin Mill
5. Lismullin Crossroads
6. Templekieran Church
   and Graveyard
7. Rath Luga
8. The Three Roads of Skryne
   (Carthys Cross 1804)
9. The Five Roads Crossroads (1806)
10. Candle Hill
11. The Priest's Crossroads (1806)
12. Oberstown Crossroads (1806)
13. Site of Maryville House
14. Ross Crossroads (1801/1804)
15. Old Road to Rathoath and Dublin

A few hundred yards beyond McCormack's farm we top the brow of a low rise and the road angles to the left – nowadays the slight deviation is scarcely noticeable, but it was much more clearly defined years ago. Though seemingly insignificant, it's an important little curve in the context of tracing the history of this road in times past, as it was here that the old road through Walterstown and the new line through Slanduff parted company for several miles. The new line of the road altered the landscape and in so doing created different features and routes for local people. As children, we travelled this way regularly in the pony trap on our way to Sunday Mass in Walterstown Chapel: about half way between the Decoy and the Glean Lane, in those days a short laneway led up a slope into the fields to the right of the road. I remember the lane clearly, yet at the time we paid it scant attention, as it appeared to be just another entry to some farmer's land – now I know that this was the old route of the road prior to 1830.

In 2007, while researching the history of nearby Glanuaigneach, known colloquially as 'the Gleann' (Glean), I called to Oliver Duane in nearby Balgeeth (*the town or place of the wind*). Oliver spoke about the history of the area and mentioned that, according to anecdote, a mill was once sited on a stream close by his house in Balgeeth (Belgeeth), which mill may have been used for grinding corn and scutching flax. In olden times many flax retting ponds (or rotting ponds) were located in the district, the remains of such a pond can still be seen at the back of his haggard. The yellow flax plants (blue flowered) were allowed to soak in the ponds and partly decay, before being 'scutched' at the mill, which process consisted of the flax being beaten, or flailed by wooden mechanised flails. This separated the valuable fibres used to produce linen, with linseed oil being obtained from the residue.

Our conversation turned eventually to the road system, as it existed in days gone by. Oliver mentioned that over the years, traces of an old road were discovered in various places while the land was being ploughed – in his view a road once led from Walterstown Chapel and headed westward towards Lismullin. Research proves that he was correct. While most of the evidence was found on the maps, some traces could still be discovered on the topography and in local folklore. So now let us take a trip along the old lost route from the Decoy to the Black Lion Inn.

This stretch of old defunct roadway supports previous assertions that in olden times many of the roads ran along the high ridges. Whilst this fact is noted vis-à-vis the ancient *Slighte*, it applied also to many of the lesser roads in more modern times. Or perhaps this road was built upon part of *An Slighe Mhidhluchra*, one of the legendary five roads of Tara, which reputedly ran northeastwards towards Ulster. Some ancient writings refer to a road named *The Royal Road* passing through the area near Balgeeth. Whatever the merits of this speculation, the old route in question traversed the high ground above the valley, whereas the new line of the same road ran along the low ground and wound through Slanduff.

From the point of deviation east of the Decoy, the old line continued eastwards between Balgeeth farmhouse and the present day road. Larkin's Map shows the Glean Lane on the left heading towards Glanuaigneach from the old line of the road. Slightly further east and to the right of the route, it indicates the lane to Balgeeth running up to the farmhouse and a group of buildings, which may have been a hamlet. In those days the two laneways were not directly in line as they are at time of writing. The same map names the area around Balgeeth as Mountstown and has only the old line of road marked thereon. This indicates that no realignment had taken place until after publication of the map in 1817, which is valuable information for dating the road alterations. The 1837 OS map shows both routes in the area: and cross-referencing the different maps indicates that the major road realignments possibly occurred between 1817 and 1837, perhaps being part of the road's development as a mail coach route.

From the Glean Lane, the old line ran along the southern ridge of the valley and descended to the crossroads at Cusackstown (Walterstown). About a hundred yards west of this crossroads a small laneway, known locally as Darby's Lane, led off to the left towards the northwest. This name derived from a family named Darby who lived behind the old castle during my youth. Larkin's Map indicates this laneway leading to a fair sized hamlet nestled to the west of the castle ruins and names the hamlet as *Mounkstown*. The 1837 OS map indicates the laneway leading from the old line of the road, crossing the new line and heading northwestward, with a branch to the right leading to the castle ruins. Some historians conclude that this old castle was built in the 13th century and was possibly a *watchtower of the Pale*. Local legends say that the Plunkett family occupied the building at one time. Some writings mention a 'capital mansion' near the medieval church at Monktown, which may be a reference to the castle. The ruined castle at Walterstown is interesting from an historical perspective, as it seems to continue the line of watchtowers and towerhouses from Assey on the river Boyne in an almost straight line towards Duleek. Perhaps this line included the long gone 'castle' at Philpotstown, which may have been a watchtower, and the disappeared castle at Balrath. If these were castles of the Pale, possibly part of a defensive line was based along this ancient road, rather than following the circuitous course of the river Boyne.

A monument to a long dead Norman Knight is located in St Mary's Protestant Church in Kentstown, which was a Catholic Church prior to the Reformation. In the 1930s a stone slab was unearthed in this ancient churchyard, upon which the effigy of an unarmoured knight was carved, together with a Latin inscription. Part of the translated text names the tomb as the burial place of *Sir Thomas Tuite, Lord Duke of Kentstown and Walterstown* and the date of his death as 1363. Legends say that the name Walterstown may derive from Walter Tuite, a forebear of Sir Thomas who supposedly ruled the lands of Kentstown in earlier times. It's possible, therefore, that the castle at Walterstown was Walter Tuite's stronghold during the earlier years of the Norman invasion. The nearby townland of Tuiterath is named after this family, who supposedly obtained the lands of Kentstown and Walterstown as part of the original grants made by Adam de Feypo (Pheypo) in the 12th century. The Civil Survey of 1654/56 states that Mountowne parish contained the townlands of Walterstown, Cusackstown, Slanduffe (Shanduffe) and Mountowne – but seems to query the name Mountowne, which it suggests should be called Monkstowne.

A study of the road layout at Walterstown (Cusackstown), as presented on Larkin's Map, shows Darby's Lane was an access road from the old line to Walterstown Castle and its attendant hamlet; named Mounkstown on the map. This map indicates the ruined casle and Mountown church as two separate entities.

The old road ran from Darby's Lane but a short distance to the crossroads at Cusackstown, nowadays the crossroads at Walterstown Chapel (the

Left: *The ruins of Walterstown Castle, eastern aspect, 2009.*
Right: *The old crossroads at Walterstown, 2009 (Cusackstown). The old schoolhouse to the left, Kitty Farrelly's house, centre, Walterstown Chapel to the right.*
Facing page: *Are these pupils of Walterstown school in the early 1950's?*

townland boundary ran through the centre of the crossroads and over the Basla Bridge). The old road entered the junction through what is now the church car park. Traces of the long gone southern section of Darby's Lane can still be discerned leading from the carpark towards the *new line* of the road to the west of the new Walterstown crossroads – in times past, the Carney and Traynor families lived in two houses located on this section. I realise that this is especially confusing to anyone not too familiar with the area; but imagine what it will be like in future years when most of the old features have disappeared beneath motorways and further developments. The old crossroads at Walterstown is complex and extremely difficult to understand from the present day perspective. The original line of the road took it through the crossroads and over the twin arched stone bridge spanning the Basla (Bosla) – on the old OS maps it's named the Basla Stream. I could find no reliable translation for this name. The road once ran straight up the hill and through the old farmyard where the Hynes family lived during my early years; then followed the high ridge on the southside of Slanduff valley towards Danestown House. There it descended to a lower level and passed to the front of the present day house in the valley (Danestown House), before ascending to higher ground and passing the old church (chapel) of Blacklion, then on to the crossroads at the former Black Lion Inn.

The layout of the crossroads at Walterstown (Cusackstown) depicted on Larkin's Map shows the road from the Decoy passing through the crossroads close by the chapel, therefore, until I cross-referenced it with the 1837 OS map I concluded that the map contained several errors. From this process, together with extensive research of the Grand Jury records, the evolution of the road network could be deduced accurately. Larkin's Map indicates the old road from Trim to Drogheda as it existed prior to many of the later realignments being made, therefore it is extremely useful in deciphering the later OS maps which indicate both lines of the road.

Now let us follow the route of each road leading from the crossroads at Cusackstown, the original crossroads at the present day Walterstown Chapel. The chapel was constructed at the old crossroads by Father Michael Reid in 1837, some say on the site of an existing church. The latter is a moot point, because Larkin's Map shows a building by the stream at the crossroads but does not mark it as a church or chapel. Local legends tell of an old church, supposedly the original chapel for the area, being located in Glean Uaigneach in penal times. Father Reid built Johnstown Chapel in the same year.

The road to the left at the crossroads led to Mountown and on to Kentstown. This road passed to the right of the graveyard, nowadays known as Mountown (Mounttown) cemetery: local folklore says that on this section of the old road lived a tailor named Rahil (Raal). An old schoolhouse supposedly stood near the graveyard, from which place the now defunct road curved northwards across the Slanduff ridge into the valley of the River Nanny, known to some as *the Nanny water*. Here it joined with the road from Johnstown, which passed through Oldtown and onwards to Kentstown. This long gone junction was located south of the bridge and to the east of the present day Fairland crossroads at the place where 'Senator' Jimmy Kelly lived during my childhood days. Fairland crossroads was formed post 1837, as the crossroads and the new road from Walterstown Chapel to Brownstown are not shown on the 1837 OS map. At the former junction near the bridge, a lane branched off to the right and ran along the southside of the Nanny towards Kentstown. This laneway led to McNamara's corn mill, which stood on the south bank of the river. All traces of this mill and lane have vanished from the landscape, but are shown on Larkin's Map, with the lane leading off the lost road from Walterstown. The Civil Survey of 1654/56 indicates that a water mill was located in the old parish of Mountowne, of which parish the Nanny formed the northern mearing. This record suggests that the mill on the southside of the Nanny was very old indeed. McNamaras owned shops in Drogheda and were involved in milling in the 19th century – they supposedly operated two other corn mills at Clavinstown, near Killeen Castle. Local legends say that the first McNamara to arrive in the district was a wounded Jacobite soldier fleeing from the Battle of the Boyne in 1690; he received succour from the local populace and settled in Kentstown. In later years, the family supposedly helped found Castleknock College in Dublin and I'm told that there's still a room there known as The McNamara Room: they were involved also in the endowment and construction of the institute for the hard of hearing in Cabra. Larkin's Map indicates the mill on this site and a headrace taken off the Nanny upstream, opposite the entrance to Fairland farmhouse near the site of the old Walterstown GAA pitch. This millrace flowed on the south side of the Nanny, passed under the road at the bridge and on to McNamara's Mill; the tailrace fell into the mainstream of the river above Brownstown Mill. The 1837 map indicates the mill, a millpond and much the same layout of the millraces shown on Larkin's Map. The 1911 OS map indicates some traces of the old headrace to the west of both the bridge and the road to Brownstown, but there's no trace of McNamara's old mill, though a millpond is shown on the site. North of the bridge, the road continues eastward along the Nanny towards Kentstown and past a laneway leading down a steep hill to another mill by the river's northern bank. In my early years this mill was known as Daly's sawmill (Brownstown Mill) and operated as such until more recent times. Both Larkin's Map and the OS maps indicate the mill – the 1911 OS map shows both a sawmill and a corn mill on the site.

Recently I came upon an old order book from Daly's Mill, it was dated 1912 and the entries were made in pencil. Browsing through this old book was like taking a trip in a time machine through times past. Seemingly, the mill was the centre of much industry in those times and manufactured a great number and variety of equipment that nowadays can be seen only at vintage shows in the countryside. I recognised many of the items from my own childhood days, but a few were strange to me. The following are orders for items made at Daly's Mill in 1912. The book is prefaced by the entry:

*Accidents*
*James Kelly Jaug (July Aug?) 13th 1913*
*Resumed work Feb 24th – 6 week incapacitated* (sic).

*March 15th 1912*
*Melford I. S. Varian olo*
*(of the firm Varian Brushes? – author's query)*
*5 Gross s.b. handles 4 ¾") (small brush handles? – author's query)*
*8 ½ Gross s.b. handles 5 9/16" £6. 1s. 6d.*
*15 Gross s.b. handles 5 ½")*
*4 Gross s.b. handles 5 ¾ ")*
*8 Gross s.b. handles 6") £13. 10s. 0d.*
*5 Gross s. b. handles 6 ¼" £ 2. 15s. 0d.*
*£22. 6s. 6p.*
*20 Weeks under same £ 1. 1s. 6d.*
*£23. 8s. 0d.*

Another order reads as follows:

*March 16th 1912:*
*Mr O. L. Finnegan Navan*

| | | |
|---|---|---|
| *3 Oak Coffin suits* | *£2. 0s 6d.* | *13/6 (crossed out)* |
| *2nd quality* | *£1. 16s. 0d.* | *12/* |
| *24 slips extra* | *5s. 0d.* | |
| *2 Elm boards  18"x 1 ¼ x5ft* | | *3s 6d.* |

-------------

*£2. 4s. 6d.*

The book includes entries from March 15th 1912 to Feb' 14th 1914 and is a fascinating insight into how things were done in those times, when events like the great lock out in Dublin took place and the prelude to World War I unfolded. Many other items manufactured from wood were listed, including: washboards, fence posts, gates, quantities of wheel felloes (felly), shafts for carts, horse drawn rakes and hay bogies (floats), dashes for churns, several types of hand rakes including bow rakes, wooden handles for all sorts of hand tools. Charges for time spent sawing for private individuals were included. There are many entries for the supply of bags of sawdust to Lord Fingall, possibly these were used for bedding horses. As stated, it was fascinating to browse through the old records of a sawmill that operated on the Nanny water in times long gone and which were diligently written by people who passed away long since.

Larkin's Map names the area above Daly's Mill and along the north side of the valley *Legnanara*, which local legends says translates to 'the place of the disaster'. I'm told that this name originates from a big flood on the Nanny water many years ago, which did great damage and swept timber from the nearby mill out to sea. The stretch of road from Daly's Mill to Kentstown was known to some as the Legnanara road – a student of Gaelic tells me that this name is most likely Log Na nGarrai, which translates to 'the hollow of the gardens'. The area to the south of the valley just west of Danestown is marked *Bahaguc*. I have no idea of the origin of this name, but it may be another version of the colloquial name *Baltog*, which I'm told is the name of some fields in the same area meaning 'the place of hills and valleys'. The OS map shows a copper mine to the right

*The waterfall at Daly's Mill, formerly the headrace that powered the mill's water turbine. 2009*

of the road between the bridge and the lane to Daly's Mill. Isaac Butler's itinerary notes on his travels to Lough Derg in the 1740s mention this copper mine and names the area as Legnaghneara. He refers to the copper ore as 'diamond stone' – which may account for an old name given to the deep glen, namely, *The Valley of the Diamond Rocks*. Local folklore tells of haunting pipe music being heard in this deep valley below Slanduff hill and how it supposedly emanates from a labyrinth of caverns connected to the mineshafts.

Apart from the disappearance of McNamara's Mill, its access lane and the road from Walterstown via Mountown cemetery, the old maps indicate the same road configuration at the bridge as pertains at time of writing. So it would seem that very little has changed here since the early 1800s.

This road, which starts in Johnstown and passes through Oldtown, crosses the bridge and runs on by the mill lane to Kentstown, once continued onwards to join with the main Dublin to Derry road at Somerville. In my view, this was part of the main road from Navan to Duleek in times past and had two links with the Navan to Dublin turnpike road. One line ran through Johnstown to Kilcarn Bridge and the other via the disappeared road from the Rath at Pastor Hill to upper Kilcarn (Rev' Phil Barry's road). Prior to construction of 'The New Bridge' across the Boyne in Navan,

(1730s to 1750s), the only 'dry' crossing points on the river near Navan were the ancient bridge at Kilcarn and Babes' Bridge near Dunmoe. The *new bridge* on the Athlumney Road was the first stone bridge to be built over the Boyne in Navan, whereas a bridge existed across the Blackwater (Poolboy or yellow pool) since medieval times. This route was therefore logical for the times.

Back at the old Walterstown crossroads, the first road to the right leads from *The Five Roads of Skryne,* which in olden times was a crossroads on the Dublin to Navan road via Ratoath. In days of yore a public house stood on the corner of this road adjacent to the present day churchyard near the little belfry. This establishment was known as Cristy Macken's pub, but though its name is still alive in the folklore of the area, I have found it difficult to discover further information about the place. I heard a story that the pub was burned down in 1916 – whether this had anything to do with the rising of that year I have no idea. Griffith's valuation of 1854 shows that Macken was a common enough name in the area at the time, but does not record a public house.

The road leading from Walterstown to *The Five Roads of Skryne* was a new line, which was mapped, cut and built in or about 1806. Starting from the old crossroads at Walterstown, this new line ran through Skryne, Oberstown (Obrestown), Colvinstown, it continued on past 'the fingerboard' forked junction for Dunshaughlin (the road across the former *red bog*) and onwards to Ratoath. This road became variously known as the new road from Navan to Ratoath and the new road from Dunshaughlin to Carricmacross through Walterstown. A new crossroads was formed at Oberstown where this line crossed yet another new road built from Batterjohn (big) to Edoxtown. The latter road was presented for in 1801 and probably built at about that time, this was the previously mentioned new line of the Summerhill to Drogheda road.

As can be deduced from the above, a great deal of road building activity took place in the vicinity of Skryne in the years between 1800 and 1808 – this must have been most confusing for travellers and locals alike in those days prior to the introduction of road maps. The formation of the five road's crossroads is partly covered by three presentments made in 1806 and 1807. The first was entered under the Barony of Skreen in the Grand

Jury Query Book for the summer assizes of 1806 and reads: *Item 280 Wher £10,, be raised as before & paid to Mr Carberry – Surveyor for marking and laying the new line of road from Oberstown to Walterstown* (sic). The second was presented to the same assizes in the same year and reads: *Item 278 Wher £162,, 6,, / wages £8,, 2,, 3 be raised as before and paid to Elias Corbally Ja's Swan & Hugh Carberry for forming, moulding & fencing 541 p's 32ft wide road from Dunshaughlin to Carricmacross through the lands of Skreen & Yellow Furze Balgeeth & Walterstown @ 6s* (sic). The third was presented to the summer assizes of 1807 under the Barony of Skreen and reads: *Item 421 Wher £324,, 12 & £4,, 9,, wages to Elias Corbally Ja's Swan & James Fox to gravel 541p from Dunshaughlin to Carricmacross through the lands of Skreen & Balgeeth & Walterstown @ 12s* (sic).

Assuming that the only road running eastwards through this area then was the Borrowaddy Road, these three presentments accounted for a *four crossroads*. The fifth leg of the five roads crossroads is the road leading northwest towards Lismullin and joining the old road from Skryne to Navan at what is nowadays known as Carthy's Cross, formerly *The Three Roads of Skryne*. From here it leads to Garlagh Cross and onwards to Navan. In the context of the times, this was obviously a new road as evidenced by its width, so where does this road fit into the picture and when was it built? The answer to this riddle appears to be contained in the following entry in the Grand Jury Query Book of 1804.

This presentment appears under the Barony of Skreen and reads: *Item 474 Wher £84 & £4,, wages be raised as before and Acc for by Jo'n Swan Elias Corbally Esq. & Hugh Carberry for making 120 Per's from Navan to Ratoath at 14s,, Pr* (sic).

The distance presented for in Irish perches equates to 840 yards, or .477 of a statute mile – when scaled onto a modern Discovery Map it comes close to matching this section of road. From the above presentments, it's almost certain that no crossroads existed at the site of the later day *Five Roads of Skryne* until the new lines were cut during the period between 1804 and 1808. Hence, the Borrowaddy Road would appear to have been the main road from Skryne to Rathfeigh and places further east – and the rock road was part of the main road from Skryne to Walterstown and

Ranaghan(n) until then (more about these two roads presently). Time and space do not permit a full account of the construction of the new line of the Summerhill to Drogheda road from Batterjohn (big) to Edoxstown, therefore, only some brief details are included. I came upon many entries in the Grand Jury Query Books for the Lent assizes of 1801 relating to the cutting of this road – these presentments were listed under the Barony of Skreen and included items numbered 527, 547, 548, 549, 550, 551, 552. Some names prominent in these presentments are: Lord Dunsany, Elias Corbally Esq., Liam & Richard Kelly, George Geoghegan, J Lynch, Brab Morris Esq. and Ja's Swan.

The cutting of these new roads created many new features in the district, including the new Glen Bridge near Corbalton Hall and the following well-known crossroads: Ballyna (Ballina) Cross, Ross Cross, Oberstown Cross, George's Cross (McKeowns), Edoxtown Cross, The Priest's Cross, The Five Roads and Carthy's Cross. The name Candle Hill may have derived from these road works. This oddly named place is located to the left of the new line between *The Five Roads* and *The Priest's Cross* and is supposedly called such because strange lights were to be seen along this section in times past. Legends say that these lights were a phenonomen known as jack-o'-lantern or will-o'-the-wisp, caused by static electricity igniting swamp gas. The building of the new road may have created the swampy ground, hence the marsh gas. Apparently, when the new Land Commission houses were built there in the late 1930s, the resulting drainage seems to have rid Candle Hill of the strange lights – they have never been seen since.

The older line of the road from Dublin through Ratoath and Skryne to Navan was routed via Trevet and Collierstown. It crossed the present day line of the Oberstown to Ross Cross road near the church and school and ran northwards to link with the old road to Meagher's Cross near the zigzag section to the west of Skryne Castle. The Taylor & Skinner maps of 1778 show this line of road, which ran on from Skryne, through Garlagh Cross and joined the Dublin to Navan turnpike road close by the old church on Dowdstown Hill. The 1650s Down Survey Barony Map of Skreen shows a pair of dotted lines running southwards from Skreen towards Trevet and marks these *The Way to Dublin*.

About halfway between the crossroads at Walterstown and *The Five Roads of Skryne*, Larkin's Map shows a building on the left side of the road and names it *The White House*. I have been unable to discover the origins of this rather curious name for a house in the midst of the Irish countryside. Locals suggest that it's possibly named such because it was painted white in times past. Perhaps Larkin's Map provides a clue in the topography of the area around the hill of the rock, which I will mention presently. I'm told that, from the second half of the 19th century to the early part of the 20th century, the property was owned by Langans of Bellewstown, then by Butterlys, who intermarried with Mulvaneys, whom I believe are the owners in more recent times. Griffith's Valuation shows that in 1854 a woman named Catherine White had a house in this area leased from a man named Langan – perhaps this is a possible source for the name?

Slightly to the west of Walterstown chapel the church bell hangs in lonely splendour on a small gazebo-like belfry in the middle of the lawn. One night many years ago the normally silent bell suddenly rang out at about three-o-clock in the morning, shattering the peace and tranquillity of the little valley and awakening many of the slumbering residents. The loud pealing of the bell caused consternation and most people were fearful to go out to investigate or to even open the curtains and peek out the windows. A group of 'the good boys', playing cards in a nearby house, suddenly lost interest in shuffling and dealing – when the echoes of the last peal ceased they quietly crept out and went home to their beds. The cause of their discomfiture being that a corpse was lying in the chapel awaiting burial the next day. Superstition being what it was then; they probably thought that the spirits of the dead were somehow responsible for the sudden ringing of the bell at such an ungodly hour. The story was told around the firesides of the area and in many a tavern, needless to say it lost nothing in the telling and some said it was the Banshee who was responsible. But the corpse or the Banshee had nothing to do with the unusual event – another bunch of good boys, who were out *lamping* rabbits, decided to ring the bell for the craic. I heard this story recently from one of the said *lampers* who rang the bell all those years ago at Walterstown Chapel and caused yet more ghost stories to be told in the district.

*The bridge over Basla Stream in Walterstown*

The other road leading to the right from the old Walterstown crossroads is known as *The Rock Road* and leads up to the hill of the rock. Immediately east of the bridge across the Basla Stream, the rock road leads off southwards between the late Kitty Farrelly's old house and a curving section of the Basla, which flows close to the chapel. It is said that Kitty's old house was an Inn during the times when the main road passed through here prior to 1830. From its quaint appearance during my childhood years I would tend to believe this tale, as it then possessed all the attributes my young mind had absorbed from many readings of Dick Turpin and Treasure Island, and such stories of yesteryear. Though both its appearance and the ideal location by the crossroads would suggest that it possibly was an Inn during times past, I have as yet found no proof that the house was ever used as such. So perhaps the history of the old house by the ancient crossroads is destined to remain forever a mystery?

The rock road turns eastwards as it passes the chapel and winds its twisty way up the hill. On past the chapel it swings sharply to the south again in a right-angled turn and commences its climb up the hill of the rock, which hill gives the name to the byroad. Larkin's Map indicates several buildings beyond this sharp corner and local legends say that an Inn was located here in times past. These tales are possibly true, because, as shown by the evolution of *The Five Roads of Skryne*, part of the rock road was once the main road from Skryne to Walterstown and beyond. No traces of these buildings remain on the landscape at time of writing.

A holy well, known as Saint Patrick's Well, was located in a field to the east of the road near the corner – a copper mine was once to be found a short distance to the south of the well. Nowadays the well site is marked by several stones lying in a saucer-shaped depression; but a local man named John Hynes, who remembers it from days of yore, tells me that it was formerly enclosed within a stone-built structure. Its outflow can be seen in a nearby ditch, which takes the water down the hill to mingle with the Basla Stream in Walterstown. Larkin's Map, though it doesn't indicate the presence of the well, shows a little stream leading off to the northeast through the fields. This is probably the same stream that powered the hydraulic ram at Danestown House, as shown on the later OS maps. But the 1837 map indicates the well and there's an interesting note in John O'Donovan's letters, which is worthy of some attention. This reads: *In Cusackstown T.L. there is a well called St Patrick's well, Tobair Patraig, at which there was flag, bearing the impression of his Knees and Crosier, it is still to be seen in a drain, into which it was removed by some person* (sic). This reference is taken from one of O'Donovan's letters, as distinct from his field notes, and was written in Navan in 1836. By flag I conclude that he was referring to a flagstone, probably once part of the well's structure – like many such things of historic note, one wonders what usage it was put to over the years and to where it disappeared?

The rock road splits at a forked junction on the hilltop. Larkin's Map shows the left branch leading to Ranaghann on the back road to Danestown, but the road link onwards to Bellew didn't exist then. The right branch of the fork leads towards Proudstown and the Borrowaddy (Barrawaddy) road. The hilltop, which we always knew as the hill of the rock, is shown on this map as *Murmod Hill*, a name not known to me until I saw it marked on Larkin's Map, therefore, I have no idea of its origin. Some local folklore names the hill as *Muire Cnoic*, which possibly translates to 'Mary's Hill' but I'm unfamiliar with its derivation. Following the right fork, a short distance past the junction we come to a place that's marked on Larkin's Map as *White Rock*. This is the clue I referred to earlier in the context of the source of the name, The White House. The place marked *White Rock* is less than a half-mile to the southeast of The White House and is on the high ground overlooking the said house – perhaps this is how the strange name came to be applied to the farmhouse close by. It's also possible that this is the source of the name of the hill known as the hill of the rock. To date, I have not seen the name Murmod Hill mentioned in writings or shown on any other maps of this area. In one of O'Donovan's letters there's a brief reference to some Gaelic Chieftain being killed in a skirmish at *The White Rock* during the rebellion of the 1640s, but the location of the said rock is not given.

To the northeast of the rock road's junction with the Borrowaddy road (Reilly's Cross), Larkin's Map shows a ruined church on the left. This appears to be marked as Proudstown Church and was located down a little laneway close to where the Reilly family (whose name is given to the nearby crossroads) lived in times past. I asked local people about this church, but none of them seem to have heard of such an establishment in the area. Proudstown House is not shown on the map, though it appears on the OS maps.

The previously mentioned Borrowaddy road runs eastwards from Skryne crossroads (the five roads) and ends at Edoxtown crossroads, on the road between Oberstown and Rathfeigh. Legends and stories abound about this road and how it obtained its strange name – some say it was part of one of the fabled five roads of Tara and that the name means *the road to the sea*. The oldest local folklore says that it's named after a black dog (*Bothar an Madra*). Apart from the dog of the Borrowaddy Road being supposedly the size of an ass, this would seem to be the Skryne/Rathfeigh version of the ghostly black dog. Like the black hound with fiery red eyes which so enlivened our childhood years around the woods and fields of Dowdstown and Bellinter. Regarding the fable of the name being derived from the term *the road to the see*, research of the Grand Jury books revealed that many roads were named such in times past. For instance, 'the road from Trim to the sea', 'the road from Drogheda to the sea', 'the road from Duleek to the sea', these are but some of the many roads in the county bearing this title in the presentment books. It's reasonable, therefore, to conclude that most roads to the east of Duleek were named thus in those times.

However, Larkin's Map may provide another possible explanation for the odd sounding name. This map shows a place named Boreaclaber located between Rathfeigh and Sharry Hill (Skerry Hill). Boreaclaber was less than a mile from the eastern end of the Borrowaddy, so maybe the road derives its name from this now defunct place name. The Gaelic word *clabar* means mud, hence the name may once have been *Bothar an Clabar,* possibly meaning 'the road to the muddy place' or 'the road of the mud'. My understanding is that the letter 'w' is not part of Gaelic, but is used in loan words – Wadi or Wady is a common enough name in North Africa and the Middle East; where it means a dry river course. Waddy can mean either a cowboy or an Aboriginal war club. Perhaps therein lies some food for thought, maybe a Gaelic speaking North African, dressed as a cowboy and brandishing an Antipodean war club, travelled this road long ago, thus giving rise to the strange name which so puzzles us nowadays!

The two roads meet a short distance to the east of the five roads and close to where the satellite relay mast was erected in the 1960s. Once again Larkin's Map throws up some strange names and features now vanished from the landscape. The area known as Candle Hill at time of writing is named 'Shaw' on the map – a family named Bradshaw being landowners in the area in times past, perhaps this is the source of the name. The map also indicates four groups of houses along the road, some of these clusters being large enough to be described as hamlets. The first of these was a group of buildings on the Candle Hill corner of the five roads, while in the area of the big mast across the road a cluster of about eight buildings is shown. Further east near the site of Walsh's old Smithy yet another cluster of houses is indicated on each side of the road and in an area also shown as Proudstown. So, whether it was *the road to the sea* or the habitat of the ghost dog of legend, the Borrowaddy road was well populated by members of the human race when William Larkin's map was surveyed in the period between 1804 and 1810.

When we drove to Sunday Mass in the pony trap – in good weather Dad tied the pony at the wall in front of Walterstown Chapel and across from the old schoolhouse. On wet and windy days we drove on over the bridge and up the old lane to the farmyard, where we parked the trap in an open shed. The farmyard lane was once the continuation of the old line of the Trim to Drogheda road – it led up a steep hill and through the yard then on into the field towards the ridge along the south side of the Slanduff valley. The continuation of this old part of the road was known locally as the Kilshinny Lane. At the time we were too busy living our childhood years to have much interest in such things as the routes of ancient roads. We helped to tie up the pony while Dad chatted to Mr Hynes who lived in the farmhouse and then we walked down the cobbled lane and over the hump-backed bridge to the chapel gates. After mass we retraced our steps, boarded the trap and drove home, little realising that we had passed along part of a route trodden by so many people down through the years.

On the old line of the Trim/Drogheda road, a short distance east of the crossroads at Walterstown Larkin's Map indicates the laneway to Slanduff leading to a group of buildings on the far side of the Basla Stream, which flows to the left of the road at this place. Further east, it also shows a large house and other buildings some distance down a lane to the right of the road. The little stream from the vicinity of St Patrick's well flows into what appears to be a pond, then continues on past the buildings to join the Basla stream close to where the later day Danestown house was built. So, according to this map, in the period 1804 to 1810 another substantial dwelling, which has now vanished, was sited near the old Rath on the Walterstown side of the present day Danestown house. This disagrees with the 1837 OS map, which shows no buildings south of the old road on the stretch between Walterstown and the old Danestown crossroads. Danestown house is shown on the 1911 OS map, and, as mentioned previously, the little stream sourced near St Patrick's well is indicated passing by the house. Traces of the old road between Kilshinny and Danestown were known locally as *the stony road*. John Farrell, who owns the land in this area, tells me that he recalls some traces of ruins on the described location and suggested that they might be the remains of an old manor house. The Verschoyle family were supposed owners of large tracts of land in the area in times past.

East of Danestown house the old road climbed to higher ground and crossed the little road running from Ranaghan(n) and Bellew towards Danestown Rath, or ring fort. This section of old road nowadays forms the entrance to the house and is shown on the Discovery map. From the old crossroads at Danestown, the road led on eastwards through the woods, where it spanned a stream on a hump-backed bridge and passed by the ancient mudwalled chapel of Blacklion. Between Danestown old crossroads and the former chapel site, a small cluster of buildings can be seen on Larkin's Map, to the south of the road, with no access indicated. On the 1837 OS map a number of buildings are indicated in the same place, with an access lane shown leading from the now defunct road.

During the summer of 2009, a local man named Seamus Duffy took me to see a ruin in the fields to the south of the old line of the road near Blacklion. The stone building was so covered with ivy it was well nigh impossible to see the actual structure, but I noticed one doorway with a stone arched transom. We could not gain access because a high wire fenced enclosure surrounded the ruin, now being put to good use as a wildbird sanctuary, instead of being demolished, the fate of many such places during the crazy days of the Celtic Tiger. This ruin is sited at the location where the aforementioned cluster of buildings is shown on the old maps – in a nearby ditch can be seen the remains of stone piers, which seem to be on the line of the access laneway shown on the 1837 and 1911 OS maps.

Local legends suggest that the people of Blacklion used this old ruin as a chapel during the period immediately following Catholic emancipation in 1829 – prior to the construction of the new Catholic Church in Kentstown in the late 1840s. These anecdotes say that this building housed the ancient waterfont, now sited in Kentstown RC church, and that in times past the laneway was lined with crab apple trees. I believe that no ecclesiastical records can be found indicating the stone building being used as a chapel – which might suggest that the font was moved from the old mud-walled Chapel of Blacklion to its present location.

East of the former chapel is a 'T' junction, which nowadays is known as the grassmeal or McAuley's crossroads because of the grassmeal factory built by McAuley's on the site of the Black Lion Inn. In times past this was named Blacklion or Burtonstown (Birtonstown) crossroads, the crossing point of the Trim/Drogheda road and the former Dublin to Derry road. At time of writing, the remains of the old road form a field entrance:

Top: *The old line, left, meets the new near Blacklion.* Below: *Building on site of Blacklion Inn (circa 1930). The road to the right is the old line of the 'Great North Road' from Dublin to Derry.*

this deeply recessed gateway leads off the present day Trim/Drogheda road between Kane's Cross and McAuley's crossroads. In olden times a schoolhouse stood on the corner to the right of the old road near Blacklion crossroads, as shown on the 1837 OS map – it's said that the long-gone village of Blacklion was sited between the crossroads and the old bridge in the woods. I note that the latest Discovery map depicts the area as Burtonstown, with no indication of the former presence of the Black Lion Inn; such is how ancient landmarks are lost to posterity.

So ends our little journey along the *lost road* from the Decoy through Walterstown.

# 15

# The New Line from the Decoy to the Black Lion Inn

The lonely glen – new crossroads at Walterstown – Slanduff, *an unknown destination* – Ballad of Slanduff hill – Danestown and Ranaghan – the Aylmer family and Balrath Castle– the ancient roads from Ranaghan to Athlumney, Johnstown and Babes' Bridge – new road from Kentstown to *the fingerpost* in Athlumney.

The following tale of Glanuaigneach is an excerpt from a series of childhood memories I penned recently

> Here as I take my solitary rounds,
> Amidst thy tumbled wall and ruined grounds,
> And, many a year elapsed, return to view
> Where once cottage stood, the hawthorn grew.

From *The Deserted Village* by Oliver Goldsmith

I'll take you on a visit to the Gleann, shown on Larkin's ancient map as Glean Uaigneach, the lonely Glen; which name is apt, as it is indeed a lonely place. Our visit is in 2006 and as I hadn't visited the place in over thirty years I was, therefore, unsure of what I might find or if anything remained of the past. The Gleann lane leads off the road from Garlagh Cross to Walterstown, about a half-mile past the Decoy and on the left as

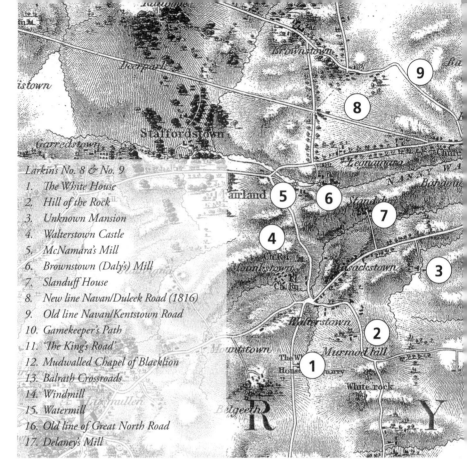

Larkin's No. 8 & No. 9
1. The White House
2. Hill of the Rock
3. Unknown Mansion
4. Walterstown Castle
5. McNamara's Mill
6. Brownstown (Daly's) Mill
7. Slanduff House
8. New line Navan/Duleek Road (1816)
9. Old line Navan/Kentstown Road
10. Gamekeeper's Path
11. 'The King's Road'
12. Mudwalled Chapel of Blacklion
13. Balrath Crossroads
14. Windmill
15. Watermill
16. Old line of Great North Road
17. Delaney's Mill

one travels towards Walterstown. On the other side and directly opposite is the lane leading up to Duane's farm in Balgeeth.

Driving up the steep hill from the valley, we pass Tobin's house on the right. The remains of Mary Kerin's stone built farmhouse are sited across the lane, gaunt ruins standing in the corner of a field, but Mary is long dead and her house crumbled away. On the left, beyond a few twists and turns in the lane we come upon the ruins of Flood's old house. Now just some whitewashed mudwalls supporting a collapsing tin roof laid over the once pristine artistry of some long dead thatcher. No trace remains of the Nissen where the Boyle brothers lived opposite Flood's house long ago. Travelling further we come to a small slate roofed house on the left. Though the windows and doors are missing the house is in surprisingly good condition, with its slated roof still intact. This is as far as we can drive, the remainder of the lane being a quagmire of mud, water and horseshit: the only sign of life being two horses looking over a gate, not one human can be seen on the landscape. Apart from these equines, the

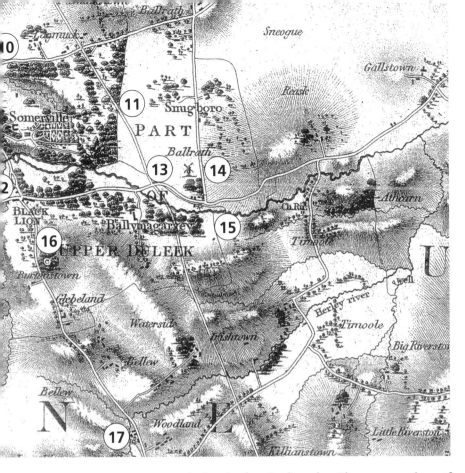

place lives up to its name *the lonely glen*. Such is the Gleann nowadays, if this is progress one might wonder how regression might be rated?

Looking back down memory lane through the misty window of time and nostalgia reminded me of the Gleann during my childhood: everything was so different back in the 1950s when I first passed along the lane with Dad in the pony trap. Tobins lived in the house atop the steep hill then as now and the Floods and Boyle brothers occupied their respective abodes. Christy and Nancy Butterly resided in the now deserted and windowless farmhouse at the end of the lane; it was thatched then before being renovated. Nancy's brother, Jim Boyle, lived further down in an old thatched house. If I recall correctly, Nancy and Jim were related to Jack Boyle and his brothers. But in those days we never called her Nancy, we knew her as Mrs Butterly, such things being more formal then when children were not allowed to address adults by their Christian names. Dad did all sorts of work for the Butterlys of the Gleann, including dosing and squeezing cattle and shearing sheep.

When finished working we went in for the 'tae' and had the usual feed, including big mugs of tea and brown bread, boiled eggs and apple tart, then sat around in the kitchen having a chat. Nancy told us many stories about her life in the Gleann in the old days and to my sorrow I have forgotten most of these. Conversely, Christy wasn't a great one to talk and could be described as taciturn and grumpy – words had to be almost dragged from him. But when wishing to show disapproval of someone, he became quite animated, wagging his finger in front of his face and saying: "that fellow's not a whole ton, no he's not a ton": because of this frequently used expression, he was nicknamed *the whole ton*. I'm told that Christy's parents once lived in the aforementioned White House near Walterstown.

Mrs Butterly kept hens opposite their house in the Glean and down a little lane where the horses gaze at us over a gate nowadays. When not too busy with Dad, we helped her in the poultry run, cleaning the henhouses, feeding the hens and gathering eggs, being well used to doing these tasks as we had hens and turkeys at home. The eggs were gathered and polished and once a week Nancy brought them in her old Morris Minor to Navan, where she sold them to various shopkeepers. The lane is now fenced off and not much trace of it remains, or any sign of the henhouses wherein resided Mrs Butterly's pride and joy, her hens and pullets of yesteryear.

On some occasions we accompanied her down into the deep part of the glen when she went down to visit her brother Jim in the thatched house. Sometimes she brought a plate of food and left it with him, he being a bachelor and living on his own. We wondered at the number of old derelict houses and sheds still standing then, well, some of them were standing and the rest were in ruins. My brother Tom recently reminded me of an old barn-like building which stood around the corner of the lane at the bottom of the narrow glen. Exploring it long ago, we discovered several old pony traps and sidecars lying there, abandoned and falling into decay.

Toadstool-like stone columns, known as corn stones, were another oddity we saw in the Gleann. These comprised two parts, the round stem or pillar hewn from limestone and standing about three feet tall: the top stones being shaped like a mushroom, rounded on top and flat on the underside; with a dish shaped depression chiselled out so that it fitted snugly atop the round pillar. In olden times several of these stones were employed to construct raised platforms upon which Ricks or Stacks of corn were built for storage of crops over the winter months. The stored corn being used for spring threshing, which I'm told was to obtain seed grain. The purpose of the platform was twofold: to keep the corn aired and dry and to prevent rats from accessing and destroying the golden grain. Though the rodents could climb up the vertical stone pillar, yet they couldn't defy gravity by crawling along the underside of the top stones. In this way they acted rather like the rat stoppers placed on ship's mooring ropes to prevent the pests boarding vessels as unpaying passengers. In later days cast iron stands were used instead of the stones to provide stilts for the corn stacks.

At the time we didn't know their purpose and wondered who had put in so much work and effort during those hungry days making decorative stones up in the Lonely Glen. But in recent times I did some research and discovered their former usage. Research also shows that these stones were used in Ireland post 1722, when brown rats first appeared on these shores. Since those early days, having seen these stones many times in my wanderings, decorating driveways and lawns, I wondered if their owners knew their usage in times past?

Downes Bridge *across the defunct Navan/Dublin railway at Kilcarthy, near Kilmessin. Note the row of cornstones to the left.*

In olden days the Gleann was an extensive hamlet, with many thatched houses and a church. Local anecdote says that a church was sited here prior to Catholic emancipation in 1829. Though no trace remains of it today, I believe that one of Sullivan's fields, in Fairland, is still called *the church field*. Perhaps this was one of the unofficial or secret chapels that flourished during the days of the penal laws. Many of these old humble houses of worship existed then and were mostly ignored by the authorities provided they remained humble structures and hidden in remote places. A perusal of Larkin's Map of 1812 shows that the place was named Glanuaigneach and at least fifteen buildings stood there at the time. A close study of this map indicates that the Gleann lane may have continued on and crossed the line of the Oldtown to Fairland road near Gossen's old laneway, then possibly passed on through Staffordstown. In more ancient times the place was supposedly part of the grange for the nearby Monastery at Mounttown (Mounktown) and housed some of the many workers of that establishment – should this be true, the Gleann is very old indeed and possibly dates back to the 12th century or earlier.

During our youthful visits, the three Boyle brothers lived in an old Nissen across the lane from Flood's house. It may come as a surprise to some that we had Nissens in those early days following World War II, but the Nissens we knew were semicircular tin huts and not Japanese cars. The three brothers were named Jack, Bilto (or Bilcher) and Tom. I didn't know Tom well, he was just an older man who wore a soft hat and said very little, a man of few words. I knew Jack well from working on the Dowdstown estate and he featured prominently in our lives during those boyhood days. In the era of the horse, Bilto had been a ploughman in Dowdstown and was reputedly very good at this skilful work, an artist so to speak.

Sometimes we visited the hut, all three brothers being batchelors things were pretty rough and ready. When sitting down at the table for a cup of tea, it wasn't unusual for us to eject a hen that might be roosting on either a chair or the table – such things were considered fairly normal in the countryside at the time. All the brothers were pretty fond of the horses and studied form in the newspapers, the finished papers usually ending up on the floor and providing a carpet.

*Round cornstones at the Lynch farm in Oldtown, 2009*

One day while having tea at harvest time in Dowdstown, Jack told a tale of when he was frying some meat in a pan upon an old stove in a dark corner of the hut. As Jack put it, "the 'mate' was very slow to cook, so I tried to cut it, but it wouldn't cut, I thought the knife was horrid blunt or the 'mate' was dammable tough". "So I carried the pan over to the window to the light and jeekers wasn't there one of Bilto's black socks in the pan, it must have fallen off the line and got mixed up with the 'mate' in the pan". Jack was normally a man of few words, but he became very animated, with his voice rising excitedly on the few occasions when he told stories. So we all had a good laugh, more at Jack's demeanour than our mental images of Bilto's old sock being chopped up and mixed with the 'mate' in the pan.

The three brothers rode their bikes everywhere, they were all hard workers and were always polite, good solid country folk and the salt of the earth. Though I can recall all of them riding their bikes on the Walterstown road, especially to Garlow Cross, my clearest memories are of Bilto. In the earlier days I remember him riding sedately along on the bike, his cap on his head and a salute for all. Later, it could be seen that the left pedal had fallen off the bike and he was pedalling awkwardly along using just one pedal, his left foot driving the crank with the pedal spindle only.

In later times the entire left crank had disappeared, it must have come adrift somewhere but the bould Bilto continued to ride his ancient machine, stubbornly refusing to give up. Though now he was using the most peculiar form of locomotion I had ever seen, back-pedalling at least half the time, putting his toe under the remaining pedal and pulling it back to the top, then pushing it down again. Having nowhere to rest his foot during these acrobatics, his left leg hung out in the air – outside of the circus it was the most peculiar and ungainly motion I ever saw being performed upon a bike and believe me I have seen quite a few. That's my last recollections of Bilto Boyle, hop-scotching his way along the Walterstown road while sitting on the saddle of his bike.

The Flood family lived in a thatched house opposite the Boyle's Nissen hut: I believe that in earlier times their original house stood close by, but had fallen down by the time of my childhood years. In our very young days just two of the family, Lizzy and Peter were still living. Several family members had died in earlier years and Lizzy passed away in 1951. This left Peter living alone in the house, I believe he died in 1967. I never really knew any of the Tobins who lived just up from the main road, but I'm told that some of the family still resided there up to 2006.

So, from being a thriving hamlet in the first third of the nineteenth century, supposedly with its own church, the lonely glen has now become the deserted glen. Indeed, during our childhood the signs of decay were evident and the people ageing. They gradually died or left the upper part of the Gleann until most traces of their presence were eliminated by progress. As stated, Peter Flood died in 1967. The Boyle brothers, whose family reputedly once owned the land as far as Walterstown Cross, all passed away and nobody came to replace them. Jim Butterly died and his sister Nancy left the Gleann, together with her husband Christy. They moved down to Johnstown and took over the house and shop once owned by 'Juicy Lynch'.

That's my story about my recollections of Glean Uaigneach as seen from the perspective of half a century ago. During my recent visit I was struck once again by the effect people have on the rural landscape. Though the two horses looking across the lane into the empty frames of Nancy Butterly's windows were friendly and nuzzled my hands in greeting, yet they were not human. And you couldn't ask them what had been here before, so a stranger might be left to wonder. But I had my memories and I didn't need to ask.

In times past, the following families reputedly lived in the Glean in addition to people mentioned previously:

- The Monaghans (or Monahans)
- The Hanlons.
- Joe Brien and family.
- The Longs.
- The Gillicks.
- Two families of Boyles – previously mentioned.
- Butterly family, Christy, Peter, May and Gerty.
- 2nd Butterly family being – Bridie and May, both married and left the Glean.
- The Barry family.

Other families lived in the Glean from time to time: conversations with local people provided the above names, which were included as a point of interest but I cannot vouch for their accuracy.

On past the Glean, the new road wound its way through the valley until it cut through an outcrop: where it turned slightly southeastwards and intersected the old road into the hamlet to the west of Walterstown castle. As mentioned, this laneway became known as Darby's lane, named after a local family who lived in a cottage at its further end.

The new Walterstown crossroads was formed by the intersection of two new road lines. For reasons explained earlier, I'm fairly sure that the new line of the Trim to Drogheda road was cut sometime between 1817 and 1837; perhaps some further scrutiny of the Grand Jury records might yield the exact date. But when was the new road cut from the old Walterstown crossroads through Fairland and on to Brownstown crossroads? According to the 1837 map it wasn't in existence then, but it was shown on the OS map of 1882, the road, therefore, was cut sometime during the forty-six year interim period.

Years ago when we were kids and passing through Walterstown new crossroads in the pony trap, Dad told us the story about Father Finn who was killed there in 1926. He was then the parish Curate and was riding a motorbike over from Johnstown to hear confessions in the chapel – his bike collided with a car coming from the Duleek direction. A great hurler and a fluent Gaelic speaker; he wore his *Fainne* proudly. Dad blessed himself when passing the spot, as he remembered the event although he was only in his early twenties when the accident occurred.

When the new line of the Trim to Drogheda road was first cut, the 'new' Walterstown crossroads was then located where, at time of writing, the lane to Mountown (Mounttown) cemetery leads off the road. The new route intersected the previously mentioned road from Walterstown chapel that passed by Mountown old church and cemetery and ran on towards the Nanny bridge near McNamara's old mill.

The remaining part of this defunct road is now an entry to the ancient churchyard, within which many interesting names are inscribed upon the tombstones. I believe that in times past Mountown was named Monktown and in early Norman times was known as Balivekerde and God knows what other names prior to that. The old church was once known as 'the chapel of the Grange' and supposedly belonged to the ancient and far-flung Grange of Skryne. The church was reputedly part of a monastic settlement originating in early Norman times and attached to St Mary's of Dublin. Some historians say that Glean Uaigneach was associated with the grange, or monastic farm for Monktown. It was supposedly owned by this order, whose influence extended far and wide in the surrounding areas. Much has been written previously by eminent historians about the ancient site, so there's nothing more that I can add to the fount of knowledge. The history of the district during Norman times is covered in the excellent book, *Skryne and the Early Normans,* by Elizabeth Hickey.

Continuing eastwards past the old cemetery, our road enters the wooded glen Slanduff, known to some as 'the black glen' or 'the dark slope' (on the Down Survey Barony Map it's marked Shanduffe). Here, the Basla Stream, flowing from the hump-backed bridge at Walterstown chapel, passes under this road for the first time. It turns eastwards and follows the glen to mingle with the 'Nanny Water' in Somerville about two miles to the east. The river passes under the road several times and flows on different sides on alternate sections of its route. The reason for the stream criss-crossing the road puzzled me as it seemed to have caused unnecessary construction of several stone bridges thereby leaving pronounced ridges on the road's surface. An older resident provided me with a simple solution to this riddle: when the new line was constructed, the extra bridges were built to provide a source of water and drainage to farms on both sides of the road. A very pragmatic method of solving problems and preventing grievances at the time when conveyances were horsedrawn and slow moving – however, in these less patient times, the bridges cause bumps on the road for vehicles speeding along at a much faster pace. The valley of Slanduff has always been sparsely populated, leastwise during the last several hundred years. This I know from my many trips through it during my own lifetime and in the past the maps show few dwellings. On its western end in the narrow part of the glen, a couple of cottages stood near the roadside during my early years. In more recent times a few modern bungalows have been built along this stretch.

To the east of the cottages we pass the entrance to Slanduff house and farmyard, which has been deserted and in ruins for many years. In the 16th century, Slanduff was owned by Dowdall's of Athlumney and known as Slaneduff: Griffith's valuation of 1854 indicates that a man named Peter Austin had 206 acres of land, a house and offices in Slanduff leased from the Earl of Milton at an annual rateable valuation of £215. It also indicates that Peter Austin leased a house to one Thomas Coffey at an annual rateable valuation of 10 shillings. Slanduff is owned nowadays by Peter Austin of Beaupark. Back in the 1960s I helped my father at sheep shearing down in the farmyard, but I can't recall much about the place now. An old brick lodge, probably built following the cutting of the new road, stands near the overgrown avenue which once ran from the old road atop the ridge to the south (Kilshinny Lane). The lodge is now deserted, but in earlier days a family named Farrell lived there and I recall having tea in the kitchen during the shearing. I still retain fond memories of the bright sunny glen and the beech woods on the high slopes above. These trees provided a magnificent and colourful backdrop, especially the soft green tints of early summer and the beautiful russet hues of autumn. The following ballad/poem about the valley was penned in 1928 by a local man named Jack Bird, who I'm told lived on the old road near Mountown cemetery

## Slanduff Hill

by Jack Bird

*Through Fairlands grove I oft times rove*
*And over Slanduff Hill*
*To view the Nanny water flowing*
*Down by Daly's Mill.*

*'Twas in my youth, to tell the truth*
*My young days I spent there*
*To mind the sheep and them to keep*
*On its pastures green and fair.*

*None can surpass the rich old grass*
*That in Kilshinny grows.*
*Where once there stood, the name of Bird*
*Now taking their last repose.*

*When I think upon those days long gone,*
*My mind with thoughts doth fill,*
*Of Birds I knew, that rambled too,*
*All over Slanduff Hill.*

*The flowers are decked of every hue*
*O'er the valleys far and wide,*
*And often times I think of them*
*When by the Nanny side.*

*Its hills are green as can be seen,*
*Its woods are charming too;*
*And the country-side both far and wide*
*From Slanduff hill you'll view.*

*The birds doth sing upon each tree,*
*Their notes both loud and shrill,*
*And the larks will play, Please God, next May,*
*All over Slanduff hill.*

But like many things in life there's a darker aspect to the beautiful valley, which perhaps matches the supposed meaning of its name, the black glen. I heard tales told that in the past the deserted glen was used for purposes other than farming. One anecdote said that following the election of the first Dáil Éireann in 1918, Sinn Fein courts were held in the valley and convicted many miscreants of minor offences – these sessions were known to activists of the period as *the court of the black hills*. Another such tale says that during the troubled era of the war of independence, 1918 to 1922, dark deeds were perpetrated in Slanduff. Which was supposedly termed *an unknown destination*, where informers from far and near were dealt with and their bodies buried on Slanduff ridge.

Local legend tells of how a military engagement occurred in Slanduff during the Irish civil war in 1922, which supposedly involved a firefight between the Free State army and anti treaty forces, known as Irregulars. This engagement became known locally as *the battle of Slanduff*. Further inquires revealed that approximately one hundred and fifty 'anti-treatyites' broke out and made good their escape from Free State custody in Dundalk Jail – about forty escapees headed southwards to camp in the glen. The remainder of the group, supposedly including the famous Frank Aikin, headed off towards Skerry Hill, near Rathfeigh, where they received succour from the local populace. Several days later the campers in the glen encountered a contingent of Free State soldiers nearby and a skirmish took place – the so-called 'Irregulars' slipped away but were captured subsequently near Dunshaughlin. Perhaps the Free State soldier killed at Oberstown crossroads, Patrick Keogh, lost his life during this skirmish. The same story also tells that during their stay they frequented Maguire's pub in Kentstown and drank the place dry. Supposedly, when asked who was paying for the drink one of them produced a revolver, placed it on the bar counter and said: "yer' man here will take care of the lot".

The road runs straight along the valley heading due east until we come to the oft' mentioned Danestown house. I have seen the name Danestown variously described as meaning "the place of profuse ferns" and it being an Old English word for a valley (dene), either of these meanings could apply to the place in question. I'm unsure of when the house was built, it doesn't show on the 1837 OS map but is depicted on the 1911 OS map.

*Slanduff - old line of the road now entrance to Danestown House*

As mentioned, the little stream flowing from the vicinity of St Patrick's well is shown on this map passing by the house where it fed a pond or water-garden. Then powered a hydraulic ram, before coalescing with the Basla Stream at the edge of the new road about two hundred yards away to the north. The house is built on the southern edge of the old line, with the defunct road shown running by the front door. The old line was used as an entry avenue to the house, running eastwards to link with the road to Ranaghann and Bellew. A small building, possibly a gate lodge, is shown at the junction that was the old Danestown crossroads prior to the new road being cut.

In times past the house was owned by Rogersons and famous for its orchards and fruit gardens at one time: during most of my lifetime the property was owned by a family named Delaney, who had many landholdings in the area and further afield, including a corn mill. A local anecdote tells of a man named Peter Kennedy, who in the 1930s, while working at some ancient ruins on Delaney's land found an oblong stone with the following inscription engraved thereon: *This forge & peers was built by Sir Walter Aylmer of mount Aylmer Bart to his lady Catherine*

*Aylmer alias H,U,S.S. daughter of Sir Sidney Barnwell of Weston after to the royal garter and royal countess of fine. ANNO DOMINI 1725* (sic). At first I thought that this stone might provide a clue to the origins of the previously mentioned large residence shown on Larkin's Map to the south of the old road close to Danestown house. But further research appears to suggest that the stone may not have been genuine. Some local historians say that several such engraved stones were found buried locally and may be samples of work done by an apprentice stonemason of former years. The Civil Survey of 1654/56 shows that Garreth Aylmer owned 120 acres of land in Danistowne parish (Danestown), perhaps the forge mentioned on the stone was on this land and located alongside the route of the lost road?

This is an opportune place to add a few words on the Aylmer family, mentioned in the Civil Survey as being papist. In earlier years this family rose to prominence in the Meath gentry when Sir Gerard Aylmer became Lord Chief Justice of Ireland. The family seat was in nearby Dollardstown from 1539 to 1641; their estates were seized by the crown because of the family's involvement in the rebellion of 1641. Garreth Aylmer of Balrath, a younger son, was supposedly one of the organisers of the said rebellion and was imprisoned and tortured in Dublin Castle as a reward for his efforts – he was pardoned and released in 1662. His home in Balrath, reputedly the long gone castle, was sacked and burned to the ground during the early years of the rebellion. In later times the family moved to Mount Aylmer, which was built nearby.

The new Danestown crossroads is situated several hundred yards eastwards of the house and is formed by the road from Ranaghan(n) and Bellew crossing the new line of the Trim to Drogheda road. To the south, Larkin's Map shows a sizeable hamlet at Ranaghann (Runaghan), a place seemingly pivotal to Norman history. I cannot find any traces of this hamlet on the subsequent OS maps of the area. As mentioned, this road links with 'the rock road' from Walterstown chapel at a 'T' junction near Ranaghann but comes to a dead end a short distance to the south. The same map shows that the later day link road through Bellew to the Dublin/Derry road via Rathfeigh didn't exist then.

# The Old and New Roads from Ranaghan towards Navan and Kilcarn

Because the ancient Norman settlement at Ranaghan is mentioned frequently in writings about the early Norman settlements in County Meath, I consider that the road network linking this place to Navan, Athlumney, Kilcarn and perhaps Babes' Bridge is worthy of mention. Nowadays the road from Ranaghan crosses the Trim to Drogheda road at the new Danestown crossroads. From there it continues on a circuitous route past Danestown Fort (ring fort) and the ancient church and graveyard close by Trinity Well, then traverses the road at the bridge on the River Nanny near *The Lion's Mouth* fountain. Beside the Protestant church, at the top of *The Minister's Hill*, it joins the cul de sac road from Kentstown to Somerville – formerly, this was the crossroads hereabouts, which was a staggered junction. In those days, the same road continued on from Kentstown through Brownstown and across Realtoge hill (Realtogue), then on through Little Follistown and Harristown to a forked junction beside the small bridge on the Johnstown side of the present day Alexander Reid crossroads (Casey's Cross). One branch of the fork led northwestwards and on through Bailis towards Violet Hill across the river from Navan (near Athlumney Castle). Prior to the construction of *The New Bridge* on the Boyne Road in the 1750s, perhaps it crossed the River Boyne at the old ford in Athlumney. Possibly a link from this old road passed through Farganstown and connected with *Babes' Bridge* (also known as Farganson's Bridge or Robber's Bridge), a medieval stone arched structure spanning the Boyne near Dunmoe. The 1837 OS map shows this bridge crossing the Boyne from Ardmulchan to Donoughmore and names it Donoughmore Bridge (in ruins) - a group of houses, named Peters Ville is depicted on the same map between Johnstown and Casey's cross. Babe's Bridge is mentioned in ancient writings as being the only bridge on the Boyne to survive a great flood in the 1330s – one arch survives at time of writing and can be seen alongside the Boyne Canal ramparts near Rowley's Lock. From the former forked junction at Alexander Read, the other branch ran southwards through Johnstown to Kilcarn Bridge. The new road from *The Finger Post* junction, near Navan, formed the crossroads in Alexander

*The surviving arch of Babe's Bridge across from Donoughmore.*

Read (Casey's Cross) and continued on to Kentstown, where it linked with the Duleek to Navan road via Oldtown: Kentstown RC church was built at this crossroads in the late 1840s. The Navan/Duleek road passed over Kilcarn Bridge then through Johnstown and Oldtown to Kentstown (see reference in Chapter 11 to Rev. Phil Barry's old road linking this road from Oldtown to the Navan/Dublin turnpike in Kilcarn). At Kentstown, the combined road ran into Sommerville to join the Dublin to Derry road at a "T" junction close by the Manor house. Most of the old and newer road layouts are shown on Larkin's Map. The present day road leading from Black Lion crossroads (the grassmeal or McAuley's Cross) and on past the lion's mouth fountain possibly didn't exist until post 1817 – I'm unsure of when the bridge over the Nanny was built. This section of road is covered in greater detail in the next chapter.

Records researched in the Grand Jury presentment books show that the previously mentioned new line from the fingerpost junction in Navan to Kentstown was cut in 1816. Several presentments were made at the Lent Assizes of 1816 for this section of road, which was named the Navan to

*This photograph was taken at the 'v' weir on the Boyne river in Navan about 1900, "The New Bridge" in the background* (Courtesy D. Halpin)

Balbriggan road. These included items numbered between 253 and 268 – one presentment of £160 0s 0d was for a new bridge in Athlumney (Smith Bridge on the 1837 OS map?). In the summer assizes of the same year a presentment, item number 218, was made for the amount of £341 10s 11d to build a bridge at Follistown. These records seem to confirm that this road was constructed in or around 1816: yet a further testament to the accuracy of Larkin's Map!

Beyond Danestown crossroads, the 'new line' of the Trim to Drogheda road continued eastwards through the woods and rejoined the old route at a forked junction about two hundred yards to the west of Black Lion crossroads. The complex evolution of the road network in this area is covered in the next chapter.

# 16

# Black Lion –
# Balrath and Ballymagarvey

Blacklion Inn and village – Great North road to Derry – mudwall chapel and *Nag's Head Fable* – Delaney's Mill – Rathfeigh's new line – Wexford insurgent column of '98 – the road from Slane to Ardee – Flemingstown Bridge and the gamekeeper's path – Kane's Cross, The Lion's Mouth Fountain and Trinity Well – The Ghosty Corner – Sean Finnegan's Quern – Ballymagarvey Churchyard and House.

Kentstown parish, of which these areas nowadays form part, would require a full book to cover adequately. Hence I will pursue my main objective of describing the various road configurations down through the years. Should the reader wish to discover more about this historic area, I recommend the book entitled *Kentstown in Bygone Days,* which is available in Navan library.

As in other places mentioned previously, such as Dowdstown and Walterstown, the changes made over the years along this section of the route are complex. I will, therefore, first provide a synopsis of the roads prior to the major alterations made in the early part of the 19th century and then cover each section individually.

The Taylor and Skinner map of 1778 shows the junction here as a four crossroads with the number 19 milestone located on the southeast corner next to the Inn. The Dublin to Derry road is depicted running from Curragha, passing Windmill Hill, then crossing the line of the Trim to Drogheda road at the crossroads, which it names *Blacklyon*. From there, the old road onwards to Derry continues northwards through the Somerville Demesne, crosses the Nanny and runs in an almost straight line towards the River Boyne at Slane. Kentstown village is not marked on this map. The road leading towards the west from Blacklyon crossroads is shown truncated and marked as the Trim road – this is the previously described old line routed along the high ground towards Walterstown. The line of the Trim to Drogheda road is not marked in its entirety on the Taylor and Skinner maps, which in this area depict only the section from Black Lion through Duleek to Drogheda. The route eastwards from Black Lion is shown crossing the Nanny at the site of the present day Ballymagarvey Bridge, then running onwards past Mount Aylmer to Duleek. The only junction indicated on this section is at the well of the Deenes, with the side road shown crossing the Nanny, probably by *the bridge of the Deenes*. In my view, the foregoing was the situation prevailing until the major road realignments were made during the early years of the 19th century.

The name *Blacklyon* seems out of context for the area and I can find no specific meaning for it in English. The most notable place bearing the name Lyon is a city in central France. It, therefore, seems likely that its use on this map is a misnomer: in this context it's noteworthy that on the same map Mount Aylmer is spelled Mount Aybner, which is incorrect. The crossroads is marked on Larkin's Map as Black Lion, but the name could be interpreted as being generic to the area. The OS maps, however, name the place as Black Lion and appear to indicate that the name applied to a building located on the southeastern sector of the crossroads, the site of the Black Lion Inn. This was especially so on the OS map of 1911, where the only building shown on the location is the old Inn standing on the apex of the corner. Beaufort's map of 1797 and J. Taylor's map of 1802 name the crossroads Black Lion and show a village close by. The Ordnance Survey field notes of 1836 state that the Black Lion Public House takes its name from a sign above the door. One local anecdote tells of how the name derived from a black line deposited on the road by sludge leaking from carts taking rotted flax to Dublin. While this may be so, it's more likely that the name Black Lion derives from the hostelry, this being a common enough name for such establishments. For instance, names such as Blackbull Inn, the Black Boar, the Red Cow and many more were commonplace then – the Taylor and Skinner map shows a place named Largay, or the Black Lion Inn, near Belcoo Bridge in County Fermanagh on the road between Enniskillen and Sligo.

It's said that an Inn is mentioned on the Civil Survey of the area in 1654/56, but I can find no such reference. Nor can I find any mention of the establishment in Griffith's valuation of 1854. The Inn certainly predates the valuation survey of 1854, in the Church of Ireland cemetery in Kentstown a tombstone bears the name of Richard Ladley and the inscription thereon says that he was the landlord of the Blacklion Inn. The date on the stone is 1801. Local legends tell of how the legendary Michael Collier of Bellewstown, colloquially known *as Collier the robber*, frequented the place in olden times. He was also reputed to have marauded around the area of the Coachman's Inn at Ballyna, near Tara on the Dublin to Navan turnpike road. While these yarns are credible enough, the other tale of the legendary English highwayman, Dick Turpin, using the Black Lion as a hideaway is rather less believable.

After Ladley's time the Inn was in the possession of the Cornwall family for a period. From 1900 the Bowen's family lived there until it was abandoned in later years, they were the last to occupy the famous old Inn, which they used as a dwellinghouse. In the early 1950s it was demolished, being blown up (or down) by explosives, supposedly because of its dangerous condition and proximity to the road. Around that time, McAuleys built a grassmeal factory on the adjacent site, which has continued in business until recent times.

The previously mentioned mudwalled chapel of Blacklion once stood on a site in the woods and fields at the southwestern sector of Sommerville, in the vicinity of Kane's Cross. This chapel seems to have been in use during penal times – though it's indicated on Larkin's Map, the precise location is difficult to determine. Several dwellings and a schoolhouse are shown here on the 1837 OS map. The area around the crossroads was, in fact, a small village. As mentioned in chapter 14, the ancient waterfont that nowadays stands in Kentstown R.C. church, was placed in Black

Lion chapel for a period in olden times. The octagonal font originated in Tymoole (Timoole) old church and was designed in 1597 by Robert Hollywood, a member of the Hollywood family that hailed from a place of the same name in North County Dublin. He was reputed to be a brother of the famous Jesuit Christopher Hollywood (1559-1626), credited with being the author of *The Nag's Head Fable* in 1604. Which fable alleged that, in the 1560s, the new Protestant Bishop of Canterbury, Matthew Parker, was indecently consecrated in the Nag's Head Tavern in Cheapside – needless to say this story caused much disharmony between the followers of the two religions. Perhaps this little snippet from the past explains the derivation of the name of a pub named *The Nag's Head*, located in the area of Hollywood Great near The Naul in north Dublin?

In October 2008 I walked in the woods near the old village of Blacklion. Paschal Marry, a local historian guided me on this visit to the site of the village of times past. He showed me the ancient stone arched bridge, now partly collapsed, which once carried the old line of the Trim/Drogheda road across the unnamed stream flowing from Ranaghan and commingling with the Nanny water close by Flemingstown Bridge. The old track of the road, though partly overgrown with trees, can be seen in the centre of the wood, heading in an east to west direction. Though we stood within a short distance of the modern road an uncanny silence permeated the site of the long lost village, of which not a trace remains. As we made our way back out to the busy noisy road, I couldn't help but wonder what the long dead inhabitants of the disappeared hamlet would think of the present day scene. And I thought of what stories they might have told of their days spent living alongside the route of the ancient road.

The old line of the Dublin to Slane road was part of the much longer route from Dublin to Derry. As far as I can ascertain it was not a tollroad, but in later years the new line of the route was defined as the Dublin and Slane turnpike, or tollroad and run by trustees for a time. There is evidence in Griffith's valuation reports on the area around Balrath to show that the new line was still classed as a turnpike road in 1854, a mere two years before all the tollroads of the period were dissolved by Parliament. This subject is covered in greater detail presently.

Alongside the former line of the great north road, between Rathfeigh

*The author atop the bridge on the old line at Blacklion.*

and Black Lion, stands an ancient watermill known to some as Rathfeigh Mill and to us in our youth as Delaney's Mill. Griffith's valuation shows that in 1854 Patrick Leany occupied the mill and the annual rateable valuation was £50. This old mill is shown on Larkin's Map of 1812 and the later OS maps but I can't find any reference to it in the Civil Survey of 1654/56, although the nearby mill at 'Masetown' (Macetown) is referred to in this document. The waters of the Hurley River (named the Herley on Larkin's Map) powered Rathfeigh Mill in times past. The mill ceased operating in 1950. Nowadays the miller's house and some of the buildings have been restored and converted, and the mill, though in a state of disrepair, is mostly intact. I believe that much of the machinery is still in place – but similar to many other old watermills, the millrace is partly dried up.

I called several times, but found nobody at home hence I couldn't view the old works for myself. The following is a condensed extract from some heritage records found on the Internet:

*Delaney's Mill – Three-storey three-bay water-powered mill, built c. 1820, probably incorporating the fabric of an earlier mill building. Entrance on east side is partly sunk into ground and is reached via flight of stone steps. This sunken entrance formed part of a gulley/drain which was used to take water away from closed sluice gates, around mill and out under later extension to north and into tailrace. Remains of timber and iron waterwheel, c. 12 feet in diameter located on south end of east façade. Remains of timber trough and sluice gate indicate waterwheel was overshot by water directed under road. Remains of four millstones are on premises.*

This description finishes with an appraisal that makes the following evaluation of the mill's historical significance: *It is very unusual for mill machinery to remain in such an intact state. Thus Delaney's Mill represents an important historical insight into the industrial practices and workings of a small scale milling operation from the mid nineteenth century onwards.*

The conclusion that the mill was built on the site of an older mill is correct, as a mill is shown here on Larkin's Map, which was surveyed between 1804 and 1812. The statement that 'the waterwheel was overshot by water directed under road' is misleading, because the headrace ran parallel to the road: I presume it was meant to convey that the water exiting the overshot wheel was directed to the tailrace, which was diverted under the road.

Here again can be seen traces of the long head and tailraces necessary for the operation of mills on rivers flowing through relatively flat terrain – this being especially so where overshot waterwheels were involved. A few hundred yards to the north the old line of the Dublin to Derry road passes over a fine stone bridge spanning the Hurley River, this bridge is known as *The Old Rathfeigh Bridge* and consists of six slightly skewed arches, built in two separate groups of three. A small stream flowing from the Bellew area mingles with the main river at the northern end of the bridge. Both Larkin's Map and the early OS maps show that the millrace started at a weir on the Hurley River about a quarter mile to the southwest of Rathfeigh, behind the church and graveyard. Local legends say that this area was named *the Taich*, possibly being derived from the Gaelic *Teasc'*, meaning to cut off. From there the headrace flowed to the east of the main river course – then through a series of flumes and sluices to the overshot wheel. The tailrace passed under the great north road via a separate small bridge to the south of the main bridge and rejoined the Hurley several hundred yards downstream. This means that the original millrace was almost one mile in length. There being a pretty good fall in the river hereabouts, in this instance the reason for the long headrace was to gain greater water elevation to drive an overshot wheel, which provides much more power than either a breastshot or undershot wheel.

During conversations with several local people whilst I was tracing the route of the old millraces at Delaney's Mill, I discovered some interesting details about the old road systems around Rathfeigh. It seems that in days of yore one of the early bypasses around an Irish village was constructed in Rathfeigh. As previously mentioned in chap' 14, the new line of the road from Summerhill and Trim to Drogheda, via Batterjohn, passed through Oberstown and swung to the right at Edoxtown crossroads. Passing by Edoxtown (old) House it ran on across the Hurley River and the mill headrace, then emerged on the great north road at what nowadays is Halligan's farmyard – this was the original crossroads of Rathfeigh. The old line continued eastwards from here, on its way to Tymoole passing a place known as *The Terminus*: perhaps this was a staging post, or post house, associated with the old coach road. For some reason this route was altered and a new line cut, which turned slightly to the left at Edoxtown crossroads and swung in a great loop to rejoin the old route a short distance to the east of The Terminus. This route alteration would seem to have been executed following completion of the OS in 1834, because the new line is not shown on either Larkin's Map or the 1837 OS map. A triple arched bridge was built to carry the new road across the Hurley, while a single arch spanned the millrace. At the place where it crossed the great north road a new crossroads was formed, which nowadays is known as the mill crossroads because it's located but a short distance from Delaney's Mill.

The reason for the cutting of the new line is uncertain, but a local anecdote claims that the death of a traveller on the old line prompted its construction. Supposedly, one night a Judge journeying along the road

*Rathfeigh old bridge on the old* Great North Road *from Dublin to Derry*

from Trim was killed, either because he was thrown from his horse or his carriage overturned at the dip in the road near the bridge on the old line. As the place of the legendary accident is but a short distance from its fabled haunt, perhaps the huge black dog of the Borrowaddy startled the horse(s) on that dark night long ago.

The old OS maps show that the aforementioned watermill at nearby Macetown had a long series of head and tailraces in olden times – this mill is shown on the 1911 OS map as Macetown Mills (corn). The headrace here was sourced from a small stream flowing from the direction of Corbalton Hall, on exiting the mill the tailrace fell into the Hurley River to the southeast of Macetown house. In 1854 Mary Flanagan occupied this mill and the annual rateable valuation was £20.

During the rebellion of 1798, it is reputed that the thousands of Croppies (Wexford Insurgent Column) who marched from Wexford

*The bridge on the old line at Rathfeigh (Hurley River)*

did so along the route of the old road. They supposedly came from Summerhill through Culmullin and camped for a while to the southwest of Dunshaughlin. They then marched to the east and joined the said road near Curragha (Curraha), from there they continued northwards through Rathfeigh, Somerville and Slane to Knightstown bog, near Wilkinstown, where they set up camp. Folklore tells of treachery and how local gentry betrayed the Croppies – of a battle being fought on Knighstown bog and of how the greatly depleted column later returned along the same route to be defeated in a battle at Ballyboughill in County Dublin. Many tales are told of various skirmishes and military confrontations of the times and the great number of Croppy graves throughout County Meath, but as my space is limited I cannot delve further into these events. The subject is covered, however, in a book entitled *March into Meath* by Eamon Doyle and published in 1997 by Duffry Press, Enniscorthy, Co' Wexford.

As stated, the old line of the road from Dublin through Black Lion crossroads and onwards through Slane and Ardee was but part of the much longer route from Dublin to Derry. The Taylor and Skinner map shows that the distance in Irish miles from Dublin to Slane was 24 miles, to Ardee 33 miles and from Ardee to Derry 79 miles and 6 furlongs – the total distance between the cities being 112 miles 6 furlongs and the route via Drogheda was longer by 1½ Irish miles. An Irish mile comprised of 2240 yards and fourteen statute miles equalled eleven Irish miles. The old route from Dublin to Slane being very different to the later day new line I will, therefore, give a brief description of the old section from Dublin to Ardee.

The starting point would appear to be in the vicinity of the present day Phibsborough, possibly between Doyle's Corner and the Mater Hospital; the map indicates No 1 milestone near this location. The old coach roads were measured from the gates of Dublin Castle, which accounts for the number one milestone being placed at Phibsborough, whilst on the Navan to Dublin turnpike it was set in Stoneybatter: the later post roads were measured from the G P O. In provincial towns and cities the early roads were marked from the Tholsell or market house. The route passed through Finglas then on through St Margarets where the No 6 milestone was located. No 7 stone was sited at a place named Chapelmidway, from here the route took the traveller to Kilsallaghan and the No 8 stone. For this area the Taylor and Skinner map includes an interesting note, which reads: *The proposed road through commons of Kilsallaghan is four furlongs shorter than Chapelmidway & Greenoge.* The map shows both routes, including two number nine milestones and a rather cryptic note, which reads: *Pass if you can.* Crossing into County Meath, the old route passed through Greenoge, Robartstown, Archerstown and onwards to Curragha, the location of milestone No 14. The route continued on to Kilmoon where a forked road to the right led northeastwards to Duleek and Drogheda, this was once part of the route from Dublin to Drogheda. The left branch continued on by Windmill Hill and on past the junction for Screen (Skryne), passed through Rathfeigh (not marked on this map) and on to Black Lion (Black Lyon) crossroads and the previously described Inn at No 19 milestone.

Crossing the line of the Trim to Drogheda road, the great road to the north entered the Somerville Demesne and ran across 'the long causeway' (or long ford) to Flemingstown (Flemington) Bridge where it crossed the River Nanny. Continuing northwards through the estate it linked with the road from Navan at a "T" junction to the west of Sommerville House, then came to another 'T' junction with a side road leading off to the east; the remains of which are known nowadays as *the gamekeeper's path*. Larkin's Map shows that in times past this long gone road was part of the line of the main route from Navan to Duleek: leaving Somerville, it ran eastward through Mullafin (old) crossroads and on towards Duleek. Within Sommerville Demesne, on the western section of this road, Larkin's Map shows a little hamlet located down a laneway to the north and names it Logmuck; which name translates to the hollow of the pigs or pig's hollow. Local legend says that this was likely the servant's quarters for the Sommerville estate. The 1837 OS map shows only part of this old road, which indicates that by then it was defunct as the line of the Navan to Duleek route – this map also indicates the old RIC Barracks located on the route of *the gamekeeper's path* through the demesne. An interesting point about this old road is that it linked with the road running northwards from Mullafin towards the old ford on the Boyne at Rossnaree – perhaps this once formed part of the ancient route between Tara and Brugh na Boinne.

The new line of the Navan to Duleek road is indicated on the 1837 OS map. This runs from beside the RC church in Kentstown, skirts Somerville Demesne and crosses the new line of the Dublin to Slane road (now the N2) at Brien's Cross (Curtises's Cross). From there it ran eastwards and joined the old line near Gaskinstown – which is much the same line followed by the present day road. As this road is not shown on Larkin's Map, it would appear to have been cut during the period 1814 to 1834.

The old line of the great north road ran northwards from Somerville towards Rathdrina, passing through places where in later days Tully's brickyard and Farrell's sawmills stood near the roadside (Scahanassey road). Larkin's Map shows a hamlet in the vicinity of Scahanassey.

Constraints of time and space don't allow further detailed discussion of this route north to Ardee, so I will make but a brief reference to its onward passage. The Taylor and Skinner map shows the road crossing the bridge at Slane but the strip map has a division in the village, which makes deciphering the route a very difficult task. The No 24 milestone is shown near the crossroads in Slane. The continuation of the map indicates that the route split just north of the village and alternative roads were apparently used from here to Ardee. The more westerly route led through a place named Grange Fortescue (perhaps later named Newtown Fortescue?) and on past Druncondra (Drumconrath) to Ardee. The easterly and slightly longer route ran through Collon then linked with the other road about a half-mile to the south of Ardee. Both roads have milestones shown along the route, starting with No 25 to the north of Slane and with No 33 shown where the routes rejoin near the junction of the Kell's road on the outskirts of Ardee.

An interesting feature in the topography at time of writing is that milestones line the route north to Drumconrath, from the junction at the Slane castle gates on the Navan to Slane road. These are triangular shaped columns, much larger than the rectangular milestones used on the Dublin to Navan turnpike road, but are similar to the stones on the old section of road from Dublin to Slane and the branch road from Kilmoon to Duleek. Some of their locations don't appear to be spaced at intervals of one Irish mile which might suggest that they were shifted during the years; I counted seven of these stones along this section of road between the castle gates and Drumconrath. A milestone, possibly the one shown on the westerly route on the T&S map and near a crossroads named Drakestown, at time of writing reads Dublin 30, Slane 8 and Collon 3. On the same road and further south towards Slane another stone reads Dublin 29, Slane 7, Drumcondra 2 and Carricmacross 9. This sequence of numbered milestones seems to coincide closely with the milestones shown on the Taylor and Skinner maps.

Flemingstown Bridge is the most tangible link with the section of the old road that ran through Somerville. In his book *The Dublin to Navan road and Kilcarn Bridge,* Peter O'Keefe mentions this bridge, the following are some direct quotations:

*This bridge is located on an abandoned section of the old Slane Road in the former Somerville estate. It spans the river Nanny. My interest in the bridge began several years ago when searching to see if the isolated bridge at Balrath clearly marked on the Down Survey maps had survived, moreover, I had come across many Grand Jury mentions of the bridge as follows:*

*Summer Assizes 1760 "Item 43, whether £8.2.5d. be raised for repairs…. To the bridge over the long ford on the Nanny water at Flemingstown on the great road from Slane to Dublin… Will require 40 perches of masonry @ 4s. a perch and raise the battlements being very dangerous for carriage and passengers" note "work done, money recd".*

*Assizes 1775, County at large, item 129, "whether £45.2.5d. be raised as before and paid to J.L. Somerville and Robt. Rice to cope the battlements of the bridge at the long ford at Flemingstrown with Ardbracken stone, 637 ft. with iron Dowels @ 2s.5d. a perch and £2.15.6d. wages* (sic).

### Additional notes by Peter O'Keefe:

*This is the only mention of Ardbracken stone I found amongst thousands of Grand Jury items that I scanned.*

*I did not record all later presentments verbatim but noted the following:*

*Lent Assizes 1807 Item 322. £9 for battlements. Summer Assizes 1812 Item 80 " We present £107.17.4d. to be raised as before and paid to Sir Marcus Somerville, John Price and Ben Carroll to build an addition to the bridge on the land of Somerville, on the road from Slane to Dublin overseer's wages £5.8.0d, Amount £113.5.4d.   In Lent Assizes1812, Item 21 provided for two extra arches and Item 94 in 1819 for an extra arch* (sic).

Peter O'Keefe concludes the article on Flemingstown Bridge as follows:

*I went to see the bridge a few years ago and found it had a main arch 14'3" span followed by a 5'6" pier then an 11'span arch followed by two smaller ones covered with briars etc. Arches 2. 3 and 4 are silted up to the springings. The river arch is 24' long consisting of a 17'3" downriver original and a 5'9" extension. There is no joint in the smaller arches. The bridge matches the presentments. The parapets are 4' high and coped and dowelled. Fig. 16 shows the downriver springings of arches 1 and 2. The name Somerville appears very frequently as Grand Jurors and trustees of turnpikes. The Slane Mail coach*

*Road followed a new alignment from 1815. The river is in a boggy level valley about 200 yards wide, hence long ford* (sic).

There is little I can add to this excellent description of the old bridge. The crossing still stands in the swampy valley of the Nanny water, but has largely faded from public awareness. I'm unsure of how old the original part of the bridge is, or who the builder was, but if it's the bridge shown on the Down Survey map the structure predates the 1640s. Because of the small scaling and no roads being marked on this map, it's difficult to be sure whether the bridge depicted is the Flemingstown crossing or the nearby bridge at Ballymagarvey. A ford or wooden bridge probably preceded the stone bridge at Flemingstown; note the reference to the long ford or causeway.

The meeting point of the old and new lines of the Trim/Drogheda road is known in local folklore as Kane's Cross. I believe this old name derives from the story of a local man named Kane, who on being tried in Trim Assizes was deported to Van Dieman's land for some 'heinous crime', such as stealing a turnip to feed his starving family.

In the years between 1803 and 1810, William Larkin, originator of Larkin's Map, was involved in surveying many road realignments around the country, including the section from Kane's Cross to Kentstown village. This was a relatively short stretch of less than a mile and involved a crossing of the Nanny water. It would seem to have been constructed in the period between 1817, the date when Larkin's Map was published, and 1837, as it's not shown on the former map but appears on the later OS map. I suspect it was part of a much larger road scheme and was built to link the new line from Kentstown to Navan with the Trim/Drogheda road at Kane's Cross. This new route (previously mentioned in chapter 15) is shown on Larkin's Map and is about five miles in length. The new line was cut from beside the later day R.C. church in Kentstown, through Brownstown and Follistown, forming new crossroads at Brownstown and Alexander Read (Casey's Cross). Larkin's Map shows the old line of this road, which ran from a forked junction south of the present day Casey's Cross, northeastwards towards Harristown hill (marked Gorse Hill on this map). It turned eastwards at a 'T' junction near the bottom of Harristown hill, (named on the 1837 map as *The Cross*) and ran eastwards across

Left: *Milestone '30' on road between Slane and Drumconrath*
Right: *Sean Finnegan and his Quern*

Realtoge (Realtogue), then through Brownstown and into Kentstown. As mentioned, this road linked with the little road running from Ranaghan through Danestown and up the minister's hill. Yet another example of how the roads of olden times ran along the high ridges and not in the valleys as in later years. On this stretch of road, near Realtoge, the 1837 OS map shows a place named *the beggars seat*, but that's definitely a story for another day.

The short section of new road runs through the woods from Kane's Cross, passes by the lion's mouth fountain, then crosses the Nanny on a four arched stone bridge at the bottom of the minister's hill. The 1837 OS map indicates the new road passing through a large gravel pit to the south of the later location of the fountain. From the bridge it ran on to form a new crossroads by Kentstown R.C. church. Nowadays this is part of the main road from Navan to Ashbourne via Balrath crossroads. The aforementioned byroad, running from Ranaghan and through Danestown 'new crossroads', uses the same bridge to cross the Nanny. I'm unsure of the construction date of this bridge, but as it's orientated to the line of the new road, it was most likely built when the new section was cut in the early years of the 19th century. The bridge has some remarkable features, including its road width and the flattened tops of the arches, which feature minimised the bumps on the road's surface.

Mention of the minister's hill reminds me of an interesting discovery I made while doing some research in the area. Sean Finnegan, a well-known member of the Kentstown pipe band and a prominent local historian, lives across the road from the 'T' junction at the top of the minister's hill. Part of his farmyard consists of some old stone buildings, local legends say that an ancient castle stood on the site long ago – supposedly this was the birthplace of St. Oliver Plunkett's mother. Several years ago, while digging in the farmyard, Sean unearthed the remains of an old rotary quern, or hand operated corn mill. It was broken into two main portions and a small triangular piece was missing, otherwise the stone basin was in good condition with four equally spaced holes drilled through the base. I thought it was a pity that such an ancient relic was broken, but folklore explains the possible reason for this. Seemingly, an ancient pagan tradition involved the burial of such querns as an offering to their gods following a bountiful harvest. The old pagans were considered by modern Christians to be misguided because they supposedly believed a quern to be a sacred object, possession of which symbolised great power. Nonetheless, the old heathens were pretty crafty: lest some of their neighbours visited the burial site and dug up the quern for their own use, they ceremoniously broke the stone basin thus rendering it useless.

The *lion's mouth* is a well-known roadside fountain and is so named because a stream of spring water issues from the mouth of a lion carved from stone. It's built on the eastside of the new road but derives its water from the famous Trinity Well, which was a pagan place of worship in former days and is located in the woods on the other side of the road near Danestown Rath and old churchyard. St Patrick supposedly spoiled their fun by sanctifying its waters when journeying to Tara to meet the High King. If only a fraction of these stories are true, the good Saint must have been exhausted by the time he reached Tara, because most parishes in County Meath have similar folklore. Maybe the signposting was equally bad in those times and he took the scenic route?

The inscription on the wall of the fountain reads: "Erected by the right

*Lion's Mouth Fountain-*

Honb! Sir Wm. Somerville, Bart 1855" (sic). Some local legends say that the fountain was erected to provide drinking water for the horses during hunting but the cynical say it was built to discourage worship at the ancient well. I have been unable to ascertain whether this means Christian or pagan worship. Another anecdote tells of how a figurine of some pagan god was found in the nearby woods. In the swampy woodlands behind the fountain and on the banks of the Nanny is a place known to some locals as *the trooper's hole*, because in times past a mounted trooper was reputedly sucked into the mire and swallowed by quicksand, together with his horse. Perhaps he was one of the soldiers of King James's army, which reputedly retreated through here following its defeat at the Battle of the Boyne in 1690.

Heading eastwards from McAuley's grassmeal factory the road starts a gradual descent into the valley of the Nanny water. In former days the northern side of the route was heavily wooded, thus obscuring the view across the valley towards Somerville house. In times past, part of this section of road was known as 'the ghosty corner', supposedly because a local man had died in the nearby woods while hunting rabbits. At time of writing, the woods have all but vanished and now there's an unobstructed view across the glen. A short distance east of the old Blacklion crossroads the only trace of the old name for the district can be seen, a local shop and service station being named the Blacklion. The proprietor of this establishment is a member of the Bowen's family, the last occupants of the former old Inn.

At the bottom of the descent and to the right of the road is Ballymagarvey church and graveyard. This is an ancient site dating back to medieval times. The church, now in ruins, is mentioned in the Civil Survey of 1654/56 as being an old church and during Bishop Dopping's visits (1682-1685) it was reported as being in ruinous condition since 1641. Nowadays the site is beautifully maintained and provides a great vista across the valley.

*Ballymagarvey graveyard and the ruins of the medieval church*

This view is greatly enhanced by the triple arched Ballymagarvey stone bridge carrying the Trim to Drogheda road across the Nanny close by the entrance gate. The Grand Jury presentment book of 1810 shows a presentment in the Lent Assizes by Rt'ble M. Sommerville, Thos' Osborne, Richard O'Brien and a man named Carroll for the building of an addition to Ballymagarvey Bridge.

Ballymagarvey House stands to the south of the old church and its rear entrance is accessed via the old churchyard lane – nowadays the front avenue leads from the N2. Larkin's Map shows the entry from the churchyard lane and some buildings are depicted on the site, the townland is named Ballymagarvey but no name is given to the house. The 1911 OS map shows some interesting details of the house and its surroundings. The only entrance shown is from the churchyard lane, no front avenue is indicated, though a lodge is shown close by the River Nanny and alongside the main road (now the N2). So it would seem that the present day grand entrance was built sometime in the interim period.

The house, which forms the southeastern corner of a quadrangle, is built on the southernmost slopes of the valley and commands a vista across the pastoral landscape of the Nanny water. To the west the scene is framed by the Knockcommera woods, this area is shown on Larkin's Map as Glebeland. At time of writing the woodland is known as Balrath woods, which provide nature trails for visitors. The quadrangle is reminiscent of a barrack's square or parade ground and slopes in a series of terraces towards the ancient churchyard. Immediately to the rear of the house a space within the enclosing buildings was occupied by a large kitchen garden, which supplied the needs of the establishment in times past. In olden times the estate was a self-sufficient entity, consisting of meadowlands, cornfields, woodlands and blue flowered fields of golden flax. The aforementioned quadrangle of stone buildings comprised inter alia the main house and farmyard, houses for the workers, lofted granaries, stables, a mill and a Smithy. I'm told that the water driven mill ground corn and may have been used for scutching flax.

The mill was located on the northwestern corner and overlooked the Nanny. Though powered by a waterwheel, there was no substantial river on the high ground above the valley to supply the millrace. Research shows that the water supply was obtained by draining the surrounding land – the gathered water being channelled through stone drains, known as 'box shores', to a millpond located to the northwest of the mill. The pond can be seen on the OS map of 1911 and if the map is closely studied traces of the headrace can be seen leading towards the mill at the corner of the quadrangle. The course of the tailrace can be traced on this map; it ran alongside the original entrance avenue and fell into the River Nanny to the east of the old churchyard immediately downstream of Ballymagarvey Bridge. I believe that during recent restoration work, many of the old stone shores were unearthed, together with some large stone built water storage cisterns.

Both house and farm buildings appear to have been constructed around 1800 and the first owner of the estate was named Mrs Osbourne, whom I

*Ballymagarvey Bridge*

believe was a member of the Protestant ascendancy of the time. Note the previous reference to Thomas Osborne in connection with building an extension to Ballymagarvey Bridge in 1810. The estate changed ownership many times over the years – some of the other owners/occupiers being as follows: Stuart Balfour (a Scottish scientist), Cloussons, Crocketts, Nobles, McCanns (millers), Leggetts (who reputedly ran a finishing school for young ladies on the premises), Captain Maguire (a noted veterinarian), and a German named Andre. The only one of these I knew was Captain Maguire: who drove an old 1930s car, if I recall correctly it was a Rover, on which I worked several times whilst employed in Navan Engineering Works in the 1960s.

At time of writing, Ballymagarvey House has been restored as a folk heritage village and is being used to host wedding events. Apparently the house was reconstructed and extended several times during different periods of its previous occupancies, which accounts for the differing levels and types of construction evident in its profile. A battlemented tower was added at some time, local historians say that this may have been built as a decorative feature for the visit of King George IV – who was supposedly a great lover of such features and drove along this road on his journey to Slane in 1821. In recent times a great deal of expense and much effort was put into restoring the house and the farmyard with its associated stone buildings: to the front, the stone bridged haw-haw presents a pleasant aspect of what the house looked like in times past. Overall, the carefully executed restoration of such a unique location is nice to see in the Ireland of today, where so much emphasis is placed on destroying many features from our past.

Travelling eastwards from Ballymagarvey and crossing the bridge, our road runs a few hundred yards before meeting the new line of the Dublin to Slane road at Balrath crossroads. For reasons explained in the next chapter, this road is known as *the King's road*.

# 17

# The King's Road,
# Balrath Cross and Journey's End

King George's Road – Ashbourne – Kilmoon to Duleek turnpike –
Balrath Crossroads, Water Mill and Windmill – Millstones – The White
Cross and Athcarne Castle – The Well and Bridge of the Deenes – The
Croppy Thorn and Morgan's curse.

The new line of road from Dublin through Ashbourne was partly designed by William Larkin, with the survey being completed about 1810 and the road cut and opened by 1815. In its day the routing of the road was the subject of some controversy. Known as the King's road or the straight road in local legends, which say that the Prince, later to be crowned King George IV, had the road realigned so that he could more rapidly visit his lover, Lady Conyngham in Slane. Like many such legends, this particular yarn doesn't stand up under close scrutiny, as the Prince (by then King George IV) apparently visited Slane for the one and only time in 1821, six years after the route was opened. There is some substance to the story however, and, like the previously mentioned intrigue with the passage of the realigned roads through Dowdstown, there appears to be considerable evidence that a similar situation prevailed on this stretch of new road. For the area around Somerville, all the shenanigans and political manoeuvrings resulted in the Slane road bypassing the demesne and new road lines forming part of the estates' perimeter.

While reading Peter O'Keefe's book *The Dublin to Navan Road and Kilcarn Bridge,* I found the following most informative references to the Dublin/Slane road. Hopefully this throws more light on some of the darker aspects of those long gone days.

**Extract from Appendix 172 pp. 752-755 of the 19th Report of the Commission of Revenue Inquiry C1929 x11. Evidence of William Duncan one of the ablest of the PO Engineers, 29 Oct. 1823.**

"Q. Had the Dublin to Drogheda road been completed according to the plan given in? No they abandoned that plan and have gone by the line I surveyed to Slane. It was not intended that the Slane road should be that to Drogheda, but to go by Monaghan (the London Derry line) but Messers. Bourne have stuck out a road for which they have got private presentments, not at all from the Post Office, that branches off and goes to Drogheda. Q. Is that a deviation below Ashbourne? It is. Then the public money has never been advanced on any part of that road? Only as far as from Dublin to Slane. Q. Did you set out the survey from Dublin to Slane? A. No, one part of it was surveyed by Mr. Larkin; I took up his survey. Q. Is the road to Ashbourne laid out according to Mr. Larkin's survey? A. Yes. Q. Has it been constructed according to your survey from Ashbourne to Slane? A. Yes I believe so; there was some part near the Boyne I did not put in execution but all the rest, as far as it was a new line, they carried into effect. Q. Did your survey in that direction extend beyond the Boyne? A. We went to the village of Slane, but we could do nothing there, for we were enclosed within domains of the Marquis of Conyngham; that would require great alteration. Q. It goes up a steep hill there? Yes, we proposed filling up of the bridge and some improvements of the hill. Q. Has there been any P.O. survey of the Mail Coach road still further north? A. Yes, there has been to Londonderry by Mr. Larkin; with respect to the road to Drogheda there was a line of road suggested by Lord Oriel, then Mr. Foster; He was anxious to keep to that line; I surveyed that also, but there seemed to be a predilection for going off more to the left, which

I did, but they have left that and gone off to Slane" (sic).

**Additional note by Peter O'Keefe:**

"Section 22 of the 1792 Post Road Act prescribed that no Grand Jury could present for any new road to be laid or any old road widened through or into any demesne or deer-park without the consent of the owner being first obtained in writing under his hand. This was mitigated somewhat by the 1805 act. The ink was scarcely dry on the print before an amendment was introduced in the following year, Section 9 of 46 G3, c 134 making the prohibition more embracing than ever by adding any field enclosed within a wall of lime and stone or brick, on or through any planted lawn or avenue or orchard planted before 17 May 1805, without the owners consent. This explains the failure to find a better line through Slane and probably much of the mystery surrounding the improvements at Dowdstown including the abandonment of the old road from the Hill of Tara to the Old Mill upriver of Kilcarn Bridge" (sic). *End of quotations from Peter O'Keefe.*

The notes from the inquiry of 1823 indicate that some political intrigue was involved in both the planning and routing of the road. From my readings and research on the matter it would seem that the finger of blame in the ancient legend is pointing in the wrong direction. John Foster of Collon (Lord Oriel) was very influential in politics and was the speaker of the Irish House of Parliament from the 1780s until 1800. In the early part of the 19th century, about 1803, he was the Irish Chancellor of the Exchequer, hence had his fingers on the purse strings, so to speak – he took a keen interest in road developments and William Larkin was reputed to be one of his proteges. Foster lived in the family demesne in Collon, therefore had a vested interest in the road being developed through that area. In 1801, upon the Act of Union disbanding the Irish House of Parliament, a trip to London was required for Irish members to attend sittings at the *Mother of Parliaments* – perhaps this provided a more substantial reason for the road realignment, than the King's tryst with his lover in Slane.

My own research of the Grand Jury presentment books uncovered the following most revealing and informative presentment to the Summer Assizes of 1815 – this was listed as item 233 and reads:

*We present £5,799,, 12,, 2 for making 2300 1/3 Perches of a new mail coach road from Dublin to Slane at the request of the Post Masters General between the Rath of Crickst'wn in the Barony of Rathtoath & Patt. Byrnes avenue in Elm Grove in the Lower Bar'y of Duleek in this county to be levied in twelve successive payments of £.483,, 6,, off the County at Large & off the several Baronies through which the said new road is to run according to the following proportions / vey County at large £.232,, 16,, 7 ½. Ratoath £.41,, 16,, 9 – Upper Duleek £.82,, 19,, 6½ - Skreen £.50,, 18,, 2 – Lower Duleek £.74,, 12,, 11 – making in the whole the sum of £.483,, 6, 0 – and we present that the said sum of £.483,, 6,, 0 being the first instalment of the said sum of £.5,799,, 12,, 2 be now part of the levy and that a similar sum be put on the levy at each subsequent Assizes until the entire sum of £.5,799,, 12,, 2 shall have been raised, and that Sir M. Sommerville B't. Ph Gorges Gus't Lambert, Fred'k & Rich'd Bourne Esq & John Clare be appointed overseers for carrying on said work into effect* (sic).

This presentment is unusually detailed and is the most informative I noted in thousands of presentments for road improvements reviewed during my research. As such it provides an excellent insight into the workings of the Grand Jury system and its methods of levying for road development during this period. The measurements were in Irish perches or 'long perches' (7 yards) – at 320 perches per mile, the distance claimed for equals 9.11 statute miles. Which represents a construction cost of £634 per mile of road – an enormous sum of money for the times, considering the new road was built through relatively flat terrain with no major engineering works required or main rivers to cross. The location of this section of road can be established fairly accurately by scaling the distances given in the presentment of 1815 onto a modern Discovery map. The record states that the section of new mail coach road was to be cut from the Rath in Crickstown (Crickst'wn in the presentment – nowadays *The Rath Cross* near Ashbourne) towards Slane for a distance of 2300 perches or 9.11 statute miles. This took the new line (now the N2) on past the aforementioned gamekeeper's path in Sommerville, through what is nowadays known as Brien's Cross – the new line rejoined the original path of The Great North Road at Rathdrina (Rathdrinagh), thereby forming a forked junction. This road junction became known in later years as The Pump. Elm Grove does not show on Larkin's Map (1812/1817) or the OS maps, but is indicated on Thomson's Map, Beaufort's Map (1797) and J. Taylor's Map of 1802 (these maps appear to originate from the same source)- the place name is shown on the said maps in the area of the later day forked junction at Rathdrina: together with a small grove of trees, which may be the source of the name Elm Grove. Although the place name seems to have fallen into disuse during the early 1800s, I'm informed that several people named Byrne live in the locality – perhaps these are descendants of Pat (t) Byrne, whose Avenue was used as a landmark for the construction of 'The King's Road' all those years ago?

It would seem that the road was completed and opened by the end of 1815 and started its life as a free road. The enabling legislation to transform the Dublin to Ashbourne road into a turnpike, or tollroad, was passed in 1827 (this possibly also covered the road to Slane and from there to Drogheda). It became one of only four privately operated tollroads in Ireland. The name of the operator for the Dublin to Ashbourne section was Mr. Frederick Bourne and the expiry date of his contract 1848. In 1832 the annual profit for the section was £1025. 8s. 4d. In the inquiry of 1823 a mention was made of Messers. Bourne being involved in the planning and construction of the road: this being a reference to the famous Bourne Brothers, Frederick and Richard, who later operated the tollroad. I note that when the new route was opened in 1815, no place named Ashbourne existed along its line. Larkin's Map of 1812-1817 does not show such a place name, but as it was mentioned in the inquiry in 1823 the name seems to have been created in the period 1817 to 1823. The location of the village is between the townlands of Milltown and Little Baltrasna (the place of the crossing), both of which appear on Larkin's Map, about one mile to the northwest of Greenoge. The section of new road, from Finglas to Rathdrina, where it rejoined the old route, appears to be an entirely new line, except for a short stretch between Ashbourne and the junction for Curraha where it appears to have run along the old line. The crossroads (now a roundabout) to the south of Ashbourne was known locally for many years as *the nine mile stone*. This name probably derives from the milestone placed on the new line – the number nine milestone on the old line was located about a mile to the east near Greenoge. Note my mention in the previous chapter of the T&S map showing two number nine milestones on the old line(s) of the road near Greenoge. A local legend tells of how Ashbourne derived its name. This says that a man named Bourne once planted an ash tree at the spot and named the place after the tree and his surname. One might wonder if this man was Frederick Bourne.

Griffith's valuation reports of 1854 have some interesting entries concerning the passage of the new road through the area of Kentstown and Balrath. Four mentions appear in that year, as follows: Under Balrath it names Messers. Edward Hogan and Thomas Flood as Occupiers and the trustees of the turnpike road as Lessors. Under Descriptions of Tenements it names 'The trustees of the Dublin & Slane Turnpike road', tolls of, (240 lineal perches) and goes on to show that the annual rateable valuation was £2. 0s. 0d.. There are similar entries, with the same names as Lessors and Lessees, for Ballymagarvey (R.V. £2), Flemingstown (R.V. £2. 5s.) and Tuiterath (R.V. £2. 5s.), with the distances being 230, 272 and 264 lineal perches respectively. Note the use of the word lineal instead of linear, the compilers were possibly distinguishing between the cubic perch (24 cubic feet) and a linear perch which was 5.5 yards (statute). It is difficult to know what exactly these entries mean, but I would suggest that they cover the new line of the road through the parish of Kentstown and show that it was a turnpike road then. The names of Hogan and Flood as occupiers might further suggest it was a privately operated tollroad and that they were either the operators, or agents for same.

The section of road from Dublin to Ashbourne was once part of the Dublin to Dunleer Mail Coach Road via Duleek and Drogheda. Some say it was opened around 1800/1802 as an alternative to the other tollroad via Balbriggan, but the statement in the enquiry of 1823 that: *Messers. Bourne have stuck out a road for which they have got private presentments, not at all from the Post Office, that branches off and goes to Drogheda*, (Kilmoon through Duleek) might suggest it was opened around 1815 and operated

*The old tollhouse (turnpike) at Kilmoon cross*

as a private tollroad. Supposedly, this route was operated in competition with this older route – some of the triangular shaped milestones are sited along the road from Kilmoon to Duleek at time of writing. Local legends tell of the milestones on the turnpike road, from Dublin to Drogheda via Duleek, being placed at distances greater than one mile – to deceive travellers into believing that the route was shorter than other tolled roads to Drogheda. The turnpike, or tollhouse, still stands at Kilmoon crossroads (on the old line opposite the road to 'the Snailbox') and the turnpike road ran through 'the Bolies' (Boolies), passed by the old staging post known as 'the Buildings' and across the River Nanny. 'The Buildings' is shown as the post office on the 1837 OS map. The Duleek bypass was possibly build after 1817 and prior to 1837, as it's not shown on Larkin's Map but appears on the 1837 OS map. Another turnpike house was located at Carranstown on the Drogheda road near the graveyard outside Duleek and is still standing at time of writing. Which suggests that the final stretch of the Trim/Drogheda road was a tollroad post 1815, with the tollhouse for the section being at Carranstown. This turnpike road was in operation in 1842, as evidenced by the writings of W.M. Thackery, who gave an account of his journey along this route in 1842.

The intersection of the Trim to Drogheda road and the new line of the Dublin to Slane road via Ashbourne formed Balrath crossroads. Balrath translates to *the place of the fort* and is located about a mile to the east of the former Black Lion crossroads. In previous days Balrath was a straight through crossroads, but at time of writing it's staggered. Some confusion can occur here as the name Balrath Cross is sometimes used to describe an old Gothic stone late 16th century wayside cross standing beside the crossroads at Balrath. Supposedly this was one of seven such crosses erected alongside the road from here to Duleek by the Aylmer family: but inscriptions on some do not support this story. The Gothic Cross was relocated to the nearby Ballymagarvey cemetery in recent times, not to avoid the confusion of the wording, but to facilitate widening of the road. Two Victorian stone houses are located on the northeastern sector of the crossroads; one of these was once an old R.I.C. barracks. The other is the Post Office and said to be built on, or very close to, the site of Balrath castle, yet another *towerhouse of the Pale*. This was formerly home to the Aylmer family and reputedly destroyed during the rebellion of 1641.

Close by the crossroads, behind the Victorian houses, is an ancient embanked fort known as a Henge. This is possibly the fort from which Balrath derives its name.

Further east the road winds through an area shaded by high trees. On the left is a three-storied country manor-style house set in beautiful gardens and on the right is the ivy-covered ruin of an old building standing near the banks of the River Nanny. The latter is the remains of Balrath water mill, built in 1782. The house, constructed in 1780, or possibly earlier, was the home of the Walsh family who once owned and operated the mill. The headrace providing water to drive the sixteen feet diameter undershot millwheel derived its source from a weir within the Somerville Demesne. The water for the mill seems to have been supplied by the weir on the Nanny water and augmented by a little stream locally named the Bohernabreena River (Brien's road river), which rises to the northwest of the old school in Kentstown. In the past a network of sluices probably existed here, so that the water might be selected from either stream during varying river levels. At time of writing the smaller river falls into the Nanny and judging by the levels it's likely that the Bohernabreena River was the main source of water used to power Balrath mill. Both Larkin's Map and the 1837 OS map indicate the line of the headrace passing under the new road (the King's Road), then running behind the buildings on the corner, later the site of the Post Office and R.I.C. barracks. It passed beneath the road to Duleek then ran along the southside of this road and on to the

Left: *Millrace skewed bridge at Balrath crossroads.*
Right: *Alfred Wood's shoeing stone at the old smithy in* The Bolies

mill. The tailrace fell into the River Nanny a short distance to the east of the mill. Most traces of this old millrace have disappeared long since, but the twin skew-built stone arched bridges under the old line of the Duleek road and near the crossroads are still in situ. I suspect they won't last much longer, as some development work in the area is likely to lead to their destruction. The mill was a corn mill, which I'm told ground wheat meal and had a kiln for drying the grain. Griffith's valuation shows that in 1854 the property consisting of a house, offices, land and a corn mill was owned by Jane Walsh and had a rateable valuation of £70. 10s. 0d. The mill closed in 1902 and is now an empty shell with no obvious sign of its previous usage being evident to the many motorists passing by.

The Civil Survey of 1654/56 indicates that a water mill was located at Balrath in those days and local historians reckon that it could predate that time. They conclude that the Aylmer family probably owned the mill in its earlier years.

I visited the site recently and was able to enter the building and walk within its ancient walls; which seem sound enough. Inside the remains of the old mill, I saw the birds flitting in and out of the empty window frames and into the dense ivy to their hidden nests. The incessant roar of heavy traffic on the nearby 'King's road' muted the music of the birdsong and I scarcely heard any sound from the River Nanny flowing nearby. Standing there amidst the remnants of the past I could imagine the thumping and splashing of the ancient wheel and the rumbling of the grinding stones, then the realisation dawned upon me that, like in the mills at Rathnally and Bective, these activities and sounds are gone forever. Leaving the scene and passing close to the old Acacia tree standing in front of the mill, I reflected once more on the meaning of the word progress and wondered where it was taking us.

On a happier note, one of the former millstones from this old watermill can be seen nearby – where it was used for many years as a shoeing stone by the well-known Blacksmith, Alfred Woods, at his forge in the Boolies.

About one hundred yards to the east of the derelict watermill a small road branches off to the left. The road leads northwards towards Mullafin (fair or white summit) and runs parallel to the new line of the Dublin to Slane road. To the left of this road stands the old tower mill or windmill of Balrath, which, at time of writing, has been converted to a modern dwelling. Some local legends say that the Walsh family built the windmill in 1780 to help with their burgeoning business at the watermill. Local historians suggest that it was built slightly later, about 1805 and the increase in business was possibly created by the Napoleonic wars. The structure is 46 feet in diameter at the base and 80 feet in height; it tapers to 12 feet at the top. Four lofted floors constituted the machinery spaces and granary and a turret held the sails and wind driven shafting. The miller could rotate the turret to take advantage of the varying wind directions. Local history says that the mill machinery was damaged by a windstorm on 'Oiche an Gaoithe Mor', the night of the Big Wind in 1839. Supposedly the four twenty foot sails (40 feet total diameter) broke their anchors and overspeeded, thus causing the machinery to overheat. Some say that the interior of the building was totally destroyed by fire at this time

There are varying accounts of the date of the damage to the machinery: Cyril Ellison's aforementioned book states that it occurred in 1889, whilst other references say 1839; the latter date (1839) being the year of the legendary 'night of the Big Wind'. Griffith's valuation would appear to partly resolve this discrepancy. It shows that in 1854 Jane Walsh owned the windmill, which the valuation report shows to be vacant, with an annual rateable valuation of £5. 0s. 0d.. Had the windmill been in operation, it's doubtful that it would have attracted such a low valuation. This, though not conclusive, would suggest that the windmill was out of commission at the time and the date referenced in Cyril Ellisson's book was possibly a misprint. Local historians tell me, however, that folklore in the area says the windmill was in operation during the later years of the 19th century, though perhaps only used intermittently, and conclude that it ceased operation around 1903. It's possible that this date may be confused with the closure date of the watermill in 1902. During restoration of the windmill tower in recent years it was found that the upper loft containing the two millstones still existed – these stones were constructed from small segments of sandstone. Though the floor was in poor condition, it was strong enough to support the heavy grinding stones, which were removed and redeployed. One is now being used as the base for a sundial and the other as a doorstep for the mill building. The fact that the wooden loft was still partly intact and there being no evidence of a major fire, would tend to conflict with local legends stating that the interior of the mill was totally destroyed by fire on the night of the Big Wind all those years ago.

Segmented millstones were constructed from various sections of stone retained within shrunk-on iron hoops and dressed accordingly – in some places the segments of these millstones were known to millers as 'harps'. The most suitable and commonly used millstones for grinding grain into flour were generally named French burr stones and were of a light brown or tan colour. The base material was formed from sandstone, therefore very porous and more easily maintained and dressed. The raw material for these millstones was obtained mostly from the Marne district in northern France, hence the name French burr. The source stones were quarried in small sections and not available in sizes large enough to form a full sized millstone of about four foot six inches diameter – which accounted for the segmented construction of the millstones. I'm told that the millstone from the Balrath windmill was for grist and was not a flour stone. Because the millstone I saw was converted to form the baseplate for a sundial I could not observe the type of drive mechanism used, but it appeared to be different to the millstones driven by waterwheels. Larkin's map shows a depiction of the windmill at Balrath and indicates the watermill by the standard cogwheel symbol.

The next junction on the road towards Duleek is to the right and leads across Nanny Bridge to the ancient church at Timoole (Tymoole), then onwards to join 'the King's road' at 'the new bridge' near Rathfeigh. Further on, a cul de sac leads off to the left to Gaulstown House. About a

*Balrath house - former home of Jane Walsh who owned Balrath corn mills in 1854*

kilometre to the east we come to a small crossroads, where stands Athcarne Cross, more commonly known as the White Cross, which gives its name to the district. This is another of the wayside Gothic Crosses sited along the stretch of road, the engraved plaque on the structure states that the cross was erected in 1675 for Sir Luke Bathe by his wife, Dame Cecilia Dowdall of the nearby Athcarne castle. Cecilia Dowdall was a member of the Dowdall family of Athlumney castle near Navan. The little road to the right, opposite the cross, leads to the site of the ancient castle while the road to the left is a cul de sac leading to a place named Sneeoge (Sniogue), meaning a small stream. The White Cross gave its name to local clubs over the years, one of these was the Duleek Cycling Club known as the White Cross Club; in 1969 an ex club member, Brian Connaughton, won *An Ras Tailteann*. This was the last year in which I competed in the race before departing to take up my seagoing career.

Leaving the area of the famous cross, we pass the short cul de sac to the left leading to Reask, then head eastwards again and come to our journey's end at the well of the Deenes. There are several versions of this place name, on Larkin's Map and the Down Survey it's spelled Deanes and on the Civil Survey and the modern Discovery map it's shown as Deenes. O'Donovan's field notes on the townland state emphatically: "Not Danes, but Deenes" and quotes the following definition: "Fearenn a' Deinigh, Mr. Dean's land" (sic). So I'll let the reader make the choice.

Aside from the name, I always knew the place as the 'T' junction with the spring well under the road nearby, where we frequently stopped to

## Athcarne Cross

A wayside cross erected c 1675 for Sir Luke Bathe by his wife Dame Cecilia Dowdall who lived in Athcarne Castle. Renaissance and Baroque influences can be seen in the figure sculpture and decoration. The east face is dominate by a very large crucifixion figure with the arms raised directly above the head and the feet resting on the skull. The west face has a Virgin and a Child in a rounded niche. At the top of the shaft there is a shield depicting the implements of Christ's Passion with the Bathe and Dowdall arms below. Angels and Maltese crosses decorate the domed cap.

SOUTH EAST MEATH
1798
BICENTENARY COMMITTEE

FR. MacMANUS MEMORIAL

Peace be round the croppies' grave,
Peace to your souls ye buried brave,
Tara's Hill when crowned and free,
Had never nobler guests than ye!

Thomas D'Arcy McGee

Sponsored by SEAN CONNELL Duleek
Also SEAMUS O'NEILL OLIVER LEVINS
GERRY SMITH GERRY MARRY Duleek

NATIONAL GRAVES

slake our thirst with the lovely cold well water during our many cycling trips along the road to Duleek and Drogheda. Sometimes we turned right, crossed 'the bridge of the Deenes' over the Nanny and beside its junction with the Hurley River (Caman). Then passed through the Bolies or Boolies (the place of the cows) and on through Ardcath and the Four Knocks to Stamullen, where St. Patrick's Cycling Club ran grass track and road cycle races.

I'm not familiar with the history of the well, nor have I found many references to it in local folklore. In times past the road junction, like many others in the countryside in those times, was a place for social activities. Here people gathered of a summer's evening and sat on the low wall atop the well to watch the world pass by on the roads. But now it's vastly different, the well is almost totally overgrown and the very survival of its stone structure is threatened by traffic cutting across the corner, now it's definitely not a place for social interaction.

Here again we encounter stories about the Wexford men of '98 and their ill-fated march into Meath in July of that year, following the defeat at Vinegar Hill. A stone has been erected on the edge of the Trim to Drogheda road, just to the east of the well. It is called The Father McManus memorial. Local legends tell of the Croppies who were captured in the area of the Deenes and summarily executed nearby. Names such as Croppy Wood, the Croppy Thorn and the Croppy Field are spoken of in the area, as in many other places in the county. The Croppy Thorn being a name given to a hawthorn tree from which some of the rebels were supposedly

From top: *The White Cross, its inscription and the monument at the well of the Deenes*

*An early Feis at Navan showgrounds* (Courtesy D. Halpin)

hanged and which was shunned for years thereafter. Like the previously mentioned *hanging tree* in the Cluide Wood in Bellinter, the old tree stood on the spot for generations until it fell down in recent years, but some say another hawthorn is sprouting from its roots. Then there's the story of Morgan's curse, the tale of a young Wexford man who was betrayed by a local family named Morgan and shot by the military, then left for dead in a field. Some time later his widowed mother, who walked from Wexford in search of her son, found his remains being eaten by one of Morgan's sows: whereupon the aggrieved woman supposedly cursed Morgan and all his descendants. Reputedly, since those times anybody living on Morgan's farm has suffered from ill luck.

So ends our little journey along some of County Meath's ancient roads. Though I travelled these routes many times during the years and by various forms of transport, yet I never made the journey previously in a literary sense. Much lost history lies along these few short miles, some of which I have been able to portray, but no doubt a great deal more is hidden amongst the ditches and woodlands. Perhaps some still exists in the form of folklore buried deep in the psyche of the more aged residents. These I would urge to relate their stories to the younger generation in the changing times of contemporary Ireland – when so much of our folklore and heritage is being blown to shreds by the harsh winds of change scything through the land.

# Postscript

# Parallels of History and the M3

### Requiem for a Lost Landscape

The great famine came in the aftermath of a road-building splurge that took place in the period between circa 1790 and 1840. More recently, the huge extravagance of the Celtic Tiger years ended in the ignominious bursting of our ego bubble and financial disaster. The demise of our charging tiger could be likened to the fate that befell *Icarus*, a figure in Greek mythology who crashed into the sea and drowned when his waxen wings melted in the hot sun above Crete; but our *tiger's* paws' of wax melted in the overheated Irish economy and the sad beast perished in the maelstrom of *N.A.M.A* (*National Assets Management Agency*). The said N.A.M.A being yet another quango, a cosy little arrangement dreamt up by unelected advisers and appointed by government; whereby Irish taxpayers bailed out greedy reckless developers and bankers; and new buzz words, such as *Bad Banks* and *Toxic Assets,* were coined and added to our vocabulary. Whilst history records the results of the great hunger during the 1840s, one wonders how the latter saga will end ... the full story remains to be told by historians of the future, yet the portents are ominous at time of writing.

The expenditure of vast amounts of money and resources on construction of roads and public buildings in the years preceding the great hunger of 1845/1850 is oftentimes confused with famine relief works; that in 1847 forced an already starving population to earn a pittance of *Trevelayan's Corn* by performing public works which included building *roads to nowhere*. Charles Edward Trevelyan (1807-1886) was assistant secretary to the treasury in the Whig Government led by Lord John Russell, Duke of Bedford, who succeeded Robert Peel in 1846 and held office until 1852; which period included the worst years of the famine. Trevelyan was a devout Christian who professed to believe that famines were sent by God to prevent the lower orders from overpopulating the earth; not exactly the best credentials for a man charged with relief of famine in Ireland! As a footnote to history, it's somewhat ironic that the former Russell Arms Hotel and Bedford Place in Navan were named in honour of a prime minister whose government oversaw the near total extinction of Irish Cottiers by starvation and disease during the Great Famine.

Grand Jury records show that under the prevailing system, pre-famine public works were financed by the Baronies and not by crown or government grants, the money for these works being extracted from tenants by means of the county and Barony cess or tax; the poorer cottiers, therefore, had less resources available for food. The population increased and social conditions deteriorated greatly during this period, while the county and Barony cess increased six fold.... was this merely a coincidence? Though many other factors contributed to the disastrous famine, the relentless increase of the cess had a huge negative impact upon the largely agrarian population of the times; many being forced into dependence upon a single-crop diet i.e. the humble spud or potato. History records the dire effects of the great famine consequent to the persistent failure of this crop, and the impact these had upon the Irish psyche: the horror and deep sense of loss remaining indelibly imprinted on the national conscience and causing a long-term schism in Anglo-Irish relations.

Several factors provided the impetus for the massive road building schemes in the late 18th and early 19th centuries, including military, upgrading the main routes to post road standards and self-aggrandizement by members of the landed gentry and ascendancy. The widespread activities of *The United Irishmen* and other disaffected groups leading to the uprising of 1798, caused much consternation and shook the British Realm to its very core: leading to the construction of military roads such as those through the Sally Gap in Wicklow and from Glengarriff in Cork through the Catha Mountains and Turner's Rock Tunnel to Kenmare in Kerry. The primary purposes of these routes were to allow the swift movement of military columns to repel invasion and suppress unrest, not for provision of succour to the populace.

The motivation behind development of post roads was more complex, but some elements were provided by the increasing social unrest. Following the dissolution of the Irish Parliament in 1801, which practically caused disenfranchisement of the vast majority of the people, it was deemed necessary to expedite communications with London and the mother parliament; hence building and upgrading of post roads was accelerated. As shown in the various routes of the turnpike/post road through Dowdstown and construction of the Dublin to Derry post road through Somerville and Slane, local members of the gentry used their position on the Grand Jury to maximise the benefits of these routes in the vicinity of their demesnes. Thus it would seem that the humbler members of the populace were paying for their own military suppression, the system that spawned it and the self-aggrandizement of their oppressors! How much has changed since then?

But to whom can we assign responsibility for the squander-mania years of the Celtic Tiger, during which so much damage was done to our landscape? The Grand Juries are long gone as are the days of the British Realm – following many years of bitter struggle we supposedly shook off the greedy clutches and oppression of the English Crown: first passing through the twilight zone of civil war and dominion status before declaring ourselves to be an independent republic in 1948. Which events changed little besides the country's name; because corruption within our systems of governance was too firmly entrenched to relinquish its greedy grasp, as evidenced by the number of costly public enquires and tribunals in progress nowadays. It could be said that the long bitter struggle was in vain, as our period of independence was short lived indeed; our fickle allegiance being now sworn to the emerging wannabe European Empire. Politicians and administrators in the public service are ever swift in trumpeting their perceived successes from the rooftops, but are very tardy in admitting to mistakes or accepting responsibility for failures such as collapse of the national economy. The so-called Celtic Tiger era was a period of inflated national ego, a greed-fest unmatched by anything that had gone before. Unfortunately, during these short few years much of our ancient culture and intrinsic values disappeared along with great swathes of arable countryside, now despoiled by high-rise glass cages and unneeded motorways.

The old adage expressing the belief that: *those who do not learn from history are destined to repeat it*, seems particularly apt when applied to road developments in Dowdstown and its environs along the Gabhra Valley in 2008. Though the gentry of former days apparently had a squabble over control of the roads in the area and much intrigue took place in the early part of the 19<sup>th</sup> century, it was but a storm in a teacup compared to events unfolding at time of writing. Fortunately, in those earlier times the landscape didn't suffer unduly as a consequence, and the area retained its pastoral excellence until recent times. Now, two hundred years later, the circumstances surrounding planning and construction of the M3 motorway and its feeder roads through this area, so close to Tara, makes the renowned arch-schemer, Niccolo Machiavelli, look like an amateur, a mere *cute hoor* in relative terms. The ill-chosen route of the new road, the conniving, political intrigue, and utter contempt shown towards genuine concerns for the pastoral and historical uniqueness of the area are beyond belief.

Part of the supposed conniving and chicanery involved inter alia the alleged 'massaging' of archaeological reports on the number and quality of historical sites in the sensitive area of the Gabhra Valley and the general area close to Tara, including Dowdstown. Supposedly, the reports to the minister of the environment were deliberately falsified, and indicated a number less than the amount requiring the reassessment or abandonment of the motorway line through the area. It was alleged by some that the number of sites shown were much fewer than the *actual* number discovered in the field – in essence the report was supposedly rigged or, as expressed in naval terms, somebody *flogged the log*. This scenario emerged recently when a newspaper published an article by an archaeologist involved in compiling the said report; resulting in a public dispute ensuing between various other 'minders of our heritage'. The whole affair being concluded in an unseemly way, and the construction of the motorway made inevitable, when the said minister, fondly known as *motor mouth* or *jaws*, signed off on the enabling legislation just hours before finishing his term of office. The succeeding minister, a self professed green, washed his hands of the affair in Pontias Pilate fashion by declaring that his hands were tied because his predecessor had signed the legislation into effect – yes indeed, Machiavelli eat your heart out!

Our so-called leaders' lack of ability to learn the lessons of history is demonstrated by the financial debacle surrounding the construction and operation of the West Link Bridge, which carries the M50 across the River Liffey. This tollbridge was built under *public private partnership* (P.P.P.) contract in the early 1990s as part of a ring road around northwest and southwest Dublin City. In its early days the route provided relief from increasing traffic congestion, but it soon became a huge bottleneck because of the poorly designed toll plaza; which caused extreme frustration for hard-pressed motorists who, as they believed, were now paying tolls for the dubious privilege of sitting in an ever-lengthening traffic jam. About 2007, the government bought back the bridge from its owners, National Toll Roads (N.T.R.), making the route *barrier free* but certainly not *cost free*.

Recent reports in the *Irish Independent* newspaper, Aug-Sep 2009, reveal some startling and disturbing details of extraordinary ineptitude within the public service in their management of this ongoing saga. The newspaper featured various excerpts from The Comptroller and Auditor General's financial report for 2009, which might suggest that the government was extremely generous in its use of taxpayers's money on this project. Some of the items highlighted were as follows: that, because the original contract did not include a termination clause, it cost the state €600 million, plus the write off of a further €140 million in VAT to buyout the tollbridge. This represented very poor value for the Irish taxpayer and a huge windfall for the private sector company whose original investment was about €12 million – which, needless to say, it recouped several times over from tolls paid by motorists, who had few other options.

But this was not the end of the sorry saga – the National Roads Authority (N.R.A.), upon being handed control of the tollbridge, added insult to injury by raising the tariff circa 40%. Collection of the tolls being assigned to a private company, with almost draconian powers to pursue errant motorists who neglected to pay their dues on time. Following the changeover, the airwaves were filled with complaints from aggrieved motorists, some of whom were threatened with arrest without due process being served, and others, who had not used the bridge, receiving demands for services not supplied. The Comptroller's report stated that the N.R.A. estimated it would extract a further one *billion Euros* from motorists in the period between 2009 and 2020.

Under the headline, *Taxpayers will have to foot bill for M3 toll shortfall,* the same newspaper outlines yet another *cosy* little arrangement with a P.P.P. for the construction and operation of the M3 motorway through the heartland of County Meath. As space does not permit inclusion of the full article, the following is a synopsis: "**Taxpayers will have to compensate the operators of the controversial M3 motorway if the number of vehicles using it falls below target.**

It is understood this is the first time such a guaranteed minimum toll income has been agreed.

There will be downward pressure on the numbers using the M3, which opens early next year, because drivers could face €11.20-a-day in tolls and there will also be a new rail service to Navan.
The Dunboyne to Clonsilla leg of the rail link to Dublin opens next year, with the full line coming on stream in 2015.

The 'minimum traffic level clause' for the M3 was included in the contract for the €650m motorway through Co Meath. It means the State will have to pay the toll operators, Eurolink, compensation if traffic flows (predicted at 60,000 drivers per day) fail to meet the agreed minimum target. But the National Roads Authority (N R A) has not revealed what this target is. Labour transport spokesman Tommy Broughan warned the State might have to compensate Eurolink if planned rail services persuade drivers to abandon their cars.

"It seems to be running counter to what would be generally accepted public transport policy. From every point of view, it seems mad," he said. There is no such 'minimum traffic' agreement for another toll road operated by the same company – the Kinnegad-Kilcock section of the Dublin-Galway route.

The National Roads Authority said the minimum traffic target was "competitive" and was based on annual rather than on weekly or monthly traffic levels. But it said it was unable to reveal it because the expert in that field was on holidays" (sic).

Other newspaper reports show that the M3 will cost Irish taxpayers a further €727.4 million in maintenance during the forty-plus years of the contract.

In my view, it is an understatement to say that the contract for the M3, as outlined in the newspaper, is a cosy little deal; which might make one wonder if the various public bodies communicate with each other. On the one hand, should the rail link to Navan be completed and succeed in reducing road traffic, a key part of the Kyoto convention to which Ireland signed up; our long suffering taxpayer is screwed once again by being obliged to compensate Eurolink for lost revenue. On the other hand, should this scenario not occur, the said taxpayer is screwed anyway by having to pay the tolls, which are likely to rise as the toll collectors maximise their advantageous position. As stated, it seems a cosy little arrangement, because, if the M3 fails in its primary objective of profiteering from hard-pressed Irish motorists, our obliging government will do the job by screwing them for extra taxes to compensate Eurolink! Should our planners prove to be as blinkered as their predecessors, and failed to learn from the financial debacle of the West Link Bridge by inserting a termination clause in the M3 contract, or perhaps some finances are sourced from N.A.M.A.'s *toxic assets*; imagine the *triple whammy* in store for taxpayers if a buyout becomes necessary – one week is considered a long time in politics, therefore, a forty year contract is a mighty long time indeed.

The shenanigans surrounding development of the M3, and new rail line to Navan, copper-fastens my earlier assertions concerning the stupidity and short-sightedness of previous government planners in allowing the destruction of the Dublin to Navan railway, and other branch lines. Some of these are now being replaced at great cost to Irish taxpayers and to our once unique landscape.

Employees of Eurolink, and their cohorts within the N.R.A. and Meath County Council, displayed an arrogant and cavalier attitude towards local residents during gouging of the M3 through Dowdstown

– unfortunately I cannot reveal details because of legal constraints. Their actions suggest, however, that within the bounds of the M3 corridor, extending from Clonee to north of Kells, the policies of Eurolink seem to override aspirations enshrined within Bunreacht Na hEireann; which are supposedly jealously guarded for the people of Ireland by statutory powers invested in the Irish Government, the N.R.A., and Meath County Council! It would seem that sovereignty over a huge swathe of our once unique landscape, including part of the Tara heritage area, has been ceded to unelected and unrepresentative groups, one a government appointed quango, and the other a corporately driven profit making enterprise.

Having walked the route many times, thereby witnessing the destruction of the landscape at close hand; the following is my opinion of the methods employed by the M3 motorway builders in gouging the route through the sensitive area around the Hill of Tara. It was run like a ruthless military campaign that brooked no nonsense or sentiment, such as care for the pastoral excellence or historical uniqueness of the area. History records much damage being done in times past by such a single-minded approach; whilst it may achieve the immediate objectives, its ill effects can live on for many generations. Whereas the delicate touch of a skilled surgeon, using a sharp scalpel, was required for such a serious operation, the so-called responsible body, the N.R.A., that faceless and powerful 'dustbin' for governmental responsibilities, seemingly assaulted the Irish countryside as though it was an enemy in battle rather than a patient. Using an approach that could be likened more to a gladiator's than a surgeon's, they attacked the pastoral landscape with broadsword and battleaxe, eviscerating and cleaving it from end to end in a display of breathtaking insensitivity verging on arrogance. In addition to destroying the landscape, gouging the path of the M3 caused the destruction of many natural centuries-old springs and the pollution of private drinking-water wells. This cavalier modus operandi being supported by apparently unlimited power and a bottomless purse – witness the previously described destruction of Dillon's Bridge as evidence of a bludgeon rather than a surgical scalpel being used.

To by pass the Hill of Tara, five other routes were postulated as prospective paths for the motorway, but I suspect that no serious consideration was given to these and they were but window dressing to give the impression of democracy being exercised. The motorway was to be constructed through the valley no matter the consequences or cost, either in terms of money or damage to the said unique environment. I believe that to achieve this result, many of the people employed on the project, at all levels, were non Irish, hence would have little or no appreciation of the area's historical significance. Supposedly, one of the top men on the project, a Scotsman, was heard boasting that if required he would have driven the motorway right through the Hill of Tara – but upon being challenged later, he denied making such a statement. The cynical would say that such people were used on the project to ensure that no sentimental issues barred the path of progress. This approach could be likened to an ancient military strategy whereby foreign mercenaries were employed to deal with recalcitrant local populations.

Equally I found a similar stratagem in the archaeological approach used by the same organisation. On various phone calls and visits to the offices, I met different personnel on each occasion, therefore, found myself having to explain the situation every time; and noted that all members of staff I spoke to were not locals, hence their knowledge of the area was scant. I was informed that no record was kept of earlier visits or communications and the previous contact seemed to have moved on. Possibly some people were following an agenda other than the professed one of recording and protecting our ancient heritage..

Had the intent been to maximise damage to the landscape in the Skane and Gabhra valleys, the operation could be deemed an outstanding success! The old line of the road across Dowdstown Bridge could have been used to straddle the motorway by building just one new bridge, with only a slight realignment of the existing road being necessary. Had the old route been realigned, as suggested, the crossing of the motorway would have been achieved where it runs in a deep cutting: thereby minimising its impact on the landscape by reducing the height of the new over-bridge, thus eliminating the need for the highly intrusive embankment and extra bridges across the Skane and Gabhra rivers – this would have maintained the line of the road close to its original path, prevented destruction of many acres of arable land and reduced the social impact upon the local community. Though this proposal would seem to be more practical from financial, social and environmental aspects, perhaps it spoiled the grandiose sweep generated by the N.R.A.'s computers, and didn't 'cut-the-mustard' for the glitzy images on PR bulletins issued by Eurolink? These pamphlets also acclaimed the many trees planted alongside the new route, which in my view are but a facile gesture, merely makeup slapped upon the ravaged features of *Dark Rosaleen* and a requiem for the destroyed woodlands and hedgerows of yesteryear.

The more cynical suggest that perhaps some other agenda was being followed here.

By using a little imagination, and showing more consideration for local residents, the environmental impact of the new roads could have been greatly reduced and a large amount of money saved. Whilst saving money was perhaps a low priority for the N.R.A. during the boom years, yet in 2008, things are totally different in the depths of a recession; when many such tales of massive overspending on publicly funded projects are bombarding the increasingly disenchanted Irish taxpayers. In recent times, the Government attempted to save miserly amounts of money by depriving old age pensioners of vital medical cards, but was balked in its attempt by the outrage of the said pensioners. Perhaps 'the powers that be' should have been looking at the ill-judged use of taxpayer's money, as evidenced by the obviously wasteful methods used in constructing motorways throughout Ireland. Part of this apparent grandiose and spendthrift approach to the use of the public's money has driven the final nail into the coffin of destruction of the once lovely Skane and Gabhra valley at Dowdstown – the charm of the beautiful place is gone forever.

In addition to the environmental damage being inflicted upon the unique area around Tara and its environs, the foolhardiness of building such infrastructure in the vicinity of rivers comes into question. The stupidity of such ventures was amply demonstrated throughout Ireland in recent times; many householders and owners of businesses having to count their costs, incurred because greedy developers, with the connivance of some corrupt officials, built upon river floodplains. Following countrywide flooding in the winter of 2009, the minister for the environment, he who washed his hands of responsibility for the M3, loudly proclaimed how he would prevent future developments upon floodplains: this tardy statement, however, was drowned out by the loud pounding of horses' hooves and slamming of stable doors, because by then, much of the available land on floodplains was occupied already by buildings and motorways. The M3 motorway has been constructed at a very low level in the valley of the Rivers Gabhra and Skane, which may leave it prone to flooding. In several places between Lismullin and Dowdstown the new road runs below the levels to which these rivers have inundated their floodplains during my own lifetime. Part of this hypothesis has been proven already in the winter of 2009 – on the former Gabhra Island, the pipe carrying the seemingly insignificant little Cardiffstown stream under the motorway proved to be inadequate to cater for its floodwaters. The completed highway, including blacktop, central barriers and railings had to be dug up to install a larger conduit; which reflects poorly on computer aided design and does not augur well for the future. To compound the problems, the constructors of the road system have built the aforementioned, and in my opinion unnecessary, raised embankment across the floodplains of both rivers, thereby making the inundation of the motorway almost a certainty at sometime in the future.

Yet, a brief study of history shows that these lessons were learned in times past – the original line of the Dublin to Navan turnpike road was built across the valleys in a similar fashion in 1729, with the road constructed at ground level. But the turnpike had to be raised and the road rebuilt on a causeway about five feet above the surrounding floodplain; which level was approximately three feet higher than the present level of the M3 blacktop. Should the new motorway become subject to flooding, the solution will not be so simple, as it would involve raising the over-bridges and the already huge embankment – in the process increasing its eyesore propensities and intrusion upon the landscape. And guess who will be obliged to carry the cost of such short-sightedness … the long suffering taxpayers of course. Experts predict that future heavier rainfall will cause more frequent inundation of floodplains, therefore, events could become very interesting indeed along the valleys of the Skane and Gabhra.

At time of writing, the foolhardiness and resulting extra costs of building a motorway through 'an alluvial plain' (in layman's terms a swamp), which constitutes much of the Gabhra valley, is obvious for even an amateur to see; witness the massive excavations made to find solid ground and the phenomenal amount of backfilling required. As one elderly resident of Bective remarked to me regarding the convoys of trucks hauling backfill to the construction sites along the motorway: "Jasus, half of County Westmeath must now be in Dowdstown and Lismullin"! Some would say 'the powers that be' are breathtakingly short sighted in their vision or perhaps blinded by power and arrogance, others that the smell of corruption taints the air. Whatever the truth of the matter, in this instance, the long-term consequences are much greater for the community and the environment. The community spirit is sundered by the bitter dispute and the motorway line now forms an impenetrable barrier through the countryside, thus splitting up entire communities. Unfortunately the pastoral environment of the area is irrevocably damaged.

But what was it all for? The use of private transport, as we know it nowadays, is destined for drastic alteration in the near future because of damage being inflicted upon the environment and dwindling oil resources. Having spent most of my adult life working in the oil and natural gas industry, I gained firsthand experience in extracting these precious fluids from ever-inhospitable locations. If used wisely, these substances could have proven to be the very elixir of life on earth; but in our own inimitable way mankind employed them to sow the seeds of our own destruction. Humankind's superior intellect supposedly raised our species above other life forms on Planet Earth; but a study of how we used coal and oil, finite and irreplaceable resources formed by many million years of solar energy, tends to cast doubts upon this supposition. Unfortunately, man's baser instinct, his insatiable greed, took precedence over his intellect; as evidenced by events occurring since the advent of the industrial revolution. Space does not permit further discussion of this extremely complex subject, but it's my belief that unless we make drastic changes and reduce our over-dependence upon petrochemical products in almost every aspect of our lifestyle; the human race faces a massive crisis and possible extinction witin a relatively short period of time.

Perhaps yet another historical parallel could be drawn from the story of a remote island in the vast expanse of the Pacific. Those who scoff at the notion of the human race becoming extinct because of environmental conditions would do well to study the grim fate that befell the population of Easter Island. This once idyllic island lies in the Pacific Ocean, about 3200 kilometres west of the South American coastline. Nowadays, evidence suggests that this island supported a Polynesian population of circa 7000 in a comfortable lifestyle for at least a millennium, but when Dutch explorers first made landfall at the island on Easter Sunday of 1722; they found a dwindling population living in squalor and resorting to cannibalism for survival. They also discovered approximately 600 massive stone statues scattered across the island. By 1877 the 400 square kilometre island had been annexed by Chile and used as a giant sheep ranch, the remaining inhabitants, consisting of circa 110 old people and children, being confined to a single village.

For many years the fate of the original inhabitants of Easter Island was the source of puzzlement amongst anthropologists, who could not envisage that primitives had sculpted the giant monuments, therefore, much conjecture ensued concerning the source of the huge statues; some writers, inevitably, attributing their manufacture to aliens from a distant planet. But scientific evidence nowadays suggests that earlier inhabitants (antecedents of the primitives) carved the giant figures from living rock, thereby causing their own downfall and eventual extinction. The reason for their demise is obviously more complex – but expressed in simple terms: they destroyed their habitat by felling the forests and using tree trunks as rollers for moving the statues to specific locations throughout the island. The denuded island, therefore, could no longer support an increasing population, which descended into cannibalism and the primitive conditions discovered by early European explorers. Additionally, due to the dearth of timber, they could not construct traditional Polynesian craft with which to escape their inevitable fate.

Perhaps this might be considered as a microcosmic insight into what mankind is doing to Mother Earth nowadays, and could be a grim warning of impending events should we continue destroying our planet, from which we cannot escape. Should we not heed the ever-increasing evidence of our environmentally destructive ways, perhaps some intergalactic explorers of the future will discover our wasted world; with the empty skeletal remains of its cities linked by silent motorways – and maybe they too will wonder at the crass stupidity that caused the extinction of human life upon the Blue Planet.

# Historical Notes

## The Grand Jury System

I was enabled to decipher the complex evolution of the older road network between Trim, Tara and Duleek because of the diligently maintained records in the Meath Grand Jury Presentment and Query Books. It's fitting, therefore, that a synopsis of this ancient system of governance is included to explain the origins of references to this body throughout the book. Information on the Meath Grand Jury was gleaned from my own research of the aforesaid records and Danny Cusack's book entitled *A History of Meath County Council.*

The Grand Jury system dates from the early 1600s and replaced what was known as the Statute System: both methods of local governance ran concurrently for some time, but the Grand Jury system took over completely until it too was superseded by County Councils in 1899.

Jeremy Bentham (1748-1832) originator of *Bentham's utilitarian philosophy,* which contended that the highest good was the happiness of the greatest number, once wrote the following of Grand Juries: *a miscellaneous company of men, selected on the presumption of possessing a certain degree of opulence, in number from twelve to twenty three; to pronounce a decision, twelve, but not less than twelve, are sufficient.*

In County Meath the High Sheriff selected the Grand Jury from the ranks of Protestant landowners and other non-Catholic gentry; members of the peerage were not included. Until 1793, Catholics were excluded by act of parliament but following the repeal of the act were seldom chosen for jury duty. The High Sheriff was appointed annually from amongst the leading county families, nominally by the Lord Lieutenant under advice from the legal profession, but was *actually* selected through political wheeling and dealing; so it would seem that little has changed over the years! The Grand Jury, which had no continuous function, was empanelled by the incumbent High Sheriff for two sessions per year; with assizes being held at Trim courthouse in spring and summer. The numerical order in which the jurors were listed was considered as a status symbol, number one being deemed the pinnacle of success. The system was dynastic, with the same powerful family names appearing on the list year after year through succeeding generations. The only notable variations being the influential offices held, such as high and sub-sheriff, Grand Jury foreman; county solicitor, county surveyor and secretary to the jury, which positions were rotated from time to time.

The following synopsis of the Grand Jury modus operandi pertains mostly to its role in maintaining roads and bridges: its original function being to rule upon the validity of civil and criminal indictments at the biannual assizes. In 1634 Parliament empowered the jury to levy a property tax to pay for building and maintaining roads and bridges; this levy became known as the county charge or cess. The cess was collected from each property owner in the Barony where road maintenance or construction was planned, with the collectors being empowered to seize goods from those persons unwilling to make payments or tardy in doing so. The power to levy cess was extended gradually by various acts of parliament beyond the narrow realm of road building; for instance, in 1708, a bill was passed allowing for the tax to cover building and maintenance of jails and courthouses. An act of 1727 specified road widths and emergency repairs to roads and bridges, also providing for presentments to the Grand Jury and the appointment of a county treasurer. In 1739, Grand Juries were empowered to pay the salaries of parish constables and to compulsorily acquire land for road building; which powers were greatly diminished in later times by section 22 of the 1792 Post Road Act. This prescribed that no Grand Jury could present for any new road to be laid or any old road widened through or into any demesne or deer-park without the consent of the owner being first obtained in writing under his hand.

The financial arrangements of the Meath Grand Jury were well-organised – authorised expenditure being covered by the county cess, which was levied upon the county as a whole, and by the Barony cess, levied on the Baronies. Road maintenance costs were borne by each Barony from its own cess, with expenditure on public works, such as bridges and county buildings, being charged to the county at large cess. Two full-time officials served the Grand Jury, a treasurer and a clerk: the clerk maintained the county records, received presentments and drafted Grand Jury orders.

In the early 1800s, central government had no department charged with responsibility for local affairs; hence no formal lines of communication existed between parliament and the local authorities in Meath. Much of the enacted legislation pertained to local government, consisting mainly of acts authorising the Grand Jury to complete projects such as improving existing routes and construction of new roads and bridges. Most of the early statutes were enabling, but as social conditions deteriorated during the early to mid-1800s, legislation became more prescriptive, with central government increasingly dependent upon Grand Juries for its enforcement.

Because of the expansion of public works, the county cess increased six-fold between the 1770s and 1830s, thereby imposing an enormous financial burden upon the landowners (tenants) of the county. This situation being further complicated by a valuation system that sometimes caused large variations in the rates imposed on different townlands within the same Barony. The injustice of this system was compounded because the cess was payable by the land occupier or tenant and not by the landowners who comprised the Grand Jury under the prevailing law. Thus, grand jurors were spending monies raised from the hard labour of their tenants, not from their own pockets. Furthermore, those MPs who could reform this iniquitous system were themselves the main beneficiaries of the status quo; therefore, legislative change was most unlikely. Catholics acquiring more land through tenancy or lease bore an increasing liability for the cess but had no say in the level of taxation or how the money was spent. The situation was not enhanced by displays of political partisanship, sectarian partiality; corruption and inefficiency evident in the workings of the Grand Juries. The system caused extreme frustration to the cess payers and grave embarrassment to central government. Less privileged Catholics perceived the Protestant minority to be an alien and numerically insignificant elite, which derived social, economic and political authority over them because of its monopoly of land ownership.

The Grand Jury system was exposed to corruption in a myriad of ways. Any landowner could make a presentment for repairs to a road or construction of a new route or bridge, and upon a certificate being drawn up and attested to by two persons before a justice of the peace it could be submitted to the Grand Jury. Many such presentments did not receive sufficient scrutiny because of constraints of time and pressure of work; therefore, most approvals were based on the influence of the applicant rather than upon the merit of his project. Insufficient checks and balances were inherent within the administration of presentments, resulting in many projects being presented for more than once and paid for several times over; thereby increasing the costs to the cess payers and lining the pockets of unscrupulous landowners and speculators. Furthermore, the system lent itself readily to quid pro quo, with landlords repairing or making new roads to their estates and sometimes processing road repair contracts favouring their tenants in order to provide money for payment of their rents.

In 1829 a contemporary writer, William Hamilton Maxwell (1792-1850), in his famous book *Wild Sports of the West* noted the following vis a vis poor roads and corruption associated with Grand Juries in the West of Ireland: "And why was this neglect? Were the proprietors of this deserted district so cold to that true spring of human action, self aggrandizement, as to omit providing an outlet for the source of their opulence? Were there no public monies allocated to these abandoned corners of the earth, and so much lavishly expended on many a useless undertaking elsewhere? Yes : large sums had been presented and *re-presented* by the Grand Juries for the last twenty years, but they have been regularly pocketed by those to whose good faith they were entrusted. Would it be believed in England, George, that this atrocious system of peculation has been carried to such an extent that roads have been passed *as completed* when their lines have been but roughly marked out – and bridges been actually paid for, the necessary accounting affidavits having been sworn to in open court, when not a stone was ever laid, and to this day the stream runs without a solitary arch to span its flood from the source to the debouchement? Ay – these delinquencies have been often and notoriously perpetrated, and none have had the courage to drag the criminals to justice" (sic).

From the above it's evident that the writer was less than enamoured with the prevailing system of road construction and local governance in Ireland. The rhetorical question posed to *George* was obviously addressed to King George 1V and seems to suggest that things were done somewhat differently in England during that era!

Although many reforms took place throughout the 19th century, Grand Juries ceased to be an organ of local government in 1898 and were replaced by County Councils in 1899. But little else changed besides the name. Considering the profusion of public enquires and tribunals being held nowadays, it is evident that corruption is alive and flourishing within our political system, where, from the upper echelons of central government to the lowest levels within local authorities; *brown* envelopes seem to be more important than *white* or *green* papers and statutory instruments.

# Meath Grand Jury list of 1803

The list was prefaced by the following heading: *Queries to the Grand Jury at a general assizes and general Goal delivery held at Trim the 22 day of March 1803* (sic).

*Grand Jury Names*

*1-Thomas Pepper Esq. 2-Robert Wade Esq. 3-Robert Waller Esq. 4-Gustavus Lambert Esq. 5-C.A. Nicholson Esq. 6-Cha's Drake Dillon Esq. 7-Walter Nugent Esq. 8-Richard Chalomer Esq. 9-Hamilton Gorge Esq. 10-John Ruxton Esq. 11-Henry Caddington Esq. 12-John Prat Winder Esq. 13-George Lucas Nugent Esq. 14-Henry Woodward Esq. 15- Anthony Blackburne Esq. 16-Georges Barnford Esq. 17-Sir Francis Hopkins Bar't 18-Thomas Everard Esq. 19-Elias Corbally Esq. 20-Skeffington Thomson Esq. 21-John Hussey Esq. 22-Thomas Taylor Rowley Esq. 23-Walter Dowdall Esq. James O'Reilly Esq. Sheriff*

# The National Roads Authority (N.R.A)

The N.R.A is a government appointed quango (an acronym of quasiautonomous nongovernmental organisation) that operates independently of the government, which finances it largely through tax revenue. Such organisations oftentimes provide smokescreens for well-paid government ministers to renege on their accountability and responsibilities to the electorate.

The self-declared responsibilities of this authority are as follows: "to secure the provision of a safe and efficient network of national roads" it has overall responsibility for the planning and supervision of construction and maintenance of national roads. In addition, the NRA has a number of specific functions under the Act, including:

- Preparing, or arranging for the preparation of road designs, maintenance programmes and schemes for the provision of traffic signs on national roads;
- Securing the carrying out of construction, improvement and maintenance works on national roads;
- Allocating and paying grants for national roads, and
- Training, research or testing activities in relation to any of its functions.

Historically, the NRA has discharged these functions through the relevant local road authorities. However, it is empowered (where it considers it would be more convenient, expeditious, effective or economical to do so) to carry out such functions directly.

The NRA has a general power to direct the road authority to "do any other thing which arises out of or is consequential on or is necessary or expedient for the purpose of or would facilitate the construction or maintenance of a national road".

The NRA may give specific directions to local authorities relating to a number of matters, including making a motorway scheme; application for a bridge order; acquiring land by compulsory purchase order; preparing an Environmental Impact Statement (EIS), and entering into contract for and/or undertaking specified construction or maintenance works.

Section 57 of the act, as amended by the Planning and Development Act, 2000, allows the NRA to prepare a scheme for the establishment of a system of tolls in respect of the use of a public road. The NRA may also enter into an agreement with another person whereby that person agrees, inter alia, to pay some or all of the costs of the construction and/or maintenance of the road and/or to upgrade and manage the road. Toll charges may be used to repay all or part of the private funding involved (sic).

The foregoing is but part of a much larger document, but this excerpt shows some of the powers ceded by the government to this organisation, which is not amenable to the Irish Electorate!

At time of writing, the management and board of the N.R.A. is comprised as follows:

**Management;**

Fred Barry, CEO.

Michael Egan, Head of Corporate Affairs and Professional Services.

Hugh Cregan, Head of PPP, Strategic Planning & Commercial Operations.

John Maher, Head of Finance and Administration.

Eugene O'Connor, Head of Engineering Operations.

**The Board**

The NRA board may comprise of up to fourteen members – thirteen ordinary members and a chairperson – appointed by the Minister of Transport. Members are appointed on the basis of their experience in relation to roads, transport, industrial, commercial, financial, or environmental matters, local government, and the organisation of workers and administration. They are directly responsible for the exercise of the NRA's functions under the Act, but can delegate these functions to committees with the approval of the Minister:

The board members are –

| | |
|---|---|
| Peter Malone, Chairman | Eugene Moore |
| Eddie Breen | Raymond Potterton |
| Frank Convery | Jenny Kent |
| Eric Fleming | Colm Lonergan |
| Fred Barry | Clifford Kelly |
| Anne Butler | Margaret O'Mahony. |

# Larkin's Map of County Meath

William Larkin was a cartographer and surveyor whose famous map of county Meath is most revealing and oftentimes provides the final pieces for solving the jigsaw-like puzzles posed by the evolving road network of long ago. The map sheets being of a very small scale are quite difficult to follow, but can be very effective when cross-referenced with the OS maps of a slightly later period. Though containing errors and some items are omitted, the map helped to solve many tantalising riddles; sometimes giving substance to folklore and occasionally consigning other local yarns to the realms of fairytales. William Larkin knew the road network of the period very well because he was involved in surveying many of the route alterations. The map was surveyed for the Meath Grand Jury in the period between 1804 and 1812 and published in 1817; it's therefore an additional bonus for those interested in local history, as it indicates many old place names, which have disappeared since. Thus Larkin's Map provides an important link to an era preceding the first Ordnance

Survey of the 1830s, during which many townland and place names were changed and some Anglicised.

Whilst researching the Grand Jury records I found several presentments for sums of money to cover the survey costs; including £400 in 1804 for launching the project. In addition to Larkin's name, other names mentioned in these presentments were John Pollock, R.S. Tighe and J.P. Winter (Winder), all were members of the Grand Jury. Though the survey was completed about 1812 the map was not engraved and printed until 1817. The estimated cost of the survey was in excess of £1200 and the engraving costs greater than £2200 – enormous sums for the time. An atlas of Larkin's Map, produced by Arnold Horner in 2007, is available in Meath County Library in Navan.

## The Irish Pale

Some dictionaries give two definitions of areas known as 'the Pale'. The first concerns a restricted area in Imperial Russia, where Jews were allowed to settle. The second, and more pertinent description to these writings reads as follows: *Pale, Part of Ireland under English rule: The area of Ireland, based around Dublin, that was controlled by England, from the 12th century, until the final conquest of the entire country in the 16th century* (sic).

The seaboard of the Irish Pale extended from south of Dublin northwards to Dundalk in County Louth. The Pale spread westward in a salient, or bulge, enclosing large areas in the later-day counties of Louth, Meath, Kildare and Dublin, including much of the Boyne Valley and parts of other counties in Leinster. In the early days of their conquest the Normans built large flat-topped Mottes, on which eminences they constructed wooden castles for defence. Later, settlements sprang up around the Mottes and these became centres of commerce. Later still, when things were more settled, stone castles were built close by, varying in size and layout from massive stone built moated-castles to the smaller towerhouses and even smaller watchtowers – these various sized structures became known as 'the castles, towerhouses and watchtowers of the Pale'. Several were constructed along the Boyne and its environs and were the target of attacks by the fiercely independent Gaelic chieftains. In later times, some were besieged during the wars of the Rebellion of 1641 and the following Cromwellian campaign. Many of the castles changed hands several times during the turbulent years of the rebellion and the land confiscations that followed the conflicts. Supposedly, in 1429, King Henry V1 offered grants of £10 to any person building specified sized castles within some areas of the Pale. *See further references on Riverstown castle in chapter six.*

# Bibliography

My principle sources of reference for this work are the following:

## Maps

- Ordnance Survey Maps of 1837, 1882, 1911. (6 inch).
- William Larkin's Map of County Meath, 1812 – 1817.
- Molls, H., *Map of Ireland, 1714,* in Nat. Lib. of Ireland.
- Pratt's map of 1702, In Nat. Lib. of Ireland.
- Petty, Sir William, (1685), *Hibernia Delineatio: Atlas of Ireland,* (Newcastle upon Tyne, 1968).
- Down Survey Barony map (1644-1656), (copies in M.C.L.).
- Longfield estate maps of Dowdstown and Kilcarn, 1822, Nat. Lib. Of Ireland.
- Taylor, G. and Skinner, A. *Maps of the Roads of Ireland,* (Shannon, 1969) (facsimile reprint of 2nd ed. 1783).(M.C.L.)
- Beaufort, Daniel Augustus, *Map of the diocese of Meath, 1797. (Meath County Library)*
- Taylor, J., *'County of Meath'* (engraved map), 1802. (M.C.L.)

Note : I came across many inaccurate maps in circulation on the internet. Some of these may derive from deliberate errors inserted on original maps as copyright protection. The most reliable maps are OS originals.

## Books

- Broderick, David, *The First Toll Roads: Irelands Turnpike Roads 1729-1858* (Cork, 2002).
- Doyle, Eamon, *The Wexford Insurgents of '98 and Their March in to Meath* (Enniscorthy, 1997)
- Duffy, Sean (ED) *Atlas of Irish History,* (Dublin, 1997).
- Ellison, Cyril, *The Waters of the Boyne and Blackwater: A Scenic and Industrial Miscellany,* (Dublin, 1983).
- Griffith, Richard, *General Valuation of Rateable Property in Ireland,* [Meath vols.], (Dublin, 1852-54).
- Gallagher, Joan, *Milestones along the journey of life,* Navan, 2003.
- Hickey, Elizabeth, *Skryne and the Early Normans,* (Navan, 1994).
- *Kentstown in Bygone Days.* (Kentstown ICA Guild, 1996).
- *Meath Grand Jury Presentment & Query Books 1790 - 1830* (National Archives, Four Courts).
- O'Donovan, John, *Ordnance Survey Field Names Books 1835-37* (typescripts Meath County Library).
- *Ordnance Survey Letters Meath,* edited by Michael Herity (Dublin, 2001).
- O'Keefe, Peter, *The Dublin to Navan Road and Kilcarn Bridge* (The Author 1994). Available M.C.L.
- Petrie, George *On the History and Antiquities of Tara Hill,* 1837.
- Reynolds, Jim, *A Life by the Boyne (M.C.L.)*
- Simington, Robert, *The Civil Survey A.D 1654-1656 County of Meath Vol. V,* (Dublin, 1940).
- Slavin, Michael, *The Book of Tara,* (Dublin, 1996).
- Steen, L.J. *The Battle of the hill of Tara: 26 May 1798* (Trim,1991).
- Wilde, Sir William, *The Beauties of the Boyne and its Tributary the Blackwater* (Dublin, 1849).